Lecture Notes in Computer Science 8472

Commenced Publication in 1973
Founding and Former Series Editors:
Gerhard Goos, Juris Hartmanis, and Jan van Leeuwen

Editorial Board

More information about this series at http://www.springer.com/series/7407

Patrick Siarry · Lhassane Idoumghar
Julien Lepagnot (Eds.)

Swarm Intelligence Based Optimization

First International Conference, ICSIBO 2014
Mulhouse, France, May 13–14, 2014
Revised Selected Papers

 Springer

Editors

Patrick Siarry
Univ. Paris-Est Créteil (UPEC), LISSI
Vitry Sur Seine
France

Julien Lepagnot
Université de Haute-Alsace, LMIA
Mulhouse
France

Lhassane Idoumghar
Université de Haute-Alsace, LMIA-INRIA
    Grand Est
Mulhouse
France

ISSN 0302-9743
Lecture Notes in Computer Science
ISBN 978-3-319-12969-3
DOI 10.1007/978-3-319-12970-9

ISSN 1611-3349   (electronic)

ISBN 978-3-319-12970-9   (eBook)

Library of Congress Control Number: 2014956195

LNCS Sublibrary: SL1 – Theoretical Computer Science and General Issues

Springer Cham Heidelberg New York Dordrecht London

Printed on acid-free paper

Springer International Publishing AG Switzerland is part of Springer Science+Business Media
(www.springer.com)

Preface

These post-proceedings include a selection of the best papers presented at the International Conference on Swarm Intelligence-Based Optimization, ICSIBO 2014, held in Mulhouse (France). ICSIBO 2014 is a continuation of the conferences OEP 2003 (Paris), OEP 2007 (Paris), and ICSI 2011 (Cergy-Pontoise).

Each submitted paper was reviewed by three members of the international Program Committee. Among the 48 submissions received, 26 were selected for oral presentation. The authors of these accepted submissions sent revised versions of their papers. From a second reviewing process, 20 revised submissions were accepted in these post-proceedings. Accordingly, the acceptance rate for the post-proceedings was 41.67%.

The aim of ICSIBO 2014 is to highlight the theoretical progress of swarm intelligence metaheuristics and their applications. Swarm intelligence is a computational intelligence technique involving the study of collective behavior in decentralized systems. Such systems are made up of a population of simple individuals interacting locally with one another and with their environment. Although there is generally no centralized control on the behavior of individuals, local interactions among individuals often cause a global pattern to emerge. Examples of such systems can be found in nature, including ant colonies, animal herding, bacteria foraging, bee swarms, and many more.

The authors were invited to present original work relevant to swarm intelligence, including, but not limited to: theoretical advances of swarm intelligence metaheuristics; combinatorial, discrete, binary, constrained, multi-objective, multi-modal, dynamic, noisy, and large-scale optimization; artificial immune systems, particle swarms, ant colony, bacterial foraging, artificial bees, fireflies algorithm; hybridization of algorithms; parallel/distributed computing, machine learning, data mining, data clustering, decision making and multi-agent systems based on swarm intelligence principles; adaptation and applications of swarm intelligence principles to real-world problems in various domains.

We would like to express our sincere gratitude to our invited speakers Maurice Clerc and Nicolas Monmarché. The success of the conference resulted from the input of many people to whom we would like to express our appreciation: the members of Program Committee and the secondary reviewers for their careful reviews that ensured the quality of the selected papers and of the conference. We take this opportunity to thank the different partners whose financial and material support contributed to the organization of the conference: Université de Haute-Alsace, Faculté des Sciences et Techniques, ROADEF, GDR-MACS. Last but not least, we thank all the authors who submitted their research papers to the conference, and the authors of accepted papers who attended the conference to present their work. Thank you all.

August 2014

Patrick Siarry
Lhassane Idoumghar
Julien Lepagnot

Organization

Organizing Committee Chairs

Patrick Siarry   Université de Paris-Est Créteil, France
Lhassane Idoumghar   Université de Haute-Alsace, France
Julien Lepagnot   Université de Haute-Alsace, France

Program Chair

Maurice Clerc   Independent Consultant, France

Website/Proceedings/Administration

MAGE Team, LMIA Laboratory, France

Program Committee

Ajith Abraham	Norwegian University of Science and Technology, Norway
Amitava Chatterjee	Jadavpur University, India
Raymond Chiong	University of Newcastle, Australia
Maurice Clerc	Independent Consultant, France
Carlos A. Coello Coello	CINVESTAV-IPN, Mexico
Pierre Collet	Université de Strasbourg, France
Jean-Charles Créput	Université de Technologie de Belfort-Montbéliard, France
Luca Di Gaspero	University of Udine, Italy
Fréderic Guinand	Université du Havre, France
Rachid Ellaia	Mohammadia School of Engineering, Morocco
Said Hanafi	Université de Valenciennes, France
Jin-Kao Hao	Université d'Angers, France
Vincent Hilaire	Université de Technologie de Belfort-Montbéliard, France
Lhassane Idoumghar	Université de Haute-Alsace, France
Jim Kennedy	Bureau of Labor Statistics, USA
Peter Korosec	University of Primorska, Slovenia
Abderrafiaâ Koukam	Université de Technologie de Belfort-Montbéliard, France
Mohamed G. Omran	Gulf University for Science and Technology, Kuwait
Fred Glover	OptTek Systems, Inc., USA

Contents

Combining PSO and FCM for Dynamic Fuzzy Clustering Problems

Yucheng Kao[(✉)], Ming-Hsien Chen, and Kai-Ming Hsieh

Department of Information Management, Tatung University,
No. 40, Sec. 3, Zhongshan N. Rd., Taipei, Taiwan
ykao@ttu.edu.tw

Abstract. This paper proposes a dynamic data clustering algorithm, called PSOFC, in which Particle Swarm Optimization (PSO) is combined with the fuzzy c-means (FCM) clustering method to find the number of clusters and cluster centers concurrently. Fuzzy c-means can be applied to data clustering problems but the number of clusters must be given in advance. This paper tries to overcome this shortcoming. In the evolutionary process of PSOFC, a discrete PSO is used to search for the best number of clusters. With a specified number of cluster, each particle employs FCM to refine cluster centers for data clustering. Thus PSOFC can automatically determine the best number of clusters during the data clustering process. Six datasets were used to evaluate the proposed algorithm. Experimental results demonstrated that PSOFC is an effective algorithm for solving dynamic fuzzy clustering problems.

Keywords: Particle Swarm Optimization · Fuzzy c-means · Data Clustering

1 Introduction

Data clustering aims to discover meaningful organization of data points in a data set in terms of their similarities and dissimilarities. A good clustering algorithm can classify a set of data points into several distinct clusters such that the members of a cluster are highly similar while the data points belonging to different clusters are dissimilar. Data clustering is an important data mining technique and has been studied in several fields such as pattern recognition, machine learning, market segmentation, bioinformatics, and so on.

Data clustering approaches can be roughly classified into two main categories: hierarchical clustering and partitional (non-hierarchical) clustering [3]. Partitional clustering methods require the number of clusters to be given beforehand and use an iterative algorithm to find out the best cluster centers for classifying data points into appropriate clusters. K-means and fuzzy c-means [2] are well-known partitional clustering methods. K-means is for crisp clustering while FCM is for fuzzy clustering. When using a partitional clustering approach, we have to provide the number of clusters and initial cluster centers in advance. Initial cluster centers can be randomly determined, but it is difficult for us to

© Springer International Publishing Switzerland 2014
P. Siarry et al. (Eds.): ICSIBO 2014, LNCS 8472, pp. 1–8, 2014.
DOI: 10.1007/978-3-319-12970-9_1

decide the best number of clusters in priori unless we understand the characteristics of data sets very well. To overcome the drawback of partitional clustering, several papers have proposed different approaches, such as genetic algorithm (GA)-based approach [1] and PSO-based approach [8].

This paper proposes a PSO-based fuzzy clustering (PSOFC) approach to deal with dynamic clustering problems. When running PSOFC, we only need to give a maximum possible cluster number in priori. In the evolutionary process, each particle selects its own best number of clusters and refines the corresponding cluster centers using fuzzy c-means. We use a clustering validity index to evaluate the clustering results of particles, which in turn are used to direct the search directions of particles. The experimental results show that PSOFC can effectively find the best clustering results, compared with current dynamic clustering algorithms.

2   Background

In this section, we introduce the PSO algorithm, fuzzy c-means, and a cluster validity measure (PBM Index).

2.1   Particle Swarm Optimization

PSO was originally proposed by Kennedy and Eberhart in 1995 [5]. The concept of PSO follows a biological swarm behavior model which was inspired by the behavior of birds searching for food sources. When birds are foraging for food, they memorize past best positions and exchange the message of best positions with each other so that all members can gradually fly toward the best target. In a PSO algorithm, a candidate solution is called a particle. Each particle memorizes two components: the personal best (pBest) and global best (gBest) positions. The former is the best position that a particle has ever visited while the latter is the best position that the whole swarm has ever experienced. A particle determines its new velocity and position according to its current velocity, its pBest position and the gBest position, as defined in Eqs. (1) and (2).

$$V_{id}^{t+1} = w^{t+1} \times V_{id}^t + c_1 \times rand() \times (P_{id}^t - X_{id}^t) + c_2 \times rand() \times (P_{gd}^t - X_{id}^t) \quad (1)$$

$$X_{id}^{t+1} = X_{id}^t + V_{id}^{t+1} \quad (2)$$

where V_i is the velocity of particle i, X_i is the position of particle i, P_i is pBest of particle i, P_g is gBest of the particle swarm, c_1 and c_2 are positive constants, $rand()$ is a random number selected from [0.0, 1.0], d is the dimension index, and t is the generation number.

The advantages of using PSO include fast convergence and fewer parameters needed to be set. Some researchers have applied PSO to data clustering [6–8].

2.2   Fuzzy c-Means Clustering Algorithm

Fuzzy c-means is a clustering method similar to K-means but the concept of fuzzy theory is incorporated to improve clustering results. That is, fuzzy c-means allows that each data point belongs to more than one cluster according to their fuzzy memberships. Assume we are going to classify n data objects into c groups, the objective function used in FCM is defined below:

$$J_m = \sum_{i=1}^{c} \sum_{j=1}^{n} u_{ij}^m \left[dist(c_i, x_j) \right]^2 \tag{3}$$

where c_i is the center vector of cluster i, x_j is data point j, u_{ij} is membership degree of point x_j related to cluster i, m is the fuzziness index and its value falls in the range of $[1, \infty]$, $dist(c_i, x_j)$ is Euclidean distance between data point j and cluster center i.

The FCM algorithm contains following main steps:

Step 1: Initialize the parameters. Note that the values of u_{ij} are subject to the following three conditions. Condition (a) means that the value of u_{ij} is a real number ranged between 0 and 1. Condition (b) indicates that for a data point, all of its u_{ij} values should be sum up to 1 . The last condition defines that the sum of u_{ij} values for a cluster should be ranged between 0 and n.
   (a) $u_{ij} \in [0, 1]$ $i = 1, 2, \ldots, c$ and $j = 1, 2, \ldots n$
   (b) $\sum_{i=1}^{c} u_{ij} = 1$ $j = 1, \ldots, n$
   (c) $0 < \sum_{j=1}^{n} u_{ij} < n$ $i = 1, \ldots, c$

Step2: Calculate the center vector of cluster i by Eq. (4).

$$c_i = \frac{\sum_{j=1}^{n} u_{ij}^m x_j}{\sum_{j=1}^{n} u_{ij}^m} \quad i = 1, \ldots, c \tag{4}$$

Step3: Update the fuzzy membership matrix U by Eq. (5).

$$u_{ij} = \frac{1}{\sum_{k=1}^{c} \left(\frac{dist(c_i, x_j)}{dist(c_k, x_j)} \right)^{2/(m-1)}} \quad i = 1, \ldots, c \text{ and } j = 1, \ldots, n \tag{5}$$

Step4: Calculate J_m using Eq. (3) and check the stop criteria. If $|J_m^{t+1} - J_m^t| < \varepsilon$, then stop the execution; otherwise go back to step 2.

2.3   Cluster Validity Measure

When solving a dynamic clustering problem, a validity index is used to determine the best clustering solution. A good validity measure considers the degrees of compactness and separation in order to ensure that the optimal number of clusters is found. This paper uses PBM Index as the cluster validity measure [9]. PBM formulas are defined as follows:

$$\text{PBM}(K) = \left(\frac{1}{K} \times \frac{E_1}{E_K} \times D_K \right)^2 \tag{6}$$

$$E_1 = \sum_{j=1}^{n} dist(c_0, x_j) \tag{7}$$

$$E_K = \sum_{k=1}^{K} E_k = \sum_{k=1}^{K} \sum_{j=1}^{n} u_{kj}^m dist(c_k, x_j) \tag{8}$$

$$D_K = \max(dist(c_p, c_q)) \ p, q = 1, \ldots, K \tag{9}$$

where K is the total number of clusters, E_1 is the sum of the distances between each data point and the geometric center of the data set (c_0), x_j is data point j, c_0 is the cluster center when the number of clusters is one, E_K is the sum of within-cluster distances of K clusters, and D_K is the maximum separation distance of each pair of cluster centers. Eq. (6) suggests that the higher the PBM Index value, the better the clustering result.

3   PSOFC Clustering Algorithm

In PSOFC, we adopt a discrete PSO algorithm to search for a best number of clusters and utilize the fuzzy c-means to find optimal cluster centers for data clustering. The clustering result is evaluated by computing cluster validity index PBM.

3.1   Solution Representation

PSOFC considers each particle as a candidate solution, which is composed of the number of clusters and several cluster centers. The number of clusters is not given in advance and must be determined at each iteration. Thus the lengths of particle solutions are varied. The number of clusters should be within a reasonable range, depending on the size of the data set. The minimum cluster number ($MinK$) is set to 2, and the maximum cluster number ($MaxK$) is set to $\sqrt{n}$ [10] [12]. The solution representation of particle i with $K_i = k$ is defined below:

$$P_i = [\ K_i = k;$$
$$(x_{i11}, x_{i12}, \ldots, x_{i1d}), (x_{i21}, x_{i22}, \ldots, x_{i2d}), \ldots, (x_{ik1}, x_{ik2}, \ldots, x_{ikd})]$$

where X_{i11} is the first dimension of the first cluster center and d is the dimension size of data points.

3.2   Initialization

First, each particle randomly determines its own cluster number K_i and initial flying velocity V_i. Here, the value of K_i is selected from the interval of $MinK$ and $MaxK$, i.e. $MinK \leq K_i \leq MaxK$. The initial velocity is randomly selected from the interval of -1 and 1. According to the specified cluster number, each particle randomly selected K_i data points from the data set as its initial cluster vectors. After that, each particle executes the fuzzy c-means clustering algorithm to refine cluster centers, and at last uses the Eq. (6) to calculate PBM value. According to the PBM values, the best particle is determined and its cluster number and cluster centers are the swarm best solution, i.e. gBest. Each particle also memorizes its current solution as pBest.

3.3 Main Steps of the Evolution Process

There are four main steps in an iteration of PSOFC, which aims to find the best number of clusters and the corresponding cluster centers.

Step 1: Evolving K_i values. As we know, determining the best number of clusters for a clustering problem is a discrete optimization problem. Therefore, a discrete PSO algorithm proposed by Jarboui et al. [4] is adopted to determine the cluster number for each particle. The main concept is to convert the number of clusters of particle i (K_i) to a virtual space using a state variable (Y_i) (see Eq. (10), to use a conventional PSO algorithm to compute the new velocity and position of state variable Y_i in the virtual space (see Eqs. (11) and (12), and then to convert the state variable with a new value back to the discrete space to get new K_i (see Eqs. (13) and (14)).

$$Y_i^t = \begin{cases} 1 & \text{if } K_i^t = P_g^t, \\ -1 & \text{if } K_i^t = P_i^t, \\ -1 \text{or } 1 & \text{if } K_i^t = P_g^t = P_i^t, \\ 0 & \text{otherwise.} \end{cases} \tag{10}$$

$$V_i^{t+1} = w^{t+1} \times V_i^t + c_1 \times rand() \times (-1 - Y_i^t) + c_2 \times rand() \times (1 - Y_i^t) \tag{11}$$

$$\lambda_i^{t+1} = Y_i^t + V_i^{t+1} \tag{12}$$

$$Y_i^{t+1} = \begin{cases} 1 & \text{if } \lambda^{t+1} > \alpha^{t+1}, \\ -1 & \text{if } \lambda^{t+1} < -\alpha^{t+1}, \\ 0 & \text{otherwise.} \end{cases} \tag{13}$$

$$K_i^{t+1} = \begin{cases} P_g^t & \text{if } Y_i^{t+1} = 1, \\ P_i^t & \text{if } Y_i^{t+1} = -1, \\ MinK \leq RN \leq MaxK & \text{otherwise.} \end{cases} \tag{14}$$

where P_g^t is the past best cluster number of the particle swarm, P_i^t is the past best cluster number of particle i, Y_i^t is the state variable of particle i, λ_i^t is the continuous version of Y_i^t, α is a threshold value, RN is an integer random number selected from the interval of $(MinK, MaxK)$.

Step 2: Selecting new cluster centers. It could happen to FCM to fall into a local optimum if initial cluster centers are not well chosen. To avoid this drawback, PSOCF changes cluster centers in different ways, depending on the value of state variable Y. If $Y_i^{t+1} = 1$, particle i will replace its cluster centers with those of the gBest particle. In addition, some cluster centers will be randomly selected and substituted with data points randomly selected from the input data set. If $Y_i^{t+1} = -1$, particle i will replace its cluster centers with those of its pBest solution. The same, several cluster centers will be randomly selected and replaced with data points randomly selected from the input data set. If $Y_i^{t+1} = 0$, particle i will replace its all cluster centers with K_i^{t+1} data points randomly selected from the input data set.

Step 3: Refining cluster centers with FCM. When new cluster centers of particle i are determined, PSOFC starts to refine the cluster centers using FCM (see Eqs. (3), (4) and (5)).

Step 4: Updating pBest and gBest. After performing FCM, PSOCF calculates PBM Index value for each particle solution. Then the algorithm updates the personal best solution for each particle and the global best solution for the whole population according to their PBM Index values. At the end of an iteration, termination condition is checked. If the maximum iteration number is reached, then stop running the algorithm; otherwise, go back to step 1 to continue next iteration.

Table 1. Dataset Information

Dataset	Number of Attributes	Number of points	Actual number of clusters
Data_4_3	3	400	4
Data_4_2	2	80	4
Data_5_2	2	250	5
Date_6_2	2	300	6
Iris	4	150	3
Breast Cancer	9	683	2

4   Experiments

In order to validate the clustering performance of the PSOFC algorithm, four artificial data sets and two real world data sets from UCI machine learning repository [11] were selected as test problems. The detailed information of these six data sets is listed in Table 1.

The POSFC algorithm was coded in Visual C#, and all experiments were run on a personal computer with Pentium IV(3.0 GHz) running Windows XP. Based on the results of preliminary experiments, the parameters of PSOFC were set as follows: $MinK = 2$, $MaxK = \sqrt{n}$ (n is the number of data points in a test data set), the population size of particles $S = 20$, the stop criteria of fuzzy c-means $\varepsilon = 0.001$, $m = 1.5$, $\alpha = 1.0 \sim 0.35$, $c_1 = c_2 = 0.5$, $w = 0.72 \sim 0.4$, the maximum number of iterations $MNI = 30$. Here $\alpha = 1.0 \sim 0.35$ denotes that the parameter will be linearly decreased from 1.0 to 0.35 during a run. To compare PSOFC with current algorithms, two dynamic clustering algorithms were selected form the literature. The first one is GCUK [1] and the second one is DCPSO [8]. The parameters of GCUK were set as follows: the number of chromosomes is 50, the number of iterations is 100, crossover rate is 0.8, mutation rate is 0.001, $MinK$ is 2, and $MaxK$ is $\sqrt{n}$. On the other hand, the parameters of DCPSO were set as follows: $N_c = 20$, $P_{ini} = 0.75$, $s = 100$, $w = 0.72$, $c_1 = c_2 = 1.49$, $V_{max} = 255$, MNI of binary PSO $= 50$ and the number of outer iterations is 2. For each of the six test data sets, 20 independent runs were performed for each of these algorithms.

The experimental results are summarized in Table 2. The results show that the performance of PSOFC is better than that of two existing algorithms in terms of the average values of objective function. Regarding the number of clusters found by these algorithms, it is obvious that PSOFC is able to provide the best number of clusters compared with GCUK and DCPSO. For example, the real-world data set Iris has two overlapped data clusters. PSOFC can correctly identify three clusters in this test problem while GCUK and DCPSO cannot.

Table 2. Experimental results

Dataset	Algorithm	Objective Function Value		Obtained Cluster number	Actual cluster number	CPU Time	
		Avg.	Stdev			Avg.	Stdev
Data_4_2	GCUK	11.7365	3.1135	2,3	4	1.3761	0.1664
	DCPSO	13.2984	1.2046	2		2.5102	0.1283
	PSOFC	**18.4572**	**0.0732**	**4**		**1.1477**	**0.0139**
Data_5_2	GCUK	21.6571	3.5126	3,5	5	4.7211	0.4276
	DCPSO	26.588	**0.0571**	5		5.0953	0.3122
	PSOFC	**26.8756**	0.0658	5		**3.7773**	**0.0328**
Data_6_2	GCUK	372.341	4.3122	3,4,5	6	5.4122	0.3017
	DCPSO	408.7406	2.0281	5		5.932	0.2043
	PSOFC	**557.411**	**0.0483**	**6**		**3.6828**	**0.0418**
Data_4_3	GCUK	651.7921	3.7683	2,3,4	4	5.2189	0.4261
	DCPSO	731.9498	0.3181	4		5.9922	0.2007
	PSOFC	**732.0347**	**0.0374**	4		**3.7336**	**0.1449**
Iris	GCUK	20.8765	1.3712	2	3	3.9118	0.2132
	DCPSO	21.3497	1.2215	2		4.2117	0.1943
	PSOFC	**27.1652**	**0.0451**	**3**		**3.5664**	**0.0587**
Breast	GCUK	169.6934	0.8976	2	2	15.5612	0.5164
Cancer	DCPSO	169.2878	0.9735	2		17.7039	**0.4952**
	PSOFC	**170.3247**	**0.0327**	2		**10.4805**	0.5321

5   Conclusion

This paper proposed a new fuzzy clustering algorithm combining PSO and FCM to deal with dynamic clustering problems. By sharing the best results among particles, the optimal number of clusters and cluster centers are easily found. From the experimental results, it can be seen that PSOFC can find the best cluster number even though the number of clusters is not given in advance. The results also demonstrate that PSOFC has the ability to provide equal or better solutions for the test problems. For the future work, it is worth to apply other validity measure indices to the same clustering problems to see if the clustering results are sensitive to different validity measure indices.

References

1. Bandyopadhyay, S., Maulik, U.: Genetic clustering for automatic evolution of clusters and application to image classification. Pattern Recognition **35**(6), 1197–1208 (2002)
2. Bezdek, J.C.: Pattern Recognition with Fuzzy Objective Function Algorithms. Plenum, NY (1981)
3. Han, J., Kamber, M., Pei, J.: Data Mining: Concepts and Techniques, 3rd edn. Morgan Kaufmann, San Francisco (2011)
4. Jarboui, B., Cheikh, M., Siarry, P., Rebai, A.: Combinatorial particle swarm optimization (cpso) for partitional clustering problem. Applied Mathematics and Computation **192**(2), 337–345 (2007)
5. Kennedy, J., Eberhart, R.: Particle swarm optimization. In: Proceedings of IEEE International Conference on Neural Networks. vol. 4, pp. 1942–1948. Perth, Australia (1995)
6. Van der Merwe, D.W., Engelbrecht, A.P.: Data clustering using particle swarm optimization. In: IEEE Evolutionary Computation, 2003. CEC'03. The 2003 Congress on. vol. 1, pp. 215–220 (2003)
7. Mir, M.G., Tadayon Tabrizi, G.: Improving data clustering using fuzzy logic and pso algorithm. In: IEEE Electrical Engineering (ICEE), 2012 20th Iranian Conference on, pp. 784–788 (2012)
8. Omran, M.G.H., Engelbrecht, A.P., Salman, A.: Dynamic clustering using particle swarm optimization with application in unsupervised image classification. Transaction on Engineering, Computing and Technology **9**, 199–204 (2005)
9. Pakhira, M.K., Bandyopadhyay, S., Maulik, U.: Validity index for crisp and fuzzy clusters. Pattern recognition **37**(3), 487–501 (2004)
10. Pan, S.M., Cheng, K.S.: Evolution-based tabu search approach to automatic clustering. IEEE Transaction on Systems Man, and Cybernetics, Part C: Applications and Reviews **37**(5), 827–838 (2007)
11. UCI: UCI Repository of Machine Learning Databases. http://archive.ics.uci.edu/ml/
12. Yang, S.L., Li, Y.S., Hu, X.X., Pan, R.Y.: Optimization study on k value of k-means algorithm. Systems Engineering Theory & Practice **26**(2), 97–101 (2006)

Metaheuristics for Solving a Hybrid Flexible Flowshop Problem with Sequence-Dependent Setup Times

Aymen Sioud$^{(\boxtimes)}$, Caroline Gagné, and Marc Gravel

Département d'informatique et de mathématique,
Université du Québec à Chicoutimi, 555 Boulevard Université,
Chicoutimi, Québec G7H 2B1, Canada
{asioud,c3gagne,mgravel}@uqac.ca

Abstract. In this paper, we propose three new metaheuristic implementations to address the problem of minimizing the makespan in a hybrid flexible flowshop with sequence-dependent setup times. The first metaheuristic is a genetic algorithm (GA) embedding two new crossover operators, and the second is an ant colony optimization (ACO) algorithm which incorporates a transition rule featuring lookahead information and past information based on archive concepts such as the multiobjective evolutionary computation. The third metaheuristic is a hybridization (HGA) of the GA and the ACO algorithms. Numerical experiments were performed to compare the performance of the proposed algorithms on different benchmarks from the literature. The algorithms are compared with the best algorithms from the literature. The results indicate that our algorithms generate better solutions than those of the known reference sets.

Keywords: ACO · Genetic Algorithm · Hybrid Metaheuristics · Scheduling · Hybrid flowshop · Makespan · Sequence-dependent setup times

1 Introduction

Among production scheduling systems, the flowshop is one of the most well-studied environments. In this configuration, all jobs follow the same routing scheme. The associated problem can be considered as a basic model for several variants of real problems. Moreover, real production systems rarely employ a single machine at each stage. Therefore, the regular flowshop problem is often extended to a set of usually identical parallel machines at each stage. That is, instead of having a series of machines, we have a series of stages. The goal here is to increase the capacity and the outflow of the production system and to reduce the impact of bottleneck stages on overall shop efficiency. It is also frequent in practice to have optional treatments for products, like polishing or additional decorations in ceramic manufacturing as examples [2, 21]. In this latter case some jobs will skip some stages. We obtain thereby the hybrid flexible flowshop.

© Springer International Publishing Switzerland 2014
P. Siarry et al. (Eds.): ICSIBO 2014, LNCS 8472, pp. 9–25, 2014.
DOI: 10.1007/978-3-319-12970-9_2

Furthermore, in many industries such as pharmaceutics, metallurgy, ceramics and automotive manufacturing, we often have setup times on equipment between two different jobs. Many authors assume that setup times are negligible, or a part of the job processing time. But explicit setup times must be included in scheduling decisions in order to model a more realistic variant of hybrid flowshop scheduling problems. These setup times may or may not be sequence-dependent. [6] reported that 70% of industrial activities include dependent setup times. More recently, [3] pointed out in 250 industrial projects that 50% of these projects contain setup dependent times and when these setup times are applied, 92% of the order deadline could be met. Production of good schedules often relies on good management of these setup times [1, 29].

The present paper considers the hybrid flexible flowshop problem with sequence-dependent setup times (SDST/HFFS) minimizing the makespan. In accordance with the notation for hybrid flowshops introduced by [26] who extended the well-known three fields notation $\alpha/\beta/\gamma$ of [8], this problem is noted as $((PM)^{(i)})_{i=1}^{m}/F_j, s_{ijk}/C_{max}$. [9] showed that the flowshop with multiple processors (FSMP) problem with only two stages ($m = 2$), which can be considered as a special case of the SDST/HFFS problem, is NP-hard, and therefore the SDST/HFFS problem studied in this paper is also NP-hard.

The $((PM)^{(i)})_{i=1}^{m}/F_j, s_{ijk}/C_{max}$ problem may be defined as a set of N jobs, $N=\{1,..., n\}$, available for processing at time zero on a set of M stages, $M=\{1,..., m\}$. At every stage i, $i \in M$, we have a set of M_i, $M_i=\{1,..., m_i\}$, identical parallel machines. Every machine at each stage can process all the jobs. Each job has to be processed in exactly one of the M_i identical parallel machines at stage i. However, some jobs will skip some stages. F_j denotes the set of stages that the job j, $j \in N$ has to visit. Furthermore, only stage skipping is allowed, so it is not possible for a given job to visit stages $\{1, 2, 3\}$ and another one to visit stages $\{3, 2, 1\}$. p_{ij} denotes the processing time of job j at stage i. Finally, s_{ijk} denotes the setup time between jobs j and k, $k \in N$ at stage i. The optimization criterion is the minimization of the maximum completion time or makespan, which is calculated as $C_{max} = max_{j \in N}\{C_j\}$.

Considering the completion time criterion for a regular flowshop problem, a simple permutation of the jobs in an array constitutes the most widely used encoding for the sequences. Nevertheless, when we handle a hybrid flowshop scheduling problem with this kind of representation, two main decisions have to be taken : (i) determine the job sequence at the beginning of each stage, and (ii) assign jobs to machines at each stage. For the HFFS problem, the job sequence at the first stage is normally determined by the outcome of the scheduling algorithms. For subsequent stages, the jobs are sorted in increasing value of their completion times in the previous stage. Furthermore, in the case of HFFS without setup times, assigning jobs at each stage to the first available machine (FAM), which results in the earliest completion time for the jobs in that stage, represents a possibility as the assigning decision. However, in the case of the SDST/HFFS we use the earliest completion time (ECT) rule which incorporates the incurred setup times between two jobs when calculating the job completion times. These completion times are calculated as $C_{ij} = max\{C_{i,j-1}, C_{i-1,j}\}+$ $S_{i,j-1,j} + p_{ij}$, where $C_{i,j-1}$ is the completion time of the previous job in the sequence that was assigned to the same machine as job j at stage i. Similarly, $C_{i-1,j}$ is the completion time of job j at the previous stage that this job visited. [17] enhance the ECT rule with the fast earliest completion time rule (FECT). This technique arranges the jobs in the same relative order when they have the same ready times at each stage. The authors show that this technique be very effective in the presence of stage skipping. We will use the FECT rule in the rest of the paper.

In this work, to solve the SDST/HFFS problem, we introduce new crossover operators in a genetic algorithm (GA), a new transition rule in an ant colony optimization algorithm (ACO) and a new hybrid metaheuristic involving the GA and the ACO. These represent the main contribution of this paper. The innovative GA and ACO are designed and developed to adapt to the treated problem. Both are then combined to create a new hybrid metaheuristic GA/ACO with features not seen in the traditional GA and ACO. All the proposed approach are essentially based on adapting their different mechanisms to the specifics of the problem studied.

The body of this paper is organized into five sections. Section 2 provides a brief literature review of the SDST/HFFS problem. Section 3 describes the proposed GA, while Section 4 and Section 5 describe the ACO algorithm and the hybrid genetic algorithm (HGA), respectively. The computational testing and discussion are presented in Section 6. Finally, we conclude with some remarks and future research directions.

2   Literature Review of SDST/HFFS

There is not much published research on the SDST/HFFS problem. To our knowledge, there are only papers proposing heuristics and/or metaheuristics for this problem. [13] introduced dispatching rules based on greedy methods, insertion heuristic and an adaption of Johnson's rule. Later, they [14] formulated an integer programming (IP) model and developed random keys genetic algorithm (RKGA). The results showed that the IP model does not easily solve the SDST/HFFS problem and that the RKGA outperforms the dispatching rules of [13] and other heuristics. All the algorithms are tested on generated problem data. [28] proposed an immune algorithm (IA) which outperform the RKGA of [14]. The authors used a real representation for individuals and the order crossover (OX) as the crossover operator. [16] proposed a simulated annealing (SA) using pair-wise and inverse interchange as moving operators. They also used the Shortest Processing Time Cyclic Heuristic of [14], showing that the SA outperforms the RKGA of [14] and the IA of [28]. [17] proposed a dynamic dispatching rule heuristic and an iterated local search (ILS). They also proposed 960 test instances and compared their approaches to the dispatching rules of [13], the RKGA of [14], the IA of [28] and the GA of [21] which is used for a different problem. The results showed that their ILS with different encoding scheme gives better results than all the other algorithms. [7] proposed an agent-based genetic algorithm using the Similar Block 2-Point Order Crossover (S2BOX) of [21] and introducing the agent-solution scheme to solve the SDST/HFFS problem.

There are studies about related problems with a more complex setting and/or variations of the SDST/HFFS problem. [21] discussed also the SDST/HFFS problem but they assumed that some machines are not eligible to perform some jobs. They proposed a genetic algorithm using new and classic crossover operators from the literature. [22] proposed two iterated greedy heuristic (IGH) for the SDST/HFFS problem with the objectives of minimizing the makespan and the weighted tardiness. In this paper the authors consider release dates for machines, machine eligibility, possibility of the setup times to be both anticipatory and non-anticipatory, precedence constraints and time lags. [11] proposed three heuristics, based on Shortest Processing Time (SPT), Longest Processing Time (LPT) and the Johnson rule, and two metaheuristics based on a genetic algorithm and simulated annealing, to solve the SDST/HFFS problem with machine availability constraints. [12] proposed an immune algorithm (IA) for solving the SDST/HFFS problem with time lags on the machines comparing it with the IP model on small instances. [18] studied a hybrid flowshop with setup times where no flexibility is considered. They proposed a variation of simulated annealing using the Taguchi method and minimizing the makespan and the maximum tardiness.

3 A Genetic Algorithm for the SDST/HFFS

Genetic algorithms are methods based upon biological mechanisms such as the genetic inheritance laws of Mendel and the natural selection concept of Darwin, where the best adapted species survive. The basic concepts of GAs have been described by [10]. He explains how to add intelligence to a program by using the crossover exchange of genetic material and transfer which is a source of genetic diversity. Indeed, this kind of metaheuristic works with a set of individuals called the population. Every chromosome is evaluated and assigned a fitness value. This evolving process exchanges genetic material and uses crossover and mutation operators to transfer it, generating new individuals called offspring. Selection and replacement processes are applied to reach better individuals over the generations,converging to an optimum in the solution search space. The effectiveness of a GA depends on the choice of its operators and parameters, but also on the specific adaptation to the problem treated. In the following sections, we explain the different choices of the GA's parameters and we describe the proposed crossover operators.

3.1 Population Encoding and Initialization

A genetic algorithm works on individuals with chromosomes, which are a representation or codification of the solutions to the problem. In this case, we have chosen an ordinal genetic representation. As shown in Figure 1, the individuals *P1*, *P2*, *O1* and *O2* are identified by sequences so that each element of the sequence is associated with a numeric identifier that represents a particular job. The population size is set to 40. The initial population is randomly generated except for one individual, which is generated using the NEH Hybrid (NEHH) rule [21], an adaptation of the well known NEH heuristic [19].

3.2   Crossover Operator

The crossover operator generates offspring in general, by coalescing two parents with the objective of generating a better sequence, in this case a better makespan C_{max}. Many crossover operators from the literature are used for the permutation flowshop, such as the Partially Mapped Crossover (PMX), OX, Order Based Crossover (OBX) or Uniform Order Based Crossover (UOBX) [15]. But for regular flowshops and especially the hybrid flowshops these crossover operators give the worst results because they break the building blocks [21]. Introducing dependent setup times and job skipping will complicate the situation even more. The crossover operators that we present aim to ensure a better conservation of the relative order and the absolute order when we deal with dependent setup times. In this work we present three new crossover operators adapted for the SDST/HFFS problem.

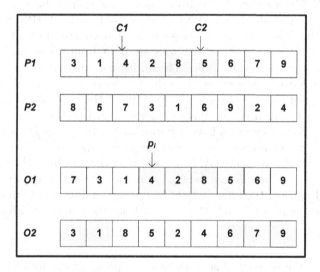

Fig. 1. Illustration of RMPX and ARMPX

The RMPX Crossover. The first crossover operator is the *Random Maximal Preservative Crossover* (RMPX) crossover introduced by [23], which shows good behavior when dealing with the dependent setup times but for a single machine. RMPX is defined as follows : (i) two parents *P1* and *P2* are considered and two distinct crossover points $C1$ and $C2$ are selected randomly, as shown in Figure 1; (ii) an insertion point p_i is then randomly chosen in the offspring $O1$, p_i being a random number in the interval $[1, n - (C2 - C1)]$; (iii) the part $[C1, C2]$ of $P1$, shaded in Figure 1, is inserted in the offspring $O1$ from p_i, from the position 4 as shown in Figure 1; and (iv) the rest of the offspring $O1$ is completed from $P2$ in the order of appearance from its first position. To generate the second offspring, we just reverse the roles of the two parents P1 and P2 and repeat the same process.

The ARMPX Crossover. The second crossover operator is the *Antagonist Random Maximal Preservative Crossover* (ARMPX), an adaptation of the RMPX crossover where in steps *(ii)* and *(iii)* we insert the parents' first and last parts instead of the part $[C1, C2]$ in the offspring (shaded in $O2$ in Figure 1). After that, the rest of the offspring is completed from the other parent in the order of appearance from its first position. As shown in Figure 1, from parents $P1$ and $P2$ we obtain the offspring $O2$ when applying the ARMPX crossover. The aim here is to preserve the two building blocks in the front and the back of the parent, and to preserve the relative order in the insertion section.

The LJMPX Crossover. The third crossover operator is the *List Jobs Maximal Preservative Crossover* (LJMPX) which works like the RMPX crossover for the first 3 steps. This crossover represent the first contribution in this paper. After inserting the cross section, two lists are built from the second parent $P2$ which contains the unscheduled jobs. The LL list contains the jobs which will be inserted to the left of this section while the RL list contains the jobs which will be inserted to the right. An approximate value of the makespan $\overline{C}_{max}$ is then calculated with a sequence containing the subsequence $[C1, C2]$ in the offspring and where the rest of the jobs have a normalized value $\overline{p}_{ij}$, using a normalized setup time $\overline{s}_{ijk}$ which represents the average processing time and setup time for the unscheduled jobs, respectively. Next, we insert the jobs from the corresponding lists one by one, minimizing the $\overline{C}_{max}$ until we obtain a complete sequence. As shown in Figure 2, the offspring $O3$ is a potential offspring from parents $P1$ and $P2$ where the lists LL and RL are built from the parent $P2$ after inserting the part $[C1, C2]$ from position p_i.

The MPOBX Crossover. The last crossover operator introduced in this paper is the *Maximum Preservative Order Block Crossover* (MPOBX) which works as follows. First, from the two parents, we insert the longest job blocks at the same positions, using four crossover points. After that, as in the LJMPX crossover, we calculate an approximate value $\overline{C}_{max}$ using the $\overline{p}_{ij}$ and $\overline{s}_{ijk}$ for the unscheduled job positions. Then we insert the remaining unscheduled jobs as in the LJMPX crossover, from a single job list. As shown in Figure 3, we insert the block $\{3, 1, 4\}$ from $P1$ and block $\{9, 7, 2\}$ from $P2$. The unscheduled job list contains jobs 5, 6 and 8. These jobs will be inserted one by one using the $\overline{C}_{max}$ value.

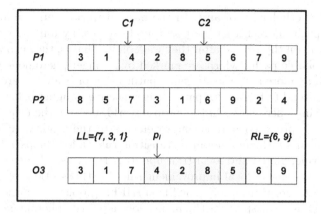

Fig. 2. Illustration of LJMPX

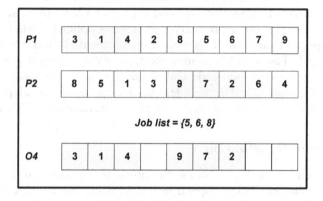

Fig. 3. Illustration of MPOBX

Finally, we set the probability p_c of crossover to 0.8. So, at each generation, $N * 0.8$ offspring will be generated. This crossover represents the second contribution in this paper.

3.3   Mutation Operator, Selection and Replacement Schemes

Mutation consists of exchanging the position of two distinct jobs randomly chosen. The probability p_m of a mutation occurring is set to 0.01. The chromosome selection for the crossover is done using a stochastic binary tournament. The replacement is elitist and uses the $(\lambda + \mu)$ scheme.

4   Ant Colony Optimization for the SDST/HFFS

The ant colony optimization (ACO) is a population based metaheuristic designed to solve combinatorial optimization problems, introduced by [4] and inspired by studies of the behavior of ants. In the natural world, ants are able to find the shortest path between their nest and food sources, by following a chemical pheromone trail on the ground after they walk on it. That is, they choose the way with more probable paths, which are marked by stronger pheromone concentrations. Indeed, as more ants use the same path, more pheromones are deposited and more ants tend to follow this path. This collective foraging behavior, deposing and following pheromones in the natural world, became the inspiring source of the ACO. [5] proposed notable improvements to the original ACO version. The improvements include a modified transition rule called the pseudo-random-proportional rule, global and local trail updating rules, use of restricted candidates list and the use of local improvement rules. In this section we describe in detail the ACO algorithm to solve the SDST/HFFS problem with the objectives of minimizing the makespan. In the main loop, after the pheromone initialization, has five steps where a ants construct a sequence of N jobs : *(i)* an initial job is set ; *(ii)* each ant builds a job sequence using the pseudo random proportional transition rule in Equations (1) and (2) ; *(iii)* a local pheromone update is performed ; *(iv)* a local improvement heuristic is applied ; and *(v)* a global pheromone update is applied. This main loop is executed until a stopping criterion is reached. The loop is executed for t_{max} cycles, as shown in Figure 4, representing a generic pseudo code embedding the new transition rule shown in Equations (1) and (2). The new transition rule has been adapted to the SDST/HFFS problem. This represents the third contribution in this paper.

4.1   Algorithm Initialization

At each iteration, given that a job i is the previous job added to the sequence, an ant chooses the next job to append by considering, among other factors, the pheromone trail intensity $\tau_{ij}(t)$ which is initialized to a small positive quantity τ_0 for all pair of jobs (i,j), i.e., $\tau_{ij}(0) = \tau_0$. Afterward, the pheromone trail will contain information based on the solution quality and the number of time that ants chose to visit job j after job i.

4.2   Setting Up the Initial Job

Each job has an initial setup time at each stage i on a machine m_i and this setup is taken into account when calculating the makespan. Therefore, to maintain diversity and for each job sequence constructed by the a ants, the first job is chosen pseudo-randomly. This choice is based on the earliest completion time on the first stage.

4.3   Building a Sequence

From an existing partial job sequence, each ant builds a sequence using the pseudo random proportional transition rule in Equations (1) and (2). In Equation (1), q is a random number and q_0 is a parameter; both are between 0 and 1.

```
/* STEP 0 : Pheromone Initialization */
for all job pair (i,j) do
    τij(0) = τ0
end for
/* Main Loop */
for t = 1 → tmax do
    /* STEP 1 : Set initial job */
    for k = 1 → m do
        Set the initial job for the ant k
    end for
    /* STEP 2 : Build a sequence */
    for i = 2 → n do
        for k = 1 → m do
            Choose the next job to insert using the Equations 1 and 2
            /* STEP 3 : Local pheromone update */
            for all chosen job pair (i,j) do
                τij(t) = pt * τij(t) + (1 − pt) * Δτij(t) where Δτij = τ0
            end for
        end for
    end for
    /* STEP 4 : Local improvement */
    for k = 1 → m do
        Apply local improvement method or-opt heuristic
    end for
    /* STEP 5 : Global pheromone update */
    for all adjacent job pair (i,j) ∈ the best sequence Q* do
        τij(t) = pt * τij(t) + (1 − pt) * Δτij(t) where Δτij = 1/L*
    end for
end for
```

Fig. 4. The ACO pseudo-code

The parameter q_0 determines the relative importance of the existing information exploitation and the new solution search space exploration. Indeed, Equation (1) states that the next job will be chosen by a greedy rule when $q \leq q_0$ or by the probabilistic rule of Equation (2) when $q > q_0$. Equation (2) describes the biased exploration rule p_{ij} also adapted to the $((PM)^{(i)})_{i=1}^{m}/F_j, s_{ijk}/C_{max}$ problem when inserting job j after job i.

In these equations, the elements $\tau_{ij}(t)$ and η_{ij} represent the pheromone trail and the visibility, respectively. Concerning the visibility, η_{ij} represents the inverse of the largest completion time among all the jobs in the list of the unselected jobs. Obviously, the completion time includes the setup times between the last scheduled job and the next one. The element $SUCC_{ij}(A_t)$ represents the past information, which is introduced by a matrix built from an archive that stores the best solutions throughout the evolution process, as in some cases in multi-objective evolutionary algorithms using the Pareto-optimal concept. This concept was first introduced in transition rules by [23]; it plays the role of a long-term memory. Here, we adapt them for our problem. From the archive we build a matrix which computes the number of times that a job j follows a job i in the

$$j = \begin{cases} arg\ max \left\{ \left[\tau_{ij}(t)\right]^{\alpha} \times \left[SUCC_{ij}(A_t)\right]^{\beta} \times \left[\eta_{ij}\right]^{\delta} \times \left[\dfrac{1}{\overline{H_{ij}}}\right]^{\phi} \right\} & if\ q \leq q_0 \\ \\ J & if\ q > q_0 \end{cases}$$

$$(1)$$

where J is chosen according to the probability p_{ij}

$$p_{ij}(t) = \frac{\left[\tau_{ij}(t)\right]^{\alpha} \times \left[SUCC_{ij}(A_t)\right]^{\beta} \times \left[\eta_{ij}\right]^{\delta} \times \left[\dfrac{1}{\overline{H_{ij}}}\right]^{\phi}}{\sum \left[\tau_{ij}(t)\right]^{\alpha} \times \left[SUCC_{ij}(A_t)\right]^{\beta} \times \left[\eta_{ij}\right]^{\delta} \times \left[\dfrac{1}{\overline{H_{ij}}}\right]^{\phi}} \qquad (2)$$

archive solutions. Finally, the element H_{ij} represents the lookahead information which use an heuristic that anticipates the choices in the transition rule. This heuristic is based on an upper bound of the makespan, using the average values of processing time $\overline{p_{ij}}$ and the normalized setup times $\overline{s_{ijk}}$ for the unscheduled jobs.

4.4   Local Trail Updating

Once the ants generate a solution, for each pair of jobs (i,j) the pheromone level on the path is updated using a local update rule as in Equation (3)

$$\tau_{ij}(t) = p \times \tau_{ij}(t) + (1 - p) \times \Delta\tau_{ij}(t) \qquad (3)$$

where $\Delta\tau_{ij} = \tau_0$ and $0 \leq p \leq 1$ is a constant parameter.

4.5   Local Improvement

After computing the makespan of the generated sequence by the ant, we apply a local improvement under probability p_{LI}. For that, we use a simple local search generating a neighborhood using a swap move.

4.6   Global Trail Updating

The pheromone trail is updated at the end of the cycle, but only for the job pairs (i,j) in the best solution with makespan C^* found in the cycle. The global update rule is executed using Equation (4)

$$\tau_{ij}(t) = p_t \times \tau_{ij}(t) + (1 - p_t) \times \Delta\tau_{ij}(t) \qquad (4)$$

where $\Delta\tau_{ij} = 1/C^*$ and $0 \leq p_t \leq 1$ is a constant parameter.

4.7   Parameter Initialization

The trail pheromone is initialized to the value $\tau_0 = (N * L_r)^{-1}$ where N is the job number and L_r is the makespan value of a randomly generated sequence. The other parameters have been assigned the following values : $p = p_t = 0.9$, the ant number $a = 10$ and $q_0 = 0.9$. The parameters α, β, ϕ and δ associated with the four matrices in the transition rule were set to identical values for all the problems. These parameters were adjusted following empirical tests on different instances. The four parameters α, β, ϕ and δ have been assigned the values 4, 2, 3 and 3, respectively. Finally, the archive size and the local improvement probability p_{LI} have been assigned the values 20 and 0.2, respectively.

5   Hybrid Metaheuristic GA/ACO for the SDST/HFFS

We introduce here a collaborative hybridization [20] at the LJMPX crossover introduced in Section 3.2. Indeed, we use the ACO algorithm introduced in Section 4 to fill either the right part or the left part or both. Inserting the jobs on the right of the cross section is similar to the operating of a classical ant. From the last inserted job i in the cross section, a job j is chosen according to the pseudo-random-proportional transition rule expressed in Equations (1) and (2) using the jobs in the right list.

Since the cross section is already set, inserting the remaining jobs on the left of this section can be done either from the first offspring position from left to right as a classical ant or inversely from the first cross section position. During the application of the crossover, we use equiprobably one of the two methods of left insertion. Finally, in the case of inserting jobs from right to left, we make some adaptations in Equations (1) and (2). The hybridization represents the fourth contribution in this paper when using new features in both GA and ACO.

6   Computational Results and Discussion

The benchmark problem set is available from http://soa.iti.es and consists of 960 problem tests. The instances are combinations of N and M, where $N = \{20, 50, 80, 150\}$ and $M = \{2, 4, 8\}$. The processing times are generated from a uniform [1, 99] distribution. The setup times are generated according to four distributions [1, 25], [1, 50], [1, 99] and [1, 125]. This corresponds to a ratio between setup and processing times of 25%, 50%, 100% and 125%, respectively. There is a group with two parallel machines per stage and groups where the number of parallel machines at each stage is sampled from a uniform distribution in the range [1, 4]. The probability of skipping a stage for each job is set at 0.10 and 0.40. All the experiments were run on an Intel Core 2.8 GHz processors and 4 GB of main memory. To evaluate the performance of the other proposed algorithm, we will conduct statistical analysis and comparisons with the results of [17], where, the authors compare an iterated local search (ILS) to several metaheuristics and heuristics as the RKGA of [14], the IA of [28], the genetic algorithm (GAR) of [21] and the dispatching rules of [13] to cite these methods among others. Many of these compared methods are adapted to the treated problem and recoded for suited comparison purposes. The authors show that the ILS and the GAR represent the best method. So we will compare our algorithm results to these methods. We know that using fixed number of evaluations of the objective function to compare different algorithms allows fair comparisons, but we do not have these information for the reference algorithms. So, we use the same stopping criterion as used in [17], i.e., time computation.

It is important to note that our experiment environment is different from that of [17]. Therefore, we use the following website references [24] and [25] to determine the performance ratio between the two computers. In order to obtain a reliable comparison, all the experiments were done with the stopping criterion set to $n^2 \times m \times 1.5 \times 0.78 \ ms$ elapsed CPU time ([17] used $n^2 \times m \times 1.5 \ ms$ elapsed CPU time as the stopping criterion for all the compared algorithms). To evaluate the different algorithms we use the performance measure in Equation (5) :

% Increase Over the Best Solution

$$= \frac{Heu_{sol} - Best_{sol}}{Best_{sol}} \times 100 \qquad (5)$$

where Heu_{sol} is the best makespan obtained by a given algorithm after 10 executions and $Best_{sol}$ is the best known makespan.

First, we produce experiments in order to compare crossover operators embedded in the GA independently : OX, PMX, UOBX [15], S2BOX, used in the GAR [21], RMPX [23], ARMPX, LJMPX and MPOBX. Each crossover operator is embedded independently in the GA presented in Section 3 with 500 generations as the stopping criterion. The result summaries are presented in Table 1. Indeed, the results represent the group instances average, and the best averages are in boldface type.

As shown in this table, the *List Jobs Maximal Preservative Crossover* (LJMPX) and the *Maximum Preservative Order Block Crossover* (MPOBX) present the best results among the eight tested, and their results are very similar except for the large instances where LJMPX allows for achieving a slightly better average. This supports the idea that these two crossover operators are more adapted to the studied problem. Indeed, using the approximate value of the makespan when fulfilling the unscheduled jobs in the sequence gives the two crossover operators more accuracy when dealing with more stages. Also, using the list jobs allows us to better optimize the setup times when choosing jobs to insert.

Furthermore, maintaining the blocks of jobs in the crossover operators improves the performance of the algorithms, i.e., the LJMPX maintains the cross section while the MPOBX maintains blocks from the two parents. Hence, both crossover operators take greater account of the relative and absolute position of jobs when maintaining blocks. Finally, as shown in Table 1, MPOBX allows us to achieve a slightly better average than LJMPX, particularly for larger instances. This can be explained by the fact that MPOBX conserve more absolute positions when maintaining blocks from parents. Moreover, LJMPX compensates this behavior by

Table 1. Comparison of different crossovers (% Increase over the best solution)

Instances	OX	PMX	UOBX	S2BOX	RMPX	ARMPX	LJMPX	MPOBX
20*2	7.82	7.27	7.43	6.93	5.13	4.39	3.78	**3.39**
20*4	5.25	8.25	8.15	3.89	5.65	5.24	2.80	**2.27**
20*8	6.87	6.40	8.44	3.09	5.71	6.31	2.85	**2.49**
50*2	8.36	6.23	9.24	9.01	5.82	4.82	3.81	**3.26**
50*4	7.33	7.39	9.53	5.85	6.69	4.24	2.74	**1.85**
50*8	9.35	12.24	8.97	3.79	6.67	4.28	**3.73**	3.75
80*2	5.29	9.31	7.84	8.28	5.64	4.19	2.90	**2.06**
80*4	8.23	8.39	9.49	7.39	6.63	5.70	**2.74**	2.84
80*8	10.27	10.43	10.19	6.53	6.56	5.95	3.78	**3.48**
120*2	8.05	7.27	9.19	10.58	7.65	7.45	**3.87**	4.02
120*4	9.30	10.39	8.97	9.04	6.62	8.23	**5.95**	6.02
120*8	10.31	13.13	10.82	10.59	8.78	9.82	**6.81**	7.21
Average	8.04	8.89	9.02	7.08	6.46	5.89	3.81	**3.55**

providing more exploration when inserting the cross section but conserving the relative order and consequently conserving the setup times between jobs especially when the setup times have a significant impact when calculating the makespan. This mechanism allows LJMPX to achieve a slightly better average for the large instances where more exploration is needed to obtain better results.

We proceed now with the comparisons of the proposed algorithms (GA, ACO and HGA) against the ILS of [17] and the GAR of [21]. These two algorithms have shown high performance in the original papers in which they were proposed [17, 21]. The authors compare these algorithms with four high performing algorithms : two genetic algorithms, immune algorithm and ant colony optimization. To sum up, the ILS and GAR algorithms showed the best results in their respective studies. The GA version retained here is the one embedding the two crossover operators LJMPX and MPOBX. The choice of the crossover to apply is made randomly, i.e., by a fair coin toss. This policy was chosen as result of computational experiments. The results are presented in Table 2; they also represent the group instances averages. The best averages are also in boldface type.

The first observation is that the new GA and ACO algorithms always provide a better average than the ILS and the GAR algorithms. Also, if we compare the GA and ACO algorithms, the first provides a better average on all the group instances except for the 20×2, 50×2, 80×2 and the 120×2 group instances where the ACO does slightly better. These group instances are those with 2 stages. It seems that the transition rule embedded in the ACO algorithm performs better in these configurations. In general, the GA has a better average than the ACO, with 0.60 and 0.76, respectively. We can also remark that there is a non negligible improvement in comparison with the ILS and the GAR averages.

Now, if we focus on the HGA algorithm results, we can see that this algorithm provides the better average for all the group instances except for the 20×2 group

Table 2. Comparison of the ILS [17], the GAR [21], the ACO, the GA and the HGA (% Increase over the best solution)

Instances	GA	ACO	HGA	ILS	GAR
20*2	0.75	**0.49**	0.51	1.70	3.82
20*4	0.51	0.69	**0.49**	1.90	3.90
20*8	0.43	0.75	**0.40**	1.70	4.02
50*2	0.69	0.61	**0.55**	2.72	4.65
50*4	0.52	0.90	**0.36**	2.98	4.73
50*8	0.66	1.12	**0.45**	3.48	5.01
80*2	0.59	0.58	**0.45**	3.29	5.29
80*4	0.48	0.74	**0.44**	2.01	4.87
80*8	0.71	1.04	**0.51**	4.87	6.03
120*2	0.58	0.57	**0.54**	3.23	5.32
120*4	0.59	0.79	**0.51**	4.36	5.05
120*8	0.67	0.89	**0.53**	5.74	7.02
Average	**0.60**	**0.76**	**0.48**	**3.16**	**4.98**
Median	**0.53**	**0.71**	**0.36**	**2.45**	**4.81**
Std	**0.53**	**0.55**	**0.48**	**2.46**	**2.39**

where the ACO obtains a better average. Also, in the same vein, the HGA significantly improves all the average results in comparison to the ILS and the GAR algorithms. Furthermore, combining both the GA and ACO mechanisms in the HGA marginally enhances the results in comparison of the GA and the ACO algorithms. If we observe the standard deviation values, we remark that those of the proposed methods (ACO, GA and HGA) are very low. This can be explained by the effect of both mechanism used in the ACO and the GA, which use an upper bound and consequently smooth over the results.

Moreover, to significantly compare the proposed algorithms, we conducted a pairwise comparison to detect significant performance differences between all the algorithms with the non-parametric Wilcoxon signed-rank test [27] for each instance using the results of our 10 runs with an error probability of 1% over the numerical results. We remind the reader here, that the Wilcoxon test does not require assumptions regarding the distribution results. Indeed, for the purpose of a pairwise heuristics comparison, the Wilcoxon test assumes that the first heuristic median M1 equals the second heuristic median M2 hypothesis is null and that M1 ≠ M2 is the alternative hypothesis.

The Wilcoxon test results are shown in Table 3 where bold values indicate where the null hypothesis is rejected. The critical values for all tests are identical and between -2.575 and 2.757. Thus, the Wilcoxon test indicates with a confidence level of 99% that the HGA algorithm statistically outperforms all other methods. Moreover, GA statistically outperforms ACO, ILS and GAR. Further more, ACO surpasses ILS and GAR. Finally, regarding the quality solutions, we obtain the following ranking : HGA-GA-ACO-ILS-GAR.

Table 3. Wilcoxon test *t-value* for the ILS [17], the GAR [21], the ACO, the GA and the HGA

	HGA	GA	ACO	ILS	GAR
HGA	--	-4.29	-10.4	-25.78	-26.71
GA		--	-6.1	-25.4	-26.7
ACO			--	-24.39	-26.66
ILS				--	-16.27
GAR					--

7   Conclusion

In this work, we have introduced three new algorithms : a genetic algorithm (GA) embedding two new crossovers, an ant colony optimization algorithm (ACO) that integrates lookahead information and archive concepts in the transition rule and a hybrid genetic algorithm (HGA) integrating the ACO in the GA crossover to minimize the makespan in a hybrid flexible flowshop with sequence-dependent setup times. The proposed approaches are essentially based on adapting different algorithm mechanisms to the specificities of the studied problem, *i.e* the crossovers in the GA and the transition rule in the ACO. Indeed, after inserting the cross section from the first parent, the two crossover operators use heuristics and lists from the second parent to insert the remaining jobs. These heuristics are replaced by the ACO algorithm in the HGA algorithm. For its part, the pseudo random proportional transition rule embedded into the ACO integrates past, present and future information to build a sequence. The numerical experiments allowed us to demonstrate the efficiency of our approaches to this problem.

Our results encourage us to use such approaches, with hybridization, for other scheduling problems in particular and other optimization problems in general. It is in this direction that our work will be directed.

References

1. Allahverdi, A., Ng, C., Cheng, T., Kovalyov, M.Y.: A survey of scheduling problems with setup times or costs. European Journal of Operational Research **187**(3), 985–1032 (2008)
2. Allahverdi, A., Soroush, H.: The significance of reducing setup times/setup costs. European Journal of Operational Research **187**(3), 978–984 (2008)
3. Conner, G.: 10 questions. Manufacturing Engineering Magazine, pp. 93–99 (2009)
4. Dorigo, M.: Optimization, Learning and Natural Algorithms. Ph.D. thesis, Politecnico di Milano, Italy (1992)
5. Dorigo, M., Gambardella, L.: Ant colony system: A cooperative learning approach to the traveling salesman problem. In: IEEE Transactions on Evolutionary Computation (1997)
6. Dudek, R., Smith, M., Panwalkar, S.: Use of a case study in sequencing/scheduling research. Omega **2**(2), 253–261 (1974)

7. Gomez-Gasquet, P., Andres, C., Lario, F.: An agent-based genetic algorithm for hybrid flowshops with sequence dependent setup times to minimise makespan. Expert Systems with Applications **39**(9), 8095–8107 (2012)

8. Graham, R.L., Lawler, E.L., Lenstra, J.K., Kan, A.G.H.R.: Optimization and approximation in deterministic sequencing and scheduling: a survey. Annals of Discrete Mathematics **5**, 287–326 (1979)

9. Gupta, J.N.D.: Two-stage, hybrid flowshop scheduling problem. The Journal of Operational Research Society **39**(4), 359–364 (1988)

10. Holland, J.H.: Adaptation in natural and Artificial Systems. MIT Press, Cambridge, MA, USA (1992)

11. Jabbarizadeh, F., Zandieh, M., Talebi, D.: Hybrid flexible flowshops with sequence-dependent setup times and machine availability constraints. Comput. Ind. Eng. **57**(3), 949–957 (2009)

12. Javadian, N., Fattahi, P., Farahmand-Mehr, M., Amiri-Aref, M., Kazemi, M.: An immune algorithm for hybrid flow shop scheduling problem with time lags and sequence-dependent setup times. The International Journal of Advanced Manufacturing Technology **63**, 337–348 (2012)

13. Kurz, M.E., Askin, R.G.: Comparing scheduling rules for flexible flow lines. International Journal of Production Economics **85**(3), 371–388 (2003)

14. Kurz, M.E., Askn, R.G.: Scheduling flexible flow lines with sequence-dependent setup times. European Journal of Operational Research **159**(1), 66–82 (2004)

15. Michalewicz, Z.: Genetic algorithms + data structures = evolution programs, 3rd edn. Springer-Verlag, London (1996)

16. Mirsanei, H., Zandieh, M., Moayed, M., Khabbazi, M.: A simulated annealing algorithm approach to hybrid flow shop scheduling with sequence-dependent setup times. Journal of Intelligent Manufacturing **22**, 965–978 (2011)

17. Naderi, B., Ruiz, R., Zandieh, M.: Algorithms for a realistic variant of flowshop scheduling. Comput. Oper. Res. **37**(2), 236–246 (2010)

18. Naderi, B., Zandieh, M., Roshanaei, V.: Scheduling hybrid flowshops with sequence dependent setup times to minimize makespan and maximum tardiness. The Internayional Journal of Advanced Manufacturing Technology **41**, 1186–1198 (2009)

19. Nawaz, M., Enscore, E.E., Ham, I.: A heuristic algorithm for the m-machine, n-job flow-shop sequencing problem. Omega **11**(1), 91–95 (1983)

20. Puchinger, J., Raidl, G.R.: Combining metaheuristics and exact algorithms in combinatorial optimization: a survey and classification. In: Mira, J., Álvarez, J.R. (eds.) IWINAC 2005. LNCS, vol. 3562, pp. 41–53. Springer, Heidelberg (2005)

21. Ruiz, R., Maroto, C.: A genetic algorithm for hybrid flowshops with sequence dependent setup times and machine eligibility. European Journal of Operational Research **169**(3), 781–800 (2006)

22. Ruiz, R., Stützle, T.: An iterated greedy heuristic for the sequence dependent setup times flowshop problem with makespan and weighted tardiness objectives. European Journal of Operational Research **187**(3), 1143–1159 (2008)

23. Sioud, A., Gravel, M., Gagné, M.: A hybrid genetic algorithm for the single machine scheduling problem with sequence-dependent setup times. Computers & OR **39**(10), 2415–2424 (2012)

24. SPEC: Intel core 2 duo p8400 @ONLINE (2009). http://www.spec.org/cpu2006/results/res2010q1/cpu2006-20100118-09344.html

25. SPEC: Intel core i7-2600 @ONLINE (2011). http://www.spec.org/cpu2006/results/res2011q3/cpu2006-20110718-17542.html

26. Vignier, A., Billaut, J.C., Proust, C.: Les problemes d'ordonnancement de type flow-shop hybride : etat de l'art. RAIRO - Operations Research - Recherche Operationnelle **33**(2), 117–183 (1999)
27. Wilcoxon, F.: Individual comparisons by ranking methods. Biometrics **1**, 80–83 (1945)
28. Zandieh, M., Fatemi Ghomi, S., Moattar Husseini, S.: An immune algorithm approach to hybrid flow shops scheduling with sequence-dependent setup times. Applied Mathematics and Computation **180**(1), 111–127 (2006)
29. Zhu, X., Wilhelm, W.E.: Scheduling and lot sizing with sequence-dependent setup: A literature review. IIE Transactions **38**(11), 987–1007 (2006)

Using Particle Swarm Optimization Method to Invert Active Surface Waves

Rashed Poormirzaee[(⊠)] and Rasoul Hamidzadeh Moghadam

Sahand University of Technology, Tabriz, Iran
rashed.poormirzaee@gmail.com, rhamidzm@yahoo.com

Abstract. The inversion of surface wave is an estimation of the earth's properties from the measured surface wave data. The surface wave inversion cannot be solved directly, requiring an optimization technique to find the most probable solution in a pool of infinite candidates. With the development of data optimization methods, fast and easier approaches can be conducted for inversion of geophysical data. This study proposes Particle Swarm Optimization (PSO) algorithm for inversion of Multichannel Analysis of Surface Wave (MASW) method as an active geophysical technique. So, first we developed PSO code in Matlab for inversion of MASW data and then the efficiency of proposed algorithm investigated by inversion of a synthetic model and a real data set. Experiments on both synthetic model and real data set demonstrate that the proposed algorithm performs well. Moreover finding shows that PSO algorithm is powerful, fast and easy for inversion of active surface waves data.

Keywords: MASW · PSO · Inversion

1 Introduction

One of the fields of studies that had been a huge effect on engineering science progress is optimization techniques. In general, optimization algorithms can be divided into two categories: deterministic algorithms, and stochastic algorithms. Deterministic algorithms follow a rigorous procedure and its path and values of both design variables and the functions are repeatable. Most conventional or classic algorithms are deterministic (e.g. Simplex method). On the other hand, the stochastic algorithms always have some randomness. For stochastic algorithms, we have in general two types: heuristic and metaheuristic, though their difference is small. Further development over the heuristic algorithms is the so-called metaheuristic algorithms. They generally perform better than simple heuristics. In addition, all metaheuristic algorithms use certain tradeoff of randomization and local search [1]. PSO algorithm is one of the global optimization methods that belong to group of metaheuristic searching algorithms. Inverse theory is an organized set of mathematical techniques for reducing data to obtain useful information about the physical world on the basis of inference drawn from observation [2]. Inversion of geophysical data consists of operating directly on those data so as to generate a view of the structure which causes

© Springer International Publishing Switzerland 2014
P. Siarry et al. (Eds.): ICSIBO 2014, LNCS 8472, pp. 26–34, 2014.
DOI: 10.1007/978-3-319-12970-9_3

them [3]. To solve an inverse problem design of three step is vital : i)parameterization of the system(i.e., discovery of a minimal set of model parameters whose values completely characterize the system), ii) forward modeling (i.e., discovery of the physical laws allowing us, for given values of the model parameters, to make prediction on the results of measurements on some observable parameters), iii)inverse modeling (i.e. use of the actual results of some measurements of the observable parameters to infer the actual values of the model parameters) [4]. Most geophysical inversion methods are based on linearized techniques to estimate the parameters of model in an iterative manner; i.e., using local optimization algorithm to modify a starting model that user defined it. At each iteration, a better estimate of the model is calculated by linearizing the problem and the best solution, minimizing a misfit function, is obtained after a few iterations [5]. Since most geophysical inverse problems are nonlinear, hence have non-linear misfit functions (e.g. RMS travel-time error), the solution is quite often trapped to local minima during the application of local optimization methods. As a result, their success depends on the initial model to the "true" global-minimum solution. But global optimization algorithms include the ability to produce solutions independent on the initial model, to explore the model space in more detail and, thus, a better chance to find the "true" global minimum solution [6, 7]. So, by finding of global minimum of misfit function the best solution of problem could be reach. Therefore using an optimization algorithm in inversion of geophysical data that satisfy above condition for finding best solution is an important issue. In geophysical surveys, there have recently been emerged several significant PSO applications. The PSO on a multilayered 1D vertical electric sounding (VES), induced polarization (IP), magnetotelluric (MT) methods both synthetic and field data have successfully been carried out by Shaw and Srivastava (2007)[8]. Naudet et al. (2008) [9] have studied water table estimation using the PSO on self-potential (SP) data. Inversion of a VES data for environmental applications by the GPSO algorithm has successfully been performed by Fernández Martínez and García Gonzalo (2008)[10]. Yuan et al. (2009)[11] have demonstrated PSO worked on seismic wavelet estimation and gravity anomalies as well. Also they concluded that the PSO inversion method have the attributes of higher convergence speed and accuracy than conventional GA and SA methods. Fernández Martínez et al. (2010) [12] present the application of a whole family of PSO algorithms to the analysis and solution of a VES inverse problem associated with a seawater intrusion in a coastal aquifer in southern Spain. Pekşen et al. (2011) [13] by application of PSO algorithm have inverted self-potential (SP) data. In recent years Rayleigh waves have attracted the interest of a constantly increasing number of researchers from different disciplines for a wide range of applications [14]. Once Rayleigh wave dispersion curve is properly identified, its inversion is the key point to obtain a reliable near-surface S-wave velocity profile. PSO is a novel and powerful technique in geophysical data interpretation. In this study, we demonstrate a PSO application on MASW data inversion. To evaluate efficiency and stability of PSO to invert MASW data, we first developed PSO code in Matlab and then investigated on a synthetic model. Finally, the PSO inversion algorithm in MASW data was applied in a case study at the part of Tabriz city in north-West of Iran for hazard assessment. Also in order to solve the forward modeling and estimate the theoretical dispersion curve the code based on the matrix algorithm developed by Herrmann (1987) [15]was used. Results from synthetic model and real data demonstrate that particle swarm optimization can be used for processing of MASW data.

2   Multichannel Analysis of Surface Waves (MASW) Method

Shallow shear-wave velocity (Vs) has long been recognized as a key factor in variable ground-motion amplification and site response in sedimentary basins [16].

In general, borehole logging is considered the standard for obtaining Vs data, but drilling and logging to the depths generally required for earthquake ground-motion investigations is very expensive, and it is becoming increasingly problematic in heavily urbanized settings [17]. This has led to the development of numerous surface acquisition methods to measure shallow Vs. Multichannel Analysis of Surface Waves (MASW) [18] is one of the most recently developed surface acquisition technique for determining shallow shear-wave velocity. The MASW method was originally developed as a land survey method to investigate the near-surface materials for their elastic properties: for example, Vs, by recording and analyzing Rayleigh-type surface waves using a vertical (impulsive) seismic source and receivers. The acquired data are first analyzed for dispersion characteristics and, from these the shear-wave velocity is estimated using an inversion technique. In land applications, the MASW method has been successfully applied to map 2D bedrock surface, zones of low strength, Poisson's ratio, voids, as well as to generate VS profiles for various other geotechnical problems [19]. Unlike other seismic methods (e.g., reflection or refraction), acquisition parameters for MASW surveys have quite a wide range of tolerance. This is because the multichannel processing schemes employed in the wavefield transformation method have the capability to automatically account for such otherwise adverse effects as near-field, far-field, and spatial aliasing effects [18]. Stephenson et al. (2005)[17] conducted a blind comparison of MASW and ReMi results with four boreholes logged to at least 260 m for shear velocity in Santa Clara Valley, California, to determine how closely these surface methods match the downhole measurements. They suggested MASW and ReMi surface acquisition methods can both be appropriate choices for estimating shear wave velocity and can be complementary to each other in urban settings for hazards assessment. Also Park and Miller (2005) [19] successfully applied MASW method for seismic characterization of wind Turbine sites in Kansas.

3   PSO Algorithm

Particle swarm optimization (PSO) is a stochastic evolutionary computation technique for optimization in many different engineering fields, which is inspired by the social behavior of individuals (called particles) in groups in nature, such as a flock (swarm) of birds searching for food [20,21]. Particle swarm optimization may have some similarities with genetic algorithms and ant algorithms, but it is much simpler because it does not use mutation/crossover operators or pheromone. This algorithm searches the space of an objective function by adjusting the trajectories of individual agents, called particles, as these trajectories form piecewise paths in a quasi-stochastic manner [1]. The particles are moving towards promising regions of the search space by exploiting information springing from their own experience during the search, as well as the experience of other particles. For this purpose, a separate memory is used where each particle stores the best position (x^*_{ij}) it has ever visited in the search space. The best position of each particle experience comprised to other ones and then the best position, which belongs to minimum of misfit function, selected as the global best(g^*). This procedure (i.e. finding x^*_{ij}, g^*) repeated for certain iteration. Finally the best global g^* is determined as the optimum solution. The movement of particles is schematically represented in Figure 1.

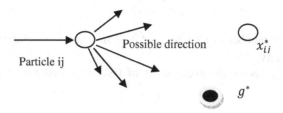

Fig. 1. Schematic representation of the motion of a particle in PSO

Particle swarm consisted of a swarm of particles each moving or flying through the search space according to velocity update (Eq.1) [20]. In equation 1 ϵ_1 and ϵ_2 are two random vectors, and each entry taking the values between 0 and 1. The Hadamard product of two matrices u $\odot$ v is defined as the entry wise product. The parameters α and β are the learning parameters or acceleration constants, which can typically be taken as, say, $\alpha \approx \beta \approx 2$ [1]. Also χ is constriction factor[20]. The new position can then be updated by equation 2. Where v_{ij} is the velocity of particle i in the jth dimension, x_{ij} is the new position of the particle i that update in its jth dimension using equation 2.

$$v_{ij} = \chi\left[v_{ij} + \alpha\epsilon_1\odot(g^* - x_{ij}) + \beta\epsilon_2\odot(x^*_{ij} - x_{ij})\right] \tag{1}$$

$$x_{ij} = x_{ij} + v_{ij} \tag{2}$$

4   PSO for Inversion of MASW Method

As the surface wave method has been drawing attention in recent days as one of the efficient tools to obtain shear-wave velocity of near-surface materials, diverse application are made in various types of geotechnical projects. MASW as an active method using an artificial seismic source, like a sledgehammer, can often achieve the goal of Vs estimation down to a few tens of meters. But the inversion stage in processing of

MASW data is the most important issue to obtain a reliable near-surface Vs profile, because of its intrinsic nonlinearity and multi dimensionality. The recent geophysical literature includes many works on development and application of inversion techniques but there are a few literatures that investigated the inversion of surface waves based methods by use of metaheuristic approaches. In this study we proposed new code using PSO algorithm to invert Rayleigh wave data for study of near surface. This code is easy and fast also allows the user to inclusion of a priori information on the different parameters. The root-mean-square (RMS) misfit between the observed and calculated value are defined as the object function (OBF) according to the following equation:

$$OBF = \sqrt{\frac{\sum_{j=1}^{n_p}(v^{obs}-v^{cal})^2}{n_p}} \tag{3}$$

Where n_p is the number of samples, v^{obs} is the observed velocity and v^{cal} is the calculated velocity.

Also figure 2 shows the pseudocode of PSO that used for inversion of MASW data.

```
1.   Swarm Initialization
2.   For i=1  to  number of particles do
3.       for j=1 to number of dimensions do
4.           Initial positions  x_{ij} and velocity v_{ij} of particles
5.           Copy  x_{ij} in x_{ij}^*
6.       End for
7.   End for
8.   Search the best global leader and record its position in g*
9.   For i=1 to number of particles do
10.      For j=1 to number of dimensions do
11.          Update  v_{ij} according to equation 1
12.          Update x_{ij} according to equation 2
13.          Mutation
14.      End for
15.      Evaluate fitness  x_{ij}  according to equation 3
16.      If fitness (x_{ij}^*) < fitness (x_{ij})
17.          Then Update x_{ij}^*
18.      End If
19.  end for
20.  Search the best global leader and record its position in g*
21.  While (loop_number< total _loop)
```

Fig. 2. Pseudocode of PSO for inversion of MASW data

5   Synthetic Dataset

The proposed method for inversion of MASW data was tested on a synthetic model. Typically, the model assumed for the interpretation of surface wave tests is a stack of homogeneous linear elastic layers over a half space. So, a synthetic model, three homogeneous layers overlying a half-space was investigated. Also the Vs and H selected for search space of algorithm, because the shear-wave velocity and layer thickness are two important parameters that influence the Rayleigh wave propagation. The particle and maximum of iteration number are 60 and 50 respectively. The Table 1 shows the model parameters and the search space of algorithm.

Table 1. Parameters of the synthetic model and search space

layer	Vp(m/s)	Vs(m/s)	Poisson	H(m)	search space	
					Vs(m/s)	H(m)
1	450	300	0.45	3	150-450	1-5
2	900	500	0.40	5	250- 750	2-7
3	1600	700	0.25	7	350-1050	3-9
4	2200	950	0.25	Half space	475-1425	-

Table 2 shows the results of synthetic model inversion and the PSO parameters. Also the synthetic model (bold line) and mean estimate values (red points) are depicted in figure 3.

Table 2. Mean model obtained from the inversion of synthetic model

parameters	Estimated	Related Error (%)	Standard deviation	PSO parameters
Vs1(m/s)	276	8.0	38.12	
Vs2(m/s)	453	9.4	56.62	
Vs3(m/s)	667	4.7	96.11	α=1.3
Vs4(m/s)	973	2.4	65.91	β=2.8
H1(m)	2.7	10.0	0.43	χ=0.729
H2(m)	5.2	4.0	0.92	
H3(m)	7.1	1.4	1.22	

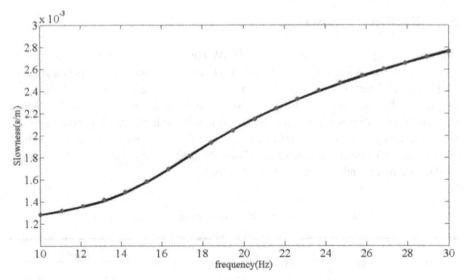

Fig. 3. Synthetic Model (bold line) and mean estimated values (red points)

6   Field Dataset

To further explore the applicability of the PSO algorithm described above, MASW
data acquired in the Tabriz city at the NW-Iran have been reanalyzed in the present
study using a PSO approach. In this study MASW method was performed with using
an OYO 12-channel seismograph and 4.5Hz geophones with a receiver spacing of
4m. Also sledge-hammer (12kg) source with offset of 4m was used to generate the
seismic signals. After obtained dispersion curve of study area Similar to the inverse
strategy of the synthetic model, we considered Vs and thicknesses (H) of layer as
variables. For evaluation of PSO inversion the obtained Vs profile was compared with
the obtained Vs profile of downhole Seismic Surveys that there are near to study area.
Table 3 shows the average velocity of borehole and average velocity that obtained by
PSO inversion of MASW. The estimated Velocity by PSO algorithm shows a good
correlation with downhole data.

Table 3. Vs from MASW and borehole (Percent Difference from Borehole in Parentheses)

Data	Vs(m/s) (top 5m)	Vs(m/s) (top 12m)	Vs(m/s) (top 18m)	Vs(m/s) (top 30m)
borehole	351	459	543	725
MASW	318 (-9)	510 (11)	590 (9)	761 (5)

7   Conclusions

Shallow shear-wave velocity (Vs) has long been recognized as a key factor in variable ground-motion amplification and site response in sedimentary basins. It is an important parameter in building codes, and the earthquake engineering community widely uses Vs in design applications. Multichannel analysis of surface waves (MASW) is an active geophysical method that has been developed recently for determining shallow Vs. MASW Data processing consists of three steps: 1) preliminary detection of surface waves, 2) extracting the signal dispersion curve, and 3) back-calculating Vs variation with depth. That this back-calculation is called inversion. But in processing of MASW, dispersion curve inversion is in fact a highly nonlinear and multimodal problem that severely challenges any inversion procedure. With the development of computer science, optimization algorithms fast and easier approaches can be conducted for inversion of geophysical data with high nonlinearity nature. In this study we introduced PSO algorithm as an efficient tool to invert MASW data. The coding for inversion of MASW data was done in Matlab. First the proposed inversion algorithm was tested on a synthetic data set. At the end, the proposed methodology to invert MASW data is applied in a case study at the part of Tabriz city in North-West of Iran for hazard assessment. The results of field dataset were in a good correlation with downhole seismic logging. The great advantages of PSO inversion algorithm are that it is fast and easy to implement and there are few parameters to adjust. Flexibility of implemented inversion algorithm is its trait. The results proved the ability and reliability of a metaheuristic approach in inversion of active surface waves for achieving to a correct Vs model with an acceptable misfit and convergence speed.

References

1. Yang, X.S.: Engineering Optimization An Introduction with Metaheuristic Applications. pp. 19–22, John Wiley & Sons (2010)
2. Menke, W.: Geophysical Data Analysis: Discrete Inverse Theory. International Geophysics series, Revised Edition **45**, 10–12 (1989)
3. Vozoff, K., Jupp, D.L.B.: Joint Inversion of Geophysical Data. Geophysic. J. R. Astr. Soc. **42**, 977–991 (1975)
4. Tarantola, A.: Inverse problem theory and methods for model parameter estimation. Society for Industrial and Applied Mathematics, pp.1–4 (2005), ISBN 0-89871-572-5 (pbk.)
5. Wathelet, M., Jongmans, D., Ohrnberger, M.: Surface wave inversion using a direct search algorithm and its application to ambient vibration measurements. Near Surface Geophysics **2**, 211–221 (2004)
6. Sen, M.K., Stoffa, P.L.: Global optimization methods in geophysical inversion. Elsevier Science (1995)
7. Soupios, P., Akca, I., Mpogiatzis, P., Basokur, A.T., Papazachos, C.: Applications of hybrid genetic algorithms in seismic tomography. J. of Applied Geophysics **75**, 479–489 (2011)
8. Shaw, R., Srivastava, S.: Particle swarm optimization: a new tool to invert geophysical data. Geophysics **72**(2), F75–F83 (2007)

9. Naudet, V., Fernández Martínez, J.L., García Gonzalo, E.: Fernández Alvarez: Estimation of water table from self-potential data using particle swarm. J.P, 1203–1207 (2008)
10. Fernández Martínez, J.L., García Gonzalo, E.: The generalized PSO: a new door to PSO evolution. J. for Artificial Evolution and Applications, 1–15 (2008)
11. Yuana, S., Shangxu, W., Nan, N.: Swarm intelligence optimization and its application in geophysical data inversion. Applied Geophysics 6(2), 166–174 (2009)
12. Fernández Martínez, J.L., García Gonzalo, E., Fernández Álvarez, J.P., Kuzma, H.A., Menéndez Pérez, C.O.: PSO: a powerful algorithm to solve geophysical inverse problems: application to a 1D-DC resistivity case. J. of Applied Geophysics 71, 13–25 (2010)
13. Pekşen, E., Yas, T.A., Kayman, Y., Özkan, C.: Application of particle swarm optimization on self-potential data. J. of. Applied Geophysics 75(2), 305–318 (2011)
14. Coccia, S., Del Gaudio, V., Venisti, N., Wasowski, N.: Application of Refraction Microtremor (ReMi) technique for determination of 1-D shear wave velocity in a landslide area. J. of Applied Geophysics 71, 71–89 (2010)
15. Herrmann, R.B.: Computer Programs in Seismology. St Louis University (1987)
16. Borcherdt, R.D.: Effects of local geology on ground motion near San Francisco Bay. Bull. Seism. Soc. Am. 60, 29–61 (1970)
17. Stephenson, W.J., Louie, J.N., Pullammanappallil, S., Williams, R.A., Odum, J.K.: Blind Shear-Wave Velocity Comparison of ReMi and MASW Results with Boreholes to 200 m in Santa Clara Valley: Implications for Earthquake Ground-Motion Assessment. Bull. Seism. Soc. Am. 95(6), 2506–2516 (2005)
18. Park, C.B., Miller, R.D., Xia, J.: Multichannel analysis of surface waves. Geophysics 64, 800–808 (1999)
19. Park, C.B., Miller, R.D.: Seismic Characterization of Wind Turbine Sites in Kansas by the MASW Method. Barr Engineering Company, Open File Report (2005)
20. Kennedy, J., Eberhart, R.C.: Particle Swarm Optimization, pp. 1942–1948. IEEE Press, Piscataway, NJ (1995)
21. Blum, C., Li, X.: Swarm Intelligence in Optimization. Natural Computing Series, pp. 43–85. Springer Heidelberg (2008)

A Fuzzy-Controlled Comprehensive Learning
Particle Swarm Optimizer

Mahamed G.H. Omran[1(✉)], Maurice Clerc[2], Ayed Salman[3], and Salah Alsharhan[1]

[1] Department of Computer Science, Gulf University for Science and Technology, Gulf, Kuwait
{omran.m,alsharhanS}@gust.edu.kw
[2] Independent Consultant, Gulf, France
maurice.clerc@writeme.com
[3] Computer Engineering Department, Kuwait University, Kuwait City, Kuwait
ayed.salman@ku.edu.kw

Abstract. An adaptive variant of Comprehensive Learning Particle Swarm Optimizer (CLPSO) is proposed in this paper. The proposed method, called Fuzzy-Controlled CLPSO (FC-CLPSO), uses a fuzzy controller to tune the probability learning, inertia weight and acceleration coefficient of each particle in the swarm. The FC-CLPSO is compared with CLPSO and SPSO2011 on 11 benchmark functions. The results show that FC-CLPSO generally outperformed CLPSO and SPSO2011 on most of the tested functions.

Keywords: Particle Swarm Optimization · Fuzzy Controller · Adaptation · Comprehensive Learning

1 Introduction

The Particle Swarm Optimizer (PSO) (Eberhart and Kennedy 1995) is a nature-inspired metaheuristic which mimics the behavior of bird flocking and fish schooling. PSO is easy to understand and implement. In addition, it requires no gradient information. PSO has been used to solve many real-world problems (Olsson 2011).

In PSO, each particle represents a candidate solution, which is a point in a D–dimensional space. A particle has a position, a velocity and a cost function. The velocity and position of the j-th dimension of the i-th particle are defined as,

$$v_{i,j}(t + 1) = wv_{i,j}(t) + c_1 r_{1,j}(t)\left(p_{i,j}(t) - x_{i,j}(t)\right) + c_2 r_{2,j}(t)\left(g_j(t) - x_{i,j}(t)\right) \quad (1)$$

$$x_{i,j}(t + 1) = x_{i,j}(t) + v_{i,j}(t) \quad (2)$$

where w is the inertia weight, c_1 and c_2 are the acceleration coefficients, $r_{1,j}$ and $r_{1,j}$ are two uniformly distributed random numbers in the interval $[0,1]$ with $j \in \{1,2,...,D\}$, $i \in \{1,2,...,N\}$ and N is the swarm size. $\vec{x_i}$ is the position of the i-th particle, $\vec{p_i}$ is the personal best position of the i-th particle and $\vec{g}$ is the best position discovered by the swarm.

© Springer International Publishing Switzerland 2014
P. Siarry et al. (Eds.): ICSIBO 2014, LNCS 8472, pp. 35–41, 2014.
DOI: 10.1007/978-3-319-12970-9_4

The basic PSO tends to converge prematurely in multi-modal functions due to poor diversity (Riget and Vesterstrøm 2002). A relatively recent variant of PSO was proposed by Liang *et al.* (2006). The proposed variant, called Comprehensive Learning PSO (CLPSO), generally has a good balance between high and low diversity. Thus, it can cope well with multi-modal functions. However, CLPSO is not the best choice for solving unimodal problems due to its slow convergence (Liang *et al.* 2006).

In this paper, a new adaptive variant of CLPSO is proposed. The proposed method, called Fuzzy-Controlled CLPSO (FC-CLPSO), uses a fuzzy controller to adapt the control parameters of CLPSO. FC-CLPSO is compared with CLPSO and the recent SPSO2011 (available at http://particleswarm.info) on 11 benchmark functions.

Section 2 provides an overview of CLPSO. FC-CLPSO is introduced in Section 3. The experimental results are presented and discussed in Section 4. Section 5 concluded the paper.

2   Comprehensive Learning Particle Swarm Optimizer (CLPSO)

The Comprehensive Learning Particle Swarm Optimizer (CLPSO) (Liang *et al.* 2006) addresses the premature convergence problem of the basic PSO by allowing each particle to learn from the personal best position of other particles. Each dimension of a particle can potentially learn from the best experience of a different particle (referred to as an *exemplar*). Hence, the velocity updating equation is modified as follows,

$$v_{i,j}(t+1) = wv_{i,j}(t) + cr_j(t)(p_{f_i(j),j}(t) - x_{i,j}(t)) \tag{3}$$

where $\vec{f_i} = [f_i(1), f_i(2), ..., f_i(D)]$ and $f_i(j) = i_1$ with $j \in \{1,2,...,D\}$ and $i_1 \in \{1,2,...,N\}$; $\vec{f_i}$ defines which particle's personal best position particle i should follow. $p_{f_i(j),j}$ can be the corresponding component of any particle's personal best position including the particle's own personal best experience. To generate $p_{f_i(j),j}$, a random number is generated. If this number is greater than a learning probability, Pc_i, this component (i.e. dimension) will learn from its own best experience, otherwise, it will learn from another particle's personal best position. If all examplars of a particle are its own personal best position, one component will be randomly chosen to learn from another particle's personal best position. If a particle failed to improve itself for m (known as the *refreshing gap*) consecutive iterations, new exemplars will be chosen for that particle. Liang *et al.* (2006) empirically determined that 7 is a good value for m. The learning probabilities are computed using,

$$Pc_i = 0.05 + 0.45 \frac{(\exp\left(\frac{10(i-1)}{N-1}\right) - 1)}{(\exp(10) - 1)} \tag{4}$$

According to Liang *et al.* (2006), different learning probabilities affect the exploration/exploitation abilities of the particles.

3   Fuzzy Controlled CLPSO (FC-CLPSO)

In the proposed method, each particle has its own learning probability, inertia weight and acceleration coefficient. A fuzzy controller is used to adapt these three control parameters (i.e. Pc_i, w and c_i). The controller takes the normalized rank of each particle as its input and generates three control parameters as outputs. The rank is determined by first sorting the swarm's particles according to their cost function. The best particle (one with the smallest error) is given a rank of 1 (i.e. $R_1 = 1$), while the worst particle (with the biggest error) is given a rank of N (i.e. $R_N = N$). The rank is then normalized to a value between 0 and 1 using,

$$r_i = 1 - \frac{R_i - 1}{N - 1}$$

The normalized ranks are then assigned as membership grades in 3 fuzzy subsets as follows: LOW, MEDIUM and HIGH. The membership functions for Pc_i, w_i and c are also defined in a similar way. There are many alternative membership functions that can be used. In this study, a Gaussian curve membership function is chosen for the input and outputs of the fuzzy controller. Figure 1 shows these membership functions.

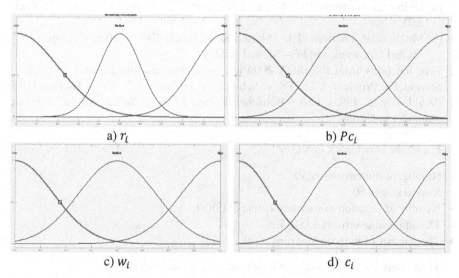

a) r_i

b) Pc_i

c) w_i

d) c_i

Fig. 1. Membership functions for inputs and outputs

The fuzzy rules of the fuzzy controller are defined as follows:

IF r_i is LOW **THEN** Pc_i is HIGH AND w_i is HIGH AND c_i is HIGH
IF r_i is MEDIUM **THEN** Pc_i is MEDIUM AND w_i is MEDIUM AND c_i is MEDIUM
IF r_i is HIGH **THEN** Pc_i is LOW AND w_i is LOW AND c_i is LOW

The rationale behind the above rules is that if a particle has a low rank this means it has a low performance, thus, it needs to learn from other particles. This can be done by increasing its Pc_i and c_i. Moreover, such a particle needs to focus more on exploring the search space, hence, its w_i should be increased. On the other hand, best particles should focus more on exploitation (i.e. local search), thus, w_i should be decreased. Moreover, such particles do not need to learn often from other particles, hence, Pc_i and c_i should be decreased.

The fuzzy controller is called whenever new exemplars are need for a particle (i.e. initially and when a particle failed to improve for m iterations).

4   Experimental Results

FC-CLPSO is compared with CLPSO and SPSO 2011. SPSO2011 is generally considered as an outstanding algorithm (Xiang *et al.* 2014). To test the performance of the different methods, 11 functions have been chosen:

1. Six functions from the CEC'2008 Special Session and Competition on large-scale global optimization (Tang *et al.* 2007):
   (a) Unimodal functions: F1 – Shifted Sphere and F2 – Shifted Schwefel's Problem 2.21.
   (b) Multimodal functions: F3 – Shifted Rosenbrock, F4 – Shifted Rastrigin, F5 – Shifted Griewank and F6 – Shifted Ackley.
2. Five functions from the ISDA'2009 test suite (Herrera and Lozano 2009): F7 - Schwefel's Problem 2.22, F8 – Schwefel's Problem 1.2, F9 – Extended f10 (Whitley *et al.* 1995), F10 – Bohachevsky and F11 – Schaffer. All functions are unimodal functions.

For all the benchmark functions:

- Number of dimensions is 30.
- Swarm size is 50.
- Number of function evaluations (*nfe*) is $5000D$.
- The admissible error is 1.00e-4.
- The number of independent runs is 30.

To measure the *effectiveness* of a method we use two metrics:

(1) The median of the best-of-run error, which is defined as the absolute difference between the best-of-the-run $f(X^*)$ value and the actual optimum $f(X')$ of a given function.
err. $= |f(X^*) - f(X')|$
(2) Success rate (SR): The number of successful runs, where a run is successful if err. $\leq$ admissible error.

All programs are implemented using MATLAB® version 8.1.0.604 (R2013a), and machine epsilon is 2.2204e-16. For the pseudo-random number generator (RNG) we have used the rand built-in function provided by MATLAB. This function implements the Mersenne-Twister RNG (Matsumoto and Nishimura 1998). We warmed the RNG by calling it 10,000 at the start of the program as suggested by Jones (2010). The non-parametric Friedman's test with $\alpha = 0.05$ and the Dunn-Sidak correction as a post-hoc test have been used to compare the difference in performance of the different algorithms. In this study, the Null Hypothesis, H_0, states that there is no difference between the *medians* of errors of the different algorithms.

Table 1 shows the median and SR of CLPSO, SPSO2011 and FC-CLPSO on the test functions. The statistically significant best solutions have been shown in **bold**. The results show that FC-CLPSO outperformed CLPSO on 8 functions while performing equally well on the rest. There is no single function where CLPSO performed better than FC-CLPSO. On the other hand, FC-CLPSO outperformed SPSO2011 on 7 functions while SPSO2011 performed better on two functions (i.e. F2 and F8). These two functions are unimodal functions.

The total number of functions solved by FC-CLPSO is 5, while CLPSO and SPSO2011 solved 2 and 4 functions, respectively.

Figure 2 shows the progress of the mean best errors found by CLPSO, SPSO2011 and FC-CLPSO over 30 runs for selected functions. The figure shows that FC-CLPSO reached better solutions faster than the other methods while SPSO2011 prematurely converged on the four functions.

In general, the results clearly shows that using the fuzzy controller to tune CLPSO's parameters improve the performance of CLPSO on most of the benchmark functions.

Table 1. Comparing CLPSO, SPSO2011 and FC-CLPSO on the test functions

f	CLPSO		SPSO2011		FC-CLPSO		p-value
	Median	*SR*	*Median*	*SR*	*Median*	*SR*	
F1	9.64e-05	93.3	9.60e-05	100	9.43e-05	100	0.3932
F2	1.16e+02	0	**1.97e-01**	0	7.79e+01	0	9.3576e-14
F3	**1.89e+02**	0	4.81e+02	0	**1.15e+02**	0	4.1186e-06
F4	8.50e+00	0	9.89e+01	0	**2.99e+00**	0	2.4603e-13
F5	7.48e-04	0	9.98e-05	53.3	**9.75e-05**	90	3.3633e-05
F6	1.17e-02	0	9.97e-05	66.7	**9.84e-05**	100	6.6018e-08
F7	1.75e-04	0	1.17e+00	0	**9.80e-05**	100	9.3576e-14
F8	1.86e+03	0	**8.58e+01**	0	1.99e+02	0	1.3924e-12
F9	4.13e+00	0	6.02e+01	0	**1.44e-01**	0	9.3576e-14
F10	8.38e-05	100	9.40e-05	80	8.74e-05	100	0.0718
F11	3.98e+00	0	6.47e+01	0	**1.02e-01**	0	9.3576e-14

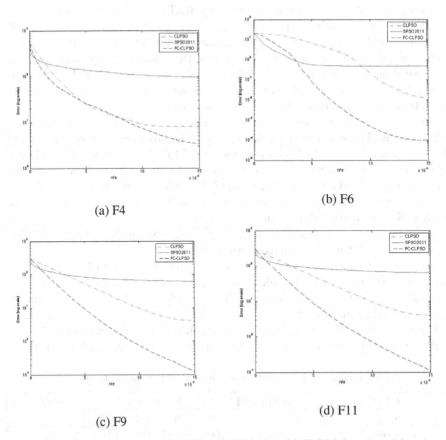

(a) F4

(b) F6

(c) F9

(d) F11

Fig. 2. Mean best error curves of CLPSO, SPSO2011 and FC-CLPSO for selected functions

5   Conclusions

A fuzzy-controlled CLPSO was proposed and compared with CLPSO and SPSO2011. The results showed that using a fuzzy controller to tune the probability learning, inertia weight and acceleration coefficient of each particle significantly improved the performance of CLPSO. Future work will investigate the proposed approach on more benchmark functions and some real-world problems. Moreover, comparison with other *state-of-the-art* methods will be conducted.

References

Eberhart, R., Kennedy, J.: A New Optimizer Using Particle Swarm Theory. In: 6th International Symposium on Micromachine and Human Science, pp. 39–43, IEEE Service Center, Piscataway, NJ (1995)

Herrera, F., Lozano, M.: Benchmark functions 7-11. Technical Report, Workshop: Evolutionary Algorithms and other Metaheuristics for Continuous Optimization Problems - A Scalability Test, http://sci2s.ugr.es/programacion/workshop/functions7-11.pdf (2009)

Jones, D.: Good practice in (pseudo) random number generation for bioinformatics applications. Technical report, UCL Bioinformatics Group (2010)

Liang, J., Qin, A., Suganthan, P., Baskar, S.: Comprehensive Learning Particle Swarm Optimizer for Global Optimization of Multimodal Functions. Transactions on Evolutionary Computation 10(3), 281–295 (2006)

Matsumoto, M., Nishimura, T.: Mersenne Twister: a 623-dimensionally equidistributed uniform pseudo-random number generator. ACM Transactions on Modeling and Computer Simulation 8(1), 3–30 (1998)

Olsson, A.: Particle Swarm Optimization: Theory, Techniques and Applications. Nova Science Pub Inc. (2011)

Riget, J., Vesterstrøm, J.: A Diversity-Guided Particle Swarm Optimizer - the ARPSO. Technical report, EVALife, Denmark (2002)

Tang, X., Yao, P.N., Suganthan, C., MacNish, Y.P., Chen, C.M., Chen, Yang, Z.: Benchmark Functions for the CEC'2008 Special Session and Competition on Large Scale Global Optimization. Technical Report, Nature Inspired Computation and Applications Laboratory, USTC, China (2007)

Whitley, D., Beveridge, R., Graves, C., Mathias, K.K.: Test driving three 1995 genetic algorithms: New test functions and geometric matching. Journal of Heuristics 1(1), pp.77–104 (1995)

Xiang, Y., Peng, Y., Zhong, Y., Chen, Z., Lu, X., Zhong, X.: A particle swarm inspired multi-elitist artificial bee colony algorithm for real-parameter optimization. Computational Optimization and Applications 57, 493–516 (2014)

Fuzzy Logic Control Optimized by Artificial Immune System for Building Thermal Condition

Jiawei Zhu[✉], Fabrice Lauri, Abderrafiaa Koukam,
and Vincent Hilaire

IRTES-SET, UTBM, 90010 Belfort Cedex, France
{jiawei.zhu,fabrice.lauri,abder.koukam,vincent.hilaire}@utbm.fr

Abstract. With the fast development of information technology and increasingly prominent environmental problems, building comfort and energy management become the major tasks for an intelligent residential building system. According to statistical studies, people spend 80% of their lives in buildings. Hence it is not surprising that they constantly seek to improve comfort in their living spaces. This paper presents a fuzzy logic controller optimized by an artificial immune system algorithm aimed at maintaining the thermal comfort while reducing energy consumption. The experimental results show the advantages of our system compared with the widely used baseline: On/Off control approach.

Keywords: Energy · Fuzzy system · Artificial immune system · Optimization

1 Introduction

According to statistical studies, people spend 80% of their lives in buildings. This explains why occupants constantly seek to improve comfort in their living spaces. In addition, environmental issues have drawn more and more attention. How to manage energy in a proper way to improve energy efficiency and reduce pollution is a subject of uttermost importance. Meanwhile, the popularization of the concept of home office makes the productivity in residential buildings economically significant.

Among all indoor comfort factors, thermal comfort attracts our special attention. According to [1], thermal comfort is the condition of mind which expresses satisfaction with the thermal environment. This definition leaves open what is meant by *condition of mind* or *satisfaction*, which implies that the judgement of comfort is a cognitive process involving many inputs including physical, physiological, psychological and other processes. Despite not being the only affecting factor, indoor temperature has physically major influence on occupants' feeling comfort. In real world, the operative temperature intervals vary with building location and type. ISO-7730 suggests temperature ranges in different types of buildings and different environmental conditions. For example, for residential

© Springer International Publishing Switzerland 2014
P. Siarry et al. (Eds.): ICSIBO 2014, LNCS 8472, pp. 42–49, 2014.
DOI: 10.1007/978-3-319-12970-9_5

buildings of category B in summer, the suggested temperature range is from $23.0°C$ to $26.0°C$, while it is between $20.0°C$ and $24.0°C$ in winter [1].

So far, most Heating, Ventilation and Air Conditioning (HVAC) systems for residential buildings usually employ a single-zone, On/Off control method which is rather simplistic [2]. Corresponding to the increasing demands for environment, energy, comfort and productivity, intelligent control methods are applied for improving thermal conditions in residential buildings [3,4]. Fuzzy control [5] is another type of intelligent control method. Comparing with classical ones, especially like Proportional Integral Derivative control (PID) that is widely used in industrial process control [6,7] due to its simplicity of structure, low-price, relative effectiveness and the familiarity of engineers, but cannot provide good enough performance in highly complex process controlling, fuzzy control can theoretically cope with complex processes [8] and is able to combine the advantages of PID control with human operator experience.

In this work, we first investigate the thermal dynamics of a building. Then a fuzzy control scheme with a meta-heuristic optimization algorithm called CLONALG, is proposed for the heating system of a residential building. This control system can make intelligent decisions of what magnitude of power the physical heating system should adopt at each time step based on the present indoor and outdoor temperatures. Due to empirical picking of fuzzy parameters initially, the target of CLONALG is to optimize these parameters to improve the performance of the fuzzy control system. The remainder of this paper is organized as follows. Section 2 describes the mathematical building thermal model. Section 3 presents the fuzzy controller used to control the heating system. Section 4 provides details about CLONALG algorithm. Section 5 explains the system design and formalizes the fuzzy system optimization process. Experimental results and analysis are given in Section 6. Finally, we conclude in Section 7.

2 Building Thermal Model

The room temperature is affected not only by auxiliary heating/cooling systems and electric appliances, but also by the solar radiation and the outside temperature. According to Achterbosch et al.[9], the heat balance of a building can be expressed as

$$\phi_h(t) + \phi_s(t) = \phi_t(t) + \phi_c(t) \tag{1}$$

where ϕ_h is the heat supplied by all internal heat sources; ϕ_s is the heat gained by solar radiation; ϕ_t is the heat loss through external contact; ϕ_c is the heat retained by the building.

The thermal system of the building can be expressed by Equations (2) - (6):

$$\frac{dT_w}{dt} = \frac{A_w}{C_w}\left[U_{wi}(T_{ai} - T_w) + U_{wo}(T_{ao} - T_w)\right] \tag{2}$$

$$\frac{dT_f}{dt} = \frac{A_f}{C_f}\left[\frac{pQ_s}{A_f} + U_f(T_{ai} - T_f)\right] \tag{3}$$

$$\frac{dT_c}{dt} = \frac{A_c}{C_c}\left[U_c(T_{ai} - T_c)\right] \tag{4}$$

$$\frac{dT_{ip}}{dt} = \frac{A_{ip}}{C_{ip}}\left[\frac{(1-p)Q_s}{A_{ip}} + U_{ip}(T_{ai} - T_{ip})\right] \tag{5}$$

$$\frac{dT_{ai}}{dt} = \frac{1}{C_{ai}}\left[Q_p + Q_e + (A_g U_g + U_v)(T_{ao} - T_{ai})\right.$$
$$+ A_w U_{wi}(T_w - T_{ai}) + A_f U_f(T_f - T_{ai}) \tag{6}$$
$$\left. + A_c U_c(T_c - T_{ai}) + A_{ip}U_{ip}(T_{ip} - T_{ai})\right]$$

In above equations: Q_e is the heat gained by using electrical equipments, Q_s is the solar radiation through glazing, Q_p is the heat supplied by the heating system, T_{ao} is the outside air temperature, T_{ai} is the inside air temperature, U is the thermal transmittance, C is the thermal capacitance, A is the area of the component, p is the fraction of solar radiation entering floor, and w, ip, f, c means external wall, internal partition, floor and ceiling respectively.

The area of each component is known after choosing the physical building model, and the properties of different building materials can be obtained from ASHRAE Handbook [10].

3   Fuzzy Logic Controller

Fuzzy Logic Controllers (FLC) have gained more and more prominence in recent years because of its ability to control devices which imitate the decision making of human being. Moreover, a FLC is efficient to cope with continuous states with the help of membership function (MF) and IF-THEN rules. In general, a FLC contains four parts: fuzzifier, rules, inference engine and defuzzifier. Firstly, a crisp set of input data is gathered and converted to a fuzzy set using fuzzy linguistic variables, fuzzy linguistic terms and membership functions. This step is known as fuzzification. Afterwards, an inference is made based on a set of rules. Lastly, the resulting fuzzy output is mapped to a crisp output using the MFs in the defuzzification step.

Specifically, in aforementioned building model the inputs include 4 elements: Q_p, Q_e, Q_s and T_{ao} and in order to simplify the problem, let's assume that Q_e and Q_s are both constant. T_{ao} can be simulated by using former weather data. Hence, the variable we need to control by our FLC is Q_p, which is the input of the building model but the output of the FLC. We define $eTai$ as the error between the indoor temperature T_{ai} and the setpoint T_{set}, and $eTao$ as the error between the outdoor temperature T_{ao} and T_{set}. Setpoint is the comfortable temperature that occupants prefer. To set the input variable(s) of the FLC there are two options: one is to consider $eTai$ solely, like common air-condition, which is naive but still possible; the other one is to take $eTai$ and $eTao$ into account together, which gathers more information and therefore performs better. In our study, we prefer the latter. Therefore, we have two input variables, $eTai$ and $eTao$ separately and one output variable, Q_p.

In practice, there are different forms of MFs such as triangular, trapezoidal, piecewise linear, Gaussian, singleton, etc. They are curves which define how each crisp input point is mapped to a degree of membership between 0 and 1. Actually, these functions can be arbitrary curves whose shapes suit us from the point of view of simplicity, convenience, speed or efficiency under the only condition of their value between 0 and 1. In our study we capitalize on the Gaussian symmetrical function (GMF), Z-shape function (ZMF) and S-shape function (SMF) [11] because of their smoothness and concise notation that each of them can be defined by two parameters. Each fuzzy linguistic variable is expressed by three MFs, namely negative, zero and positive.

In fact, choosing MF types is not a tough job which is often out of empirical analysis. However, it is difficult to choose optimal fuzzy parameters for these MFs to design an optimal FLC. Usually people do this empirically too. In this study, we will use an AIS algorithm to find a near optimal set of parameters for the FLC. The proposed method involves arbitrarily picking an initial set of parameters and then finding a set of near optimal parameters by shifting the peak locations and tuning the deviations of fuzzy sets of antecedent MFs and consequent MF. We will discuss how to implement it in detail in Section 5.

4   Artificial Immune System Architecture

It has been proved that the human adaptive immune system possesses three capabilities: recognition, adaptation and memory [12]. When the human body is invaded by a specific pathogen or antigen, it will be recognized and bound by specific immunoglobulins or antibodies, which are secreted by B cells, to be tagged for attack by other part of the immune system or neutralised to death.

Figure 1 shows the antigen recognition and clonal selection process. An antibody, Ab, can recognize and bind an antigen, Ag, when Ab matches the structure of Ag. The regions of the antibodies that match the antigens are called paratopes, while the counterpart regions of the antigens are called epitopes. In this figure, Ab1 can match Ag1 but not Ag2, while Ab2 can neither match Ag1 nor Ag2, so Ab1 has higher affinity than Ab2 for encountering antigens. Higher affinity means higher probability of being selected and higher strength of clone and mutation. By continuous cloning and mutating existing ones, new generation of antibodies will be produced and among them new types of antibodies which may better match existing or new antigens are generated, for example Ab1' which can match both Ag1 and Ag2. This presents the adaptation capability of the immune system. Even if all antigens are destroyed, some relevant B cells will differentiate into memory cells. Therefore, if the same antigens reappear, the immune response will act sooner.

Inspired by the properties of human immune system, a variety of algorithms, such as Negative Selection, Clonal Selection, Immune Networks, and Dendritic Cell, have been designed to tackle different problems. The CLONALG algorithm

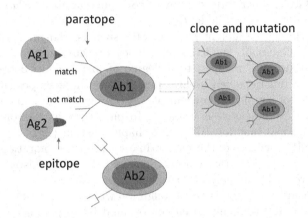

Fig. 1. Antigen Recognition, Clone and Mutation of Antibody

[12], which belongs to Clonal Selection, we use to search the near optimal fuzzy parameters for the FLC is described below:

(1) Generate a set (P) of candidate solutions, composed of the subset of memory cells (M) added to the remaining (Pr) population (P = Pr + M);
(2) Determine (Select) the n best individuals of the population (Pn), based on an affinity measure;
(3) Reproduce (Clone) these n best individuals of the population, giving rise to a temporary population of clones (C). The clone size is an increasing function of the affinity with the antigen;
(4) Submit the population of clones to a hypermutation scheme, where the hypermutation is proportional to the affinity of the antibody with the antigen. A maturated antibody population is generated (C*);
(5) Re-select the improved individuals from C* to compose the memory set M. Some members of P can be replaced by other improved members of C*;
(6) Replace d antibodies by novel ones (diversity introduction). The lower affinity cells have higher probabilities of being replaced.

5   System Design and Optimization

Based on the aforementioned model and technique, in this section we discuss the system design and the optimization of the fuzzy system. At every certain time interval, the thermal sensors of the building can record indoor and outdoor temperatures and sent them as inputs to the fuzzy controller. According to the MFs and rules of the fuzzy controller, after the fuzzifier-inference-defuzzifier process the physical heating appliance in the building will be notified a magnitude of heating power. Because the MFs defined empirically can not perform very well, therefore optimizing the fuzzy controller is a must step and this is the target of the artificial immune system, which in this application is a meta-heuristic algorithm named CLONALG. For the reason that the variation of outdoor temperature is continuous and rather slow, we can capitalize on a specific sinusoidal curve to simulate one day's outdoor temperature variation, and use CLONALG to tune fuzzy controller to make good decisions for general real-time weather situations.

Now we move on to this optimization problem formalization. Assume that there are m input variables $[x_1, x_2, ..., x_m]$ and one output variable y. The total number of fuzzy sets N is calculated as follows: $N = \sum_{i=1}^{m} n_i + n_o$, where m is the number of input variables, n_i and n_o are the number of fuzzy sets for ith linguistic input variable and the linguistic output variable. A set P with size of $2N$ contains the peak location and deviation of every fuzzy set, that is: $P = [\boldsymbol{\mu}_{in}, \boldsymbol{\sigma}_{in}, \boldsymbol{\mu}_{out}, \boldsymbol{\sigma}_{out}]$, where $\boldsymbol{\mu}_{in} = [\mu_1^1, \mu_2^1, ..., \mu_{n_1}^1, ..., \mu_{n_i}^i]$, $\boldsymbol{\sigma}_{in} = [\sigma_1^1, \sigma_2^1, ..., \sigma_{n_1}^1, ..., \sigma_{n_i}^i]$, $\boldsymbol{\mu}_{out} = [\mu_1^o, ..., \mu_{n_o}^o]$, and $\boldsymbol{\sigma}_{out} = [\sigma_1^o, ..., \sigma_{n_o}^o]$, for all $i = 1, 2, ..., m$. The objective of the method is to minimize the difference between the inference output y and the desired output y^*, in our case are controlled Q_p and desired Q_p separately, with respect to P: $C = \min_P (y - y^*)^2$, where: $y = f(x_1, x_2, ..., x_m, P)$, and $y^* = f(x_1, x_2, ..., x_m)$. We can see that the objective function C depends not only on P but also the inputs. In order to eliminate the dependence of the inputs, we use the Root Mean Square Error (RMSE), such that: $RMSE(y) = \sqrt{E((y_t - y_t^*)^2)} = \sqrt{\frac{\sum_{t=1}^{T}(y_t - y_t^*)^2}{T}}$, where T is the number of points of the whole trajectory. Therefore the objective function becomes: $C = \min_P \left[\alpha \sqrt{\frac{\sum_{t=1}^{T}(y_t - y_t^*)^2}{T}} \right]$. All else being known, at a time t indoor temperature only depends on the output power of the heating system (we can see this in Equation (6)). Therefore at every time t, indoor temperature is a function of the output power of the heating system, recorded as: $T_{ai}^t = g^t(Q_p^t)$. Moreover, because $g^t(\cdot)$ is linearly monotonically increasing, the final objective function can be expressed as follows: $C = \min_P \left[\alpha \sqrt{\frac{\sum_{t=1}^{T}(g^t(y_t) - g^t(y_t^*))^2}{T}} \right]$. Hence, after the minimization process, the FLC with fuzzy parameters in P is optimized.

6 Experiments

We first empirically pick μ and σ for all MFs of input and output variables. Then these parameters are optimized by CLONALG. Due to CLONALG can not guarantee to obtain optimal values, we run CLONALG for 30 times and take their mean values as near-optimal parameters for the fuzzy controller: $\boldsymbol{\mu}_{in} = [0, -0.4, 0, 0, -0.54, 0]$, $\boldsymbol{\sigma}_{in} = [-0.61, 0.1, 0.508, -6.952, 5.333, 6.426]$, $\boldsymbol{\mu}_{out} = [22, 18, 22]$, and $\boldsymbol{\sigma}_{out} = [10.89, 1.889, 26.24]$. In Figure 2(a), actual recorded weather data obtained from EERE [13] is used as the outdoor air temperature, which is depicted by a dashed blue line. From the simulation result, it can be found that during this period, the indoor temperature, which is delineated by a green line, is able to be kept at $22°C$. Even during the first three days' extremely cold weather, the indoor temperature is retained at the setpoint.

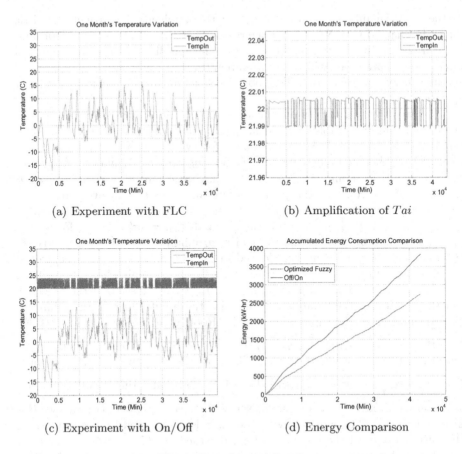

Fig. 2. Experimental Results

Figure 2(b) shows the amplification of the room temperature, and one can see that the variation of this temperature is almost within $\pm0.01°C$. Moreover, the simulation result with On/Off control is described in Figure 2(c). For this control method, the heating system turns on when the room temperature is below $20°C$, while it turns off when above $24°C$. In order to keep a comfort temperature, the heating system has to turn on and off frequently, which will jeopardize the physical system and reduce its service life. Finally, the accumulated energy consumption comparison between the optimized FLC and the On/Off control is shown in Figure 2(d). We can see that compared with the On/Off control which uses 3830 $kW \cdot hr$ in total, the optimized FLC uses 2742 $kW \cdot hr$ in total, so that it consumes 1088 $kW \cdot hr$ less energy.

7   Conclusion

This paper has presented a fuzzy logic controller optimized by an artificial immune system algorithm to keep thermal comfort while consuming less energy in residential buildings. The experimental results show that by employing this controller, the indoor temperature can be more stable and thus more comfortable than the classical On/Off control and consumes less energy. However, the work conducted here is still a preliminary step towards a completely autonomous HVAC system. In future work, the comparison with other optimization algorithms like PSO will be made. Furthermore, other systems such as a lighting system and a ventilation system, will be taken into account together. Certainly this is also a good application for multi-agent paradigm. Based on the multi-agent framework, agent-to-agent communication, cooperation and coordination can be employed to provide a more comfortable residential environment and consume less energy.

References

1. ISO7730: Ergonomics of the thermal environment - analytical determination and interpretation of thermal comfort using calculation of the pmv and ppd indices and local thermal comfort criteria (2005)
2. Paris, B., Eynard, J., Grieu, S., Polit, M.: Hybrid pid-fuzzy control scheme for managing energy resources in buildings. Applied Soft Computing 11(8), 5068–5080 (2011)
3. Moon, J.W., Kim, J.J.: Ann-based thermal control models for residential buildings. Building Environment 45(7), 1612–1625 (2010)
4. Zhu, J., Lauri, F., Koukam, A., Hilaire, V., Simoes, M.G.: Improving thermal comfort in residential buildings using artificial immune system. In: 2013 IEEE 10th International Conference on Ubiquitous Intelligence and Computing(UIC). (December 2013), pp. 194–200 (2013)
5. Kruse, R., Gebhardt, J.E., Klowon, F.: Foundations of Fuzzy Systems. John Wiley and Sons Inc, New York (1994)
6. Kaya, İ., Tan, N., Atherton, D.P.: Improved cascade control structure for enhanced performance. Journal of Process Control 17(1), 3–16 (2007)
7. Thomas, B., Soleimani-Mohseni, M., Fahln, P.: Feed-forward in temperature control of buildings. Energy and Buildings 37(7), 755–761 (2005)
8. Menon, R., Menon, S., Srinivasan, D., Jain, L.: Fuzzy logic decision-making in multi-agent systems for smart grids. In: 2013 IEEE Symposium on Computational Intelligence Applications In Smart Grid (CIASG), pp. 44–50 (2013)
9. Achterbosch, G., de Jong, P., Krist-Spit, C., van der Meulen, S., Verberne, J.: The development of a comvenient thermal dynamic building model. Energy and Buildings 8(3), 183–196 (1985)
10. ASHRAE: ASHRAE Handbook: Fundamentals. American Society of Heating, Refrigerating, and Air-Conditioning Engineers (2005)
11. Mandal, S.N., Choudhury, J.P., Chaudhuri, S.: In search of suitable fuzzy membership function in prediction of time series data. International Journal of Computer Sciences Issues 9(3), 39–45 (2012)
12. de Castro, L.N., Von Zuben, F.J.: Artificial immune systems: Part i-basic theory and applications. Universidade Estadual de Campinas, Dezembro de, Tech. Rep (1999)
13. EERE: Weather Data Golden-NREL 724666 (TMY3). Energy Efficiency and Renewable Energy, U.S. Department of Energy (2012)

Smooth Trajectory Planning for Robot Using Particle Swarm Optimization

Riad Menasri[✉], Hamouche Oulhadj, Boubaker Daachi, Amir Nakib,
and Patrick Siarry

LISSI Laboratory, University Paris-Est Créteil, 122 rue Paul Armangot,
94400 Vitry Sur Seine, France
{riad.menasri,oulhadj,daachi,nakib,siarry}@u-pec.fr

Abstract. In this work, we deal with a class of problems of trajectory planning taking into account the smoothness of the trajectory. We
assume that we have a set of positions in which the robot must pass.
These positions are not assigned in the time axis. In this work, we propose a formulation of this problem, where the total length of the trajectory and the total time to move from the initial to the final position are
minimized simultaneously. In order to ensure effective results and avoid
abrupt movement, we should ensure the smoothness of the trajectory not
only at the position level but also at the velocity and the acceleration levels. Thus, the position function must be at least two times differentiable.
In our case, we use a polynomial function. We formulate this problem
as a constraint optimization problem. To resolve it, we adapt the usual
particle swarm algorithm to our problem and we show its efficiency by
simulation.

Keywords: Trajectory planning · Smooth trajectory · Particle swarm
optimization

1 Introduction

In the recent years, optimization techniques are largely applied to deal with the
problem of trajectory planning. Indeed, in many applications in industries, this
problem became more and more difficult because of the robot's environment
which is very constrained and other factors to take into account like the energy
consumption, the smoothness of trajectory, etc. That is why the use of the optimization became necessary to find an optimal solution and to satisfy all these
factors. Thus, many techniques were developed [1–3].

In the problem of trajectory planning, many contexts can be defined. Indeed,
according to the kind of the robot, some researchers were interested by trajectory planning for mobile robot [4,5], others for manipulators (redundant or not
redundant)[6–8]. Adding to this, many points can be treated like obstacle avoidance, smoothness of the result trajectory, kinematic and dynamic constraints,
etc. The result of the developed techniques in this field were the whole trajectory

© Springer International Publishing Switzerland 2014
P. Siarry et al. (Eds.): ICSIBO 2014, LNCS 8472, pp. 50–59, 2014.
DOI: 10.1007/978-3-319-12970-9_6

for the robot or only a set of configurations in which the robot must pass. In the last case, the smoothness is not treated.

One of the problems treated in trajectory planning is the smoothness of trajectory. This aspect of the result is important because it allows to the robot to move without abrupt movements. Thus, the mechanical structure of the robot and the actuators will be preserved. Some researchers were interested especially by this aspect. Thus, they did not deal with the whole of the trajectory planning problem but only with the smoothness of the result trajectory. So, the problem of trajectory planning became a problem of interpolation. Many techniques were developed like the use of cubic spline [9], B-splines [10,11], trigonometric functions [12,13], etc. The use of trigonometric functions is interesting in the sense that guarantees a smooth curves even at the acceleration level. Indeed, to ensure a good movement of the robot, we must ensure a smooth curve at the position, the velocity and the acceleration levels. If the control points (nodes to interpolate) are near, the interpolation becomes more difficult. In this case, the use of techniques based on polynomial functions like the cubic spline is more interesting. Indeed, with these functions, it is easier to modify the available data. The common points of all these techniques is that to apply them, we need the available data to be in two dimensions (in general position versus time). However, some results of trajectory planning were only in one dimension. In this case, we can not apply directly the classical method to find the whole trajectory. In this work, we were interested by this kind of methods. We proposed a formulation of this problem and a technique to resolve it.

The rest of the paper is structured as follows : the section 2 gives more details about the problem treated and its formulation. The section 3 shows the technique used to resolve the problem. The section 4 shows the simulation results. We conclude this paper in section 5.

2   Problem Statement

As mentioned before, there are a lot of techniques to deal with the problem of trajectory planning. Some of them give the whole trajectory. Thus, we have the variation of the position versus time. Other techniques give only a set of configurations in which the robot must pass. Thus, we do not have the variation of the position versus time. Adding to this, the data are represented only in one dimension. Indeed, some works give only a set of positions like in [14–16]. In this case, we can not apply the classical methods of interpolation. So, the result is not complete in the sense that we do not have the total time to move from the initial to the final position and the smoothness of the result curves is not ensured. In this work, we were interested by this kind of methods and we propose a technique to complete these results. In order to have a smooth movement for the robot, we must ensure a smooth trajectory at the acceleration level. As the available data are represented in one dimension, we can not use directly the classical method. So, we can assign to each position a value on the time axis and after that, apply the classical methods or compute simultaneously the time values and the whole curves. We chose the second way because the criteria that we defined were related. We chose to use polynomial functions because it is easier to modify the available data.

2.1   Fourth Order Polynomial Function

In order to ensure a smooth curve at the acceleration level, we should use at least a fourth order polynomial function. This point is guaranteed by all trigonometric functions. We use polynomial functions because it is easier to modify the data. Indeed, if the control points are near, it is more difficult to interpolate. With the polynomial functions, we multiply the original data by a factor and at the end, we divide the result by the same factor. Thus, we use a fourth order polynomial function to interconnect each pair of successive knots. The figure 1 shows the use of these functions : $P_i(t)$ and $P_{i+1}(t)$ are fourth order polynomial functions.

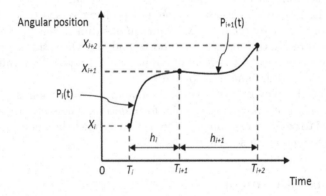

Fig. 1. The use of the fourth order polynomial function

$$P_i(t) = a_0^i + a_1^i \cdot t + a_2^i \cdot t^2 + a_3^i \cdot t^3 + a_4^i \cdot t^4$$
$$P_{i+1}(t) = a_0^{i+1} + a_1^{i+1} \cdot t + a_2^{i+1} \cdot t^2 + a_3^{i+1} \cdot t^3 + a_4^{i+1} \cdot t^4$$

According to the representation in the above figure, we have at the beginning only the values of X_i, X_{i+1} and X_{i+2}. Our goal is to associate to these values, the best values on the time axis and to determine the coefficients of the functions P_i and P_{i+1} in order to have smooth movements while moving from one point to another.

2.2   Criteria

In the proposed formulation, we use three criteria. The first one is used to minimize the total time to move from the initial to the final position, its expression is :

$$F_1 = \sum_{i=1}^{N-1} h_i^2 \tag{1}$$

Where

$$h_i = T_{i+1} - T_i$$

With N is the total number of control points . h_i is the time between two successive control points (figure 1).

To minimize the joints travelling distance, we use the next criterion:

$$F_2 = \sum_{i=1}^{N-1} \dot{q}_i^2 \tag{2}$$

With $\dot{q}_i$ is the angular velocity (joint velocity). In fact, for a function $y = g(x)$ the curve length is defined by Eq.3 and, consequently, the simplified expression in Eq.4 is adopted to minimize the curve length distance:

$$\int \left[1 + \left(\frac{dg}{dx} \right)^2 \right] dx \tag{3}$$

$$\int \left(\frac{dg}{dx} \right)^2 = \int \dot{g}^2 dx \tag{4}$$

The last criterion is used to minimize the ripple in the time evolution of the robot trajectory, its expression is:

$$F_3 = \sum_{i=1}^{N-1} \ddot{q}_i^2 \tag{5}$$

With $\ddot{q}_i$ is the angular acceleration (joint acceleration).

2.3   Constraints

The constraints used in our formulation are the continuity at the position, the velocity and the acceleration. According to the figure 1, the constraints are:

$$P_i(T_{i+1}) = P_{i+1}(T_{i+1})$$

$$\dot{q}_i(T_{i+1}) = \dot{q}_{i+1}(T_{i+1})$$

$$\ddot{q}_i(T_{i+1}) = \ddot{q}_{i+1}(T_{i+1})$$

P, $\dot{q}$, $\ddot{q}$ represent the curves of the position, the velocity and the acceleration respectively. To ensure that the curve of position passes as close to the knots, we define an inequality constraint for each knot. For instance, for the knot with the value X_i, we have:

$$|P_i(T_i) - X_i| \leq R$$

With a very small value of R. In adding these constraints, we have the initial and the final conditions.

2.4   Formulation

Using the criteria 1, 2, 5 and the constraints described before, the formulation of the problem is:

$$\min \; F = \alpha \cdot F_1 + \beta \cdot F_2 + \gamma \cdot F_3 \qquad (6)$$

$$\text{subject to} \; \begin{cases} Continuity\ conditions \\ Initial\ and\ final\ conditions \end{cases}$$

With α, β, γ are weighting parameters. $\alpha + \beta + \gamma = 1$.

3   Problem Resolution

The proposed formulation is very constrained and its complexity increases with the number of knots (control points). Indeed, if we have many knots, the number of constraints increases and it will be difficult to satisfy all of them. That is why we chose to use a population based metaheuristic.

3.1   Particle Swarm Optimization

Particle swarm optimization is a stochastic population based metaheuristic inspired by social behavior patterns of organisms that live and interact within groups. In particular, it incorporates swarming behaviors observed in flocks of birds, schools of fishes, or swarms of bees, and even human social behavior, from which the swarm intelligence paradigm has emerged [17]. The based model of particle swarm consists of a swarm of particles, which are initialised with a population of random candidate solutions. They move iteratively in the search space to find a new solution. Each particle has a position represented by a position vector x_i (i is the index of the particle), and a velocity represented by a velocity vector v_i. Each particle remembers its own best position so far in a vector p_i. The best position vector among the swarm so far is then stored in a vector p_g. During the iteration time t, the update of the velocity from the previous velocity to the new velocity is determined in Eq.7 . The new position is then determined by the sum of the previous position and the new velocity according to Eq.8 :

$$v_i(t+1) = w.v_i(t) + c_1.r_1.(p_i(t) - x_i(t)) + c_2.r_2.(p_g(t) - x_i(t)) \qquad (7)$$

$$x_i(t+1) = x_i(t) + v_i(t+1) \tag{8}$$

Where c_1 is a positive constant, called coefficient of the self-recognition component, c_2 is a positive constant, called coefficient of the social component. r_1 and
r_2 are random numbers in the interval $[0,1]$. The variable w is called the inertia
factor, of which value is in the interval $[0,1]$.

3.2   Particles Size

The size of particles depends on the numbers of knots that we take at the beginning. For instance and according to the case represented in the figure 1, the
particle is represented in the figure 2:

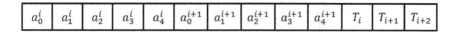

Fig. 2. Representation of the particle

4   Simulation

To test the proposed method, we took three values of angular position. We fixed
the parameters of the algorithm according to the convergence analysis done in
[18], this choice is represented in table 1:

Table 1. Fitting of algorithm parameters

Parameters	Values
Population size	100
Iteration number	300000
coefficient w	0.729
$c_1 = c_2$	1.494

We use the maximum of iterations number as condition to stop the algorithm.
The whole population is initialized randomly. At each iteration, the algorithm
provides a solution in which the values of time and the coefficients are found
simultaneously. We take $R = 0.08$, the initial and the final conditions are equal
to zero for both velocity and acceleration.

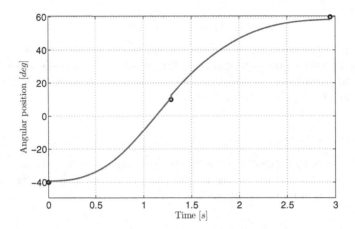

Fig. 3. Angular position

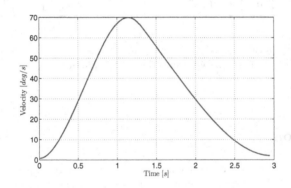

Fig. 4. Angular velocity

The result is illustrated in the figures 3, 4 and 5. In this case, we take the weighting parameters $\alpha = 0.35, \beta = 0.35, \gamma = 0.3$ for the objective function.

At the position level, we can say globally that we obtain a smooth trajectory and the result curve passes near the defined knots which are represented by a small black circle.

At the velocity level, we obtain a smooth curve. We also remark that we respect the initial and final conditions.

At the acceleration level, we remark that we respect the initial and final conditions, we obtain a smooth curve globally.

The results in the above figures present one case with an arbitrary choice of the weighting parameters. Thus, we can obtain other curves with other parameters. In real applications, we have a limitation in velocity and acceleration that we do not exceed. So, we can manipulate the weighting parameters in order to respect these limitations. For instance, we show the result of mean of velocity for two arbitrary

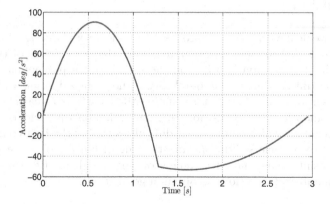

Fig. 5. Angular acceleration

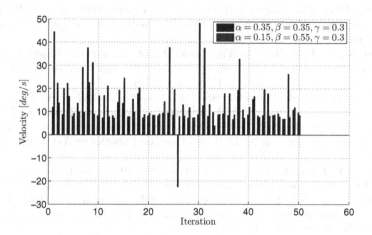

Fig. 6. Mean of velocity

choices of the weighting parameters. As we use stochastic parameters, we run the algorithm fifty times. the results are represented in figure 6 :

According to the results presented in figure 6, we have 36 % of the test results in which we have high mean of velocity for the weighting parameters $\alpha = 0.35, \beta = 0.35, \gamma = 0.3$ compared to those obtained with the weighting parameters $\alpha = 0.15, \beta = 0.55, \gamma = 0.3$. This result can be explained by the fact that in the second case, we increase the value of β. Thus, we give more importance to minimize the velocity.

With this kind of test, we can have an idea about the choice of the weighting parameters in order to respect the limitation in velocity or in acceleration.

5 Conclusion

In this work, we deal with a class of problems of trajectory planning. We propose a formulation to this problem in order to ensure the smoothness of the result trajectory. This formulation is based on the use of fourth polynomial function which are twice differentiable. The complexity of the proposed formulation is that we search simultaneously to assign a value on the time axis to each predefined position and smooth curve. Thus, for each new value on the time axis, all the result curves change, which causes great difficulties to find the best combination of them. We use particle swarm optimization algorithm to solve the problem. Simulations results show the effectiveness of this metaheuristic. However, we need a high number of iterations to obtain a good result.

References

1. Da Graa Marcos, M., Tenreiro Machado, J.A., Azevedo-Perdicoulis, T.-P.: Multi-objective approach for the motion planning of redundant manipulators. Applied Soft Computing **12**, 589–599 (2012)
2. Hauser, K., Ng-Thow-Hing, V.: Fast Smoothing of Manipulator Trajectories using Optimal Bounded-Acceleration Shortcuts. In: IEEE Intl. Conf. of Robotics and Automation (ICRA), Anchorage, USA (May 2010)
3. Solteiro Pires, E.J., de Moura Oliveira, P.B., Tenreiro Machado, J.A.: Manipulator trajectory planning using a MOEA. Applied Soft Computing **7**, 659–667 (2007)
4. Kuffner, J.J., LaValle, S.M.: RRT-COnnect: an efficient approach to single-query path planning, In: Proc. 2000 IEEE Int'I Conf. on Robotics an Automation, ICRA (2000)
5. Clark, C.M.: Probabilistic road map sampling strategies for multi-robot motion planning. Robotics and Autonomous Systems **53**, 244–264 (2005)
6. Liu, H., Lai, X., Wu, W.: Time-optimal and jerk-continuous trajectory planning for robot manipulators with kinematic constraints. Robotics Computer-Integrated Manufacturing **29**, 309–317 (2013)
7. Daachi, B., Madani, T., Benallegue, A.: Adaptive neural controller for redundant robot manipulators and collision avoidance with mobile obstacles. Neurocomputing **79**, 50–60 (2012)
8. Le Boudec, B., Saad, M., Nerguizian, V.: Modeling and adaptive control of redundant robots. Mathematics and Computers in Simulation **71**, 395–403 (2006)
9. Gasparetto, A., Zanotto, V.: Optimal trajectory planning for industrial robots. Advances in Engineering Software **41**, 548–556 (2010)
10. Shukla, A., Singla, E., Wahi, P., Dasgupta, B.: A direct variational method for planning monotonically optimal paths for redundant manipulators in constrained workspaces. Robotics and Autonomous Systems **61**, 209–220 (2013)
11. Gasparetto, A., Zanotto, V.: A new method for smooth trajectory planning of robot manipulators. Mechanism and Machine Theory **42**, 455–471 (2007)
12. S. Benyue and Z. Liping, Manipulator Trajectory Planning Based on the Algebraic-Trigonometric Hermite Blended Interpolation Spline, 2012 International Workshop on Information and Electronics Engineering, 29 (2012) 2093–2097
13. Xian, C.: Cubic trigonometric Bézier spline interpolation. Journal of Jiamusi University **27**(3), 445–448 (2009)

14. Da Graa Marcos, M., Tenreiro Machado, J.A., Azevedo-Perdicoulis, T.-P.: Trajectory planning of redundant manipulators using genetic algorithms, Common Nonlinear Sci Numer Simulat, 14 (2009) 2858–2869
15. Tian, L., Collins, C.: An effective robot trajectory planning method using a genetic algorithm. Mechatronics **14**, 455–470 (2004)
16. Menasri, R., Nakib, A., Oulhadj, H., Daachi, B., Siarry, P., Hains, G.: Path planning for redundant manipulators using metaheuristic for bilevel optimization and maximum of manipulability. In: IEEE International Conference on Robotics and Biomimetics (ROBIO) Shenzhen, China (December 2013)
17. Talbi, E.G.: Metaheuristic. John Wiley & Sons Inc, From Design to Implementation (2009)
18. Trelea, I.: Cristian. The particle swarm optimization algorithm: convergence analysis and parameter selection, Information processing letters **85**(6), 317–325 (2003)

Multi-level Parallelization for Hybrid ACO

Omar Abdelkafi, Julien Lepagnot[(✉)], and Lhassane Idoumghar

LMIA, Université de Haute-Alsace (UHA), E.A. 3993, 4 rue des frères lumière,
68093 Mulhouse, France
{omar.abdelkafi,julien.lepagnot,lhassane.idoumghar}@uha.fr

Abstract. The Graphics-Processing-Unit (GPU) became one of the
main platforms to design massively parallel metaheuristics. This advance
is due to the highly parallel architecture of GPU and especially thanks
to the publication of languages like CUDA. In this paper, we deal with
a multi-level parallel hybrid Ant System (AS) to solve the Travelling
Salesman Problem (TSP). This multi-level is represented by two parallel platforms. The first one is the GPU, this platform is used for the
parallelization of tasks, data, solution and neighborhood-structure. The
second platform is the MPI which is dedicated to the parallelization of
programs. Our contribution is to use these two platforms to design a
hybrid AS with a Local Search and a new heuristic.

Keywords: Parallel hybrid metaheuristics · TSP · GPU · MPI

1 Introduction

Hybrid metaheuristics [1][2][3] are one of the most efficient classes of algorithms.
The idea is to combine metaheuristics [4] and other techniques for optimization. With the combination of different techniques, these methods can require a
longer computation time than others. This is one of the reasons that lead the
community to propose parallel hybrid metaheuristics [5]. Another reason is the
evolution of highly parallel architectures like the GPU. This evolution is due to
the explosion of the industry of video games and his greedy demand for graphic
power. Indeed, with the advent of CUDA, the use of GPU for non-graphic applications has become easier and hybrid metaheuristics have taken advantage of this
evolution.

There are many levels of parallelization. For the Ant Colony Optimization
(ACO) [6] applied to the TSP in the context of a single colony, the parallel execution of ants in the tour construction phase was initiated by Bullnheimer et al.
[7]. Also in this same context, in 2013, Cecilia et al. [8] used the data parallelization in the update of pheromone to get the best performance from the GPU. In
the context of multiple colonies, Stutzle [9] introduced the execution of multiple
colonies in parallel with cooperation between colonies to improve the quality
of solutions using the parallelization of programs. In CUDA programming, the
execution on GPU is conducted by the kernel. It is a code called from the CPU

© Springer International Publishing Switzerland 2014
P. Siarry et al. (Eds.): ICSIBO 2014, LNCS 8472, pp. 60–67, 2014.
DOI: 10.1007/978-3-319-12970-9_7

(the host) and duplicated on GPU (the device) to run in a parallel way. The kernel is executed in a *grid*, which is a set of *blocks* where every block is a set of *threads*.

In this work, we propose a hybrid ACO through one of the first variant of this method named the Ant System (AS) [10]. Our first contribution is to propose a new design for AS multi-colonies using GPU and MPI and the second contribution is to hybridize this method with a parallel local search (PLS) providing the intensification of the search and a new heuristic to improve results.

The rest of the paper is organized as follows. In section 2, we introduce the background needed for ACO and TSP to help the understanding of this proposition. We describe in section 3 the design of our multi-level parallel hybrid AS before we discuss the results of our experimentation in section 4. Finally, in section 5, we conclude the paper and we propose some perspective.

2   Background

The TSP is an NP-hard problem and one of the most studied combinatorial problems. It consists in finding the least-cost Hamiltonian circuit between a set of cities starting and ending with the same city. In general, TSP can be represented by a complete undirected graph G = (V, E). The set V= {1, ..., n} is the vertex set, E={$(i, j) : i, j \in V, i < j$} is an edge set. c_{ij} is defined on E as the Euclidean distance between two vertices i and j.

Intuitively in the natural behaviors, the ants search the food randomly in the first tour construction. They move from one point to another until they find food. Once it is done, ants get back to the starting point. This corresponds to the initialization. In the search process, ants depose pheromone along the path they take. The quantity of pheromone is implemented by equation (1):

$$\tau_{ij} = \tau_{ij} + \sum_{k=1}^{N} \Delta\tau_{ij}^{k} \quad \forall(i, j) \in E \tag{1}$$

where $\Delta\tau_{ij}^{k}$ is the sum of pheromone which ant k deposits when it uses the edge between i and j. It depends on the length of the tour C^k constructed by the ant k; $\Delta\tau_{ij}^{k}$ is defined in equation (2):

$$\Delta\tau_{ij}^{k} = \frac{1}{C^k} \tag{2}$$

Another characteristic of the pheromone in the natural behavior is the evaporation: the pheromone evaporates over time. This characteristic is implemented with a parameter $0 < \rho \leq 1$ in equation (3):

$$\tau_{ij} = (1 - \rho)\tau_{ij}, \quad \forall(i, j) \in E \tag{3}$$

The second step is the tour construction. In the natural behaviors, the ants follow the pheromone to find the best tour. To implement this concept, a probability is defined in equation (4) where $n_{ij} = \frac{1}{c_{ij}}$, α and β are parameters and N_i^k is feasible neighborhood. A complete survey on ACO can be found in [6].

$$\Delta p_{ij}^k = \frac{[\tau_{ij}]^\alpha [n_{ij}]^\beta}{\sum_{l \in N_i^k} [\tau_{il}]^\alpha [n_{il}]^\beta} \qquad (4)$$

3 Design of the Parallel Hybrid ACO

The most straightforward way to design parallel AS or ACO in general is the parallelization of ants. This kind of parallelization is called the task parallelization and this is our first parallel level. The idea is very simple and used in most of the parallel ACO algorithms. Every ant is represented by a thread and every thread performs the tour construction in parallel with other ants. Inside the kernel, the ant chooses the next city to visit among the cities not selected yet and according to the probability computed by equation (4). The *CURAND library* allows the generation of a different random tour for every ant. The classical roulette wheel is used to select the next city to visit.

For the pheromone update part(see equation 1), using task parallelization can lead to concurrent access problems, i.e. if several ants update the pheromone of the same arc at the same time. The only solution in this case is to use atomic instructions but it decreases dramatically the performance. Hence, we are rather using data parallelism proposed by [8].

The level of data parallelization is used for the kernel of Update pheromone (see algorithm 1), the Evaporation pheromone (see algorithm 2) and the Update probability (see algorithm 3).

Algorithm 1. The Update pheromone kernel:

1: *Input*: **Pants**: the population of ants; **fants**: the fitness of ants; **pheromone**: the matrix of pheromone; **cities**: the size of the instance; **ants**: the size of the population;
2: Get the index of the thread idx; /*each idx represent one couple of cities*/
3: **for** i:=1 to ants **do**
4:     distance = fants[i];
5:     **for** j:=1 to cities **do**
6:         **if** the arc between i and j == idx **then**
7:             pheromone[idx]=pheromone[idx]+($\frac{1}{distance}$);
8:         **end if**
9:     **end for**
10: **end for**

Algorithm 2. The Evaporate pheromone kernel:

1: *Input*: **pheromone**: the matrix of pheromone;
2: Get the index of the thread idx; /*each idx represent one couple of cities*/
3: pheromone[idx]=(1-ρ) × pheromone[idx];

Algorithm 3. The Update probability kernel:

1: *Input*: **pheromone**: the matrix of pheromone; **probabilities**: the matrix of probabilities; **cij**: the matrix of distances; **cities**: the size of the instance;
2: Get the index of the thread idx; /*each idx represent one couple of cities*/
3: /*control if the cities of the couple are the same*/
4: **if** cij[idx] $\neq$ 0 **then**
5:     arc = $(pheromone[idx])^\alpha \times (\frac{1}{cij[idx]})^\beta$
6:     all = 0
7:     position = $\lfloor \frac{idx}{cities} \rfloor$ /*Get the position of the couple in the matrix*/
8:     /*when j=position, cij[(position $\times$ cities)+j]=0*/
9:     **for** $j \in \{0, 1, \ldots, position - 1, position + 1, \ldots, cities\}$ **do**
10:       all += $(pheromone[(position \times cities) + j])^\alpha \times (\frac{1}{cij[(position \times cities)+j]})^\beta$
11:     **end for**
12:     probability[idx] = $\frac{arc}{all}$
13: **end if**

Our idea to hybridize ACO is to use a Parallel Local Search and a new heuristics that we name smart ants. These algorithms are added to AS, but it can be used for all the variants of ACO. The PLS is applied to a group of ants after the Tour construction. It is a classical local search but the differences are the evaluation and generation of neighborhood executed in parallel with the GPU. It consists in representing every item of the solution by a thread, which leads to a parallel execution of neighbors generation. The thread generates and evaluates the neighbor of its item and searches the best possible switch. At the end of the parallel execution, the algorithm searches the best results of all the threads. This is the third level of parallelization.

The aim of the smart ant heuristic is to improve results. It executes as much iterations as the size of the instance without considering the start city which is static and unchangeable. The figure 1 shows a small example of the heuristic using 4 cities which mean 3 iterations and every vector represents an ant. In every iteration i we search the best ant inside the colony. For example in iteration 2 of the figure 1, the best ant is the third ant which have the index 2 because it starts from 0. All the ants follow the movement of ant_2 at the position 2 indicated by the arrow in the figure 1. The city in this position for ant_2 is city number 3. By consequence, ant_0 and ant_1 move their cities to get the city 3 in position 2. This is why we name it smart ants, because they have the intelligence to adjust their tour. All the ants perform this heuristic in parallel so we use the level of parallel tasks. As we can see with this heuristic, after a certain number of iterations, all the ants have the same tour. By consequence, this heuristic leads the search to stagnancy. To escape from this stagnancy, one improvement is added. The switch is not performed when the two cities to switch are adjacent (example in figure 1 the iteration 1 for ant_0).

The last step of our approach is to use MPI to execute our method on many GPU. This step introduces a new level of parallelization: the level of parallel programs. Actually, different colonies will be executed in parallel through many processes. For example, if we execute 3 processes, we will duplicate our algorithm

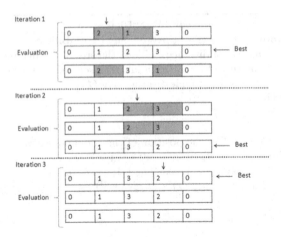

Fig. 1. Smart ants

3 times. By consequence, 3 colonies will be executed in parallel. MPI gives to our design another advantage: we can exchange information between processes in order to improve the results. To exchange information, the algorithm regularly chooses the best solution found in one process and updates the pheromone of the matrix located in the next process using a ring topology. The data parallelization is not suitable this time. Since inside the solution every city is visited only once, a new level of parallelization between cities is applied which is the solution level parallelization. For all the couple of cities used in the tour, the pheromones of these couples are updated in parallel. The atomic operation is not needed because each couple appears only once in a tour.

4   Experimental Results

4.1   Platform and Tests

In our experimentation, we use a cluster of 12 graphic cards NVIDIA Geforce GTX680. The benchmark used is a set of well known instances from the TSPLIB [11] with a size between 51 and 150 cities. All the results are expressed as a percentage deviation from the optimum. All the optimal solutions can be found in the online benchmark library TSPLIB.

4.2   The Smart Ants Heuristic

Table 1 shows the performance of the proposed algorithm with and without the smart ants (SA) heuristic for one colony. 25 tests are performed for every instance with 100 iterations. SA heuristic improves the average results of the 25 tests in the 5 instances.

Table 1. Evaluation of the smart ants heuristic

Instances	AVG with SA	AVG without SA
Eil51	3.13%	3.81%
Berlin52	2.50%	3.14%
Eil76	5.64%	6.35%
Pr76	4.85%	6.14%
KroA100	4.67%	5.26%

4.3   The Parallel Multiple Colonies Using MPI

We use the cluster with 12 GPU. 10 tests for each instance are performed for 10 instances from TSPLIB. Table 2 reports the best results (MIN), the worst results (MAX), the average results (AVG) and the average time required for the 10 tests. The parameters used are $\alpha = 1$; $\beta = 2$; $\rho = 0,5$. 300 iterations are executed for each colony and every one of them contains 256 ants. 12 processes are executed one per machine in the cluster. The number of colonies executed in parallel is 12. Every 10 iterations the processes exchange their best solutions using a ring topology. 60% of the average results are between 0 and 3%. From the 10 instances, 9 average results are inferior to 5%.

Table 2. The multi-level parallel hybrid AS

Instances	MIN (%)	MAX (%)	AVG (%)	Time (s)
Eil51	0.99	3.02	1.98	10.57
Berlin52	0.03	2.33	1.07	14
St70	1.53	3.2	2.61	25.96
Eil76	2.83	5.04	4.21	28.02
Pr76	1.99	3.55	2.76	31.44
Rat99	3.53	7.8	6.19	35.7
KroA100	2.41	3.61	3.17	55.92
Bier127	1.25	2.58	1.87	87.72
Ch130	1.86	3.11	2.51	72.2
Ch150	2.84	3.75	3.42	76.8

The next experiment has the aim to see the behavior of the cluster when the objective function is evaluated equally between one GPU and 8 GPU. In this experiment, the same number of ants is used in the two cases. Table 3 presents the average results of 10 tests for 4 instances. AVG 1 is the average for the first case, AVG 2 is the average for the second case and ACC is the acceleration of the cluster compared to one GPU. With these conditions, the parallel design with the cluster improves the results and gives accelerations between 1.22 and 1.84 times compared to one GPU.

The final experiment is to compare our approach to other methods from the literature. In table 4, works from the literature are used for the evaluation. 4 approaches are selected. [12] is an ACO algorithm for TSP and [13][14][15] are other approaches to solve TSP for 5 instances. [*] is our approach and the results are the percentage deviation from the optimum. The Friedman test [16], performed on these 5 problems with $\alpha = 5\%$, shows that we can reject the null hypothesis, i.e. there is at least one algorithm whose performance is different

Table 3. MPI accelerations

Instances	AVG 1(%)	AVG 2 (%)	ACC
Berlin52	2.72	1.04	×1.73
Pr76	5.4	3.08	×1.40
Bier127	2.53	2.18	×1.22
Ch150	4.43	3.91	×1.84

from at least one of the other algorithms. To know which algorithms are different, we perform paired comparisons. The critical value is C=3.67. The paired comparisons (see Table 5) show that the results obtained by [*] are different from those obtained by the four other approaches. From the above analysis, we can see that our hybrid algorithm is better and outperforms the other four metaheuristics.

Table 4. Literature comparison

Instances	[*]	[12]	[13]	[14]	[15]
Eil51	1.98	7.98	2.89	2.69	3.43
Berlin52	1.07	7.38	7.01	5.18	5.81
Eil76	4.21	12.08	4.35	3.41	5.46
Bier127	1.87	15.32	3	2.2	3.41
Ch130	2.51	24.15	2.82	2.82	2.82

Table 5. Paired comparisons

Instances	[12]	[13]	[14]	[15]
[*]	19	10	4	12
[12]	-	9	15	7
[13]	-	-	6	2
[14]	-	-	-	8

5 Conclusion and Perspectives

This work has two main objectives. The first one is to design a parallel ACO which can run in a cluster of GPU. The second objective is to improve the quality of solutions and to be as close as possible to the global optimum.

For the first objective, we use Five levels of parallelization. The first one is the parallelization of tasks performed by the GPU, which helps us to parallelize ants for the tour construction and the smart ant heuristic. The second level is the parallelization of data performed by GPU, which help us to update and evaporate the pheromones and to update the probabilities. The third level is the parallelization of the neighborhood structure performed also by GPU. This level is essentially used to parallelize the neighborhood inside the PLS. The fourth level is the solution level parallelization, performed by the GPU and used to update the pheromone when the best solution is exchanged between colonies. Finally, the last level is the parallelization of programs performed by MPI. It allows us to parallelize different colonies and to diversify the search as much as possible. For the second objective we hybridize the AS: we use two techniques. The first one is to add the PLS for the intensification of the search. The second technique is to test a new heuristics named smart ant to improve results.

In our future works, we plan to apply the proposed algorithm to other combinatorial problems like the quadratic assignment problem. Another perspective is to reuse the same design for other swarm intelligence methods like the particle swarm optimization.

References

1. Blum, C., Puchinger, J., Raidl, G.R., Roli, A.: Hybrid metaheuristics in combinatorial optimization: A survey. Applied Soft Computing **11**(6), 4135–4151 (2011)
2. Lepagnot, J., Idoumghar, L., Fodorean, D.: Hybrid Imperialist Competitive Algorithm with Simplex approach: Application to Electric Motor Design, In: 2013 IEEE International Conference on Systems Man and Cybernetics (SMC) pp. 2454–2459, Manchester UK (October 2013)
3. Aouad, M.I., Idoumghar, L., Schott, R., Zendra, O.: Sequential and Distributed Hybrid GA-SA Algorithms for Energy Optimization in Embedded Systems, In: The IADIS International Conference Applied Computing 2010, pp. 167–174 (2010)
4. Blum, C., Roli, A.: Metaheuristics in Combinatorial Optimization: Overview and Conceptual Comparison. ACM Computing Surveys **35**, 268–308 (2003)
5. Cotta, C., Talbi, E.G. Alba, E.: Parallel Hybrid Metaheuristics, in Parallel Metaheuristics: A New Class of Algorithms. John Wiley and Sons (2005)
6. Dorigo, M., Stutzle, T.: Ant Colony Optimization. Bradford Company, USA (2004)
7. Bullnheimer, B., Kotsis, G., Strauss, C.: Parallelization strategies for the ant system. Applied Optimization **24**, 87–100 (1997)
8. Cecilia, J.M., Garcia, J.M., Nisbet, A., Amos, M., Ujaldon, M.: Enhancing data parallelism for Ant Colony Optimization on GPUs. J. Parallel Distrib. Comput. **73**, 42–51 (2013)
9. Stützle, Thomas: Parallelization Strategies for Ant Colony Optimization. In: Eiben, Agoston E., Bäck, Thomas, Schoenauer, Marc, Schwefel, Hans-Paul (eds.) PPSN 1998. LNCS, vol. 1498, p. 722. Springer, Heidelberg (1998)
10. Dorigo, M.: Optimization: learning and natural algorithms, Ph.D. Thesis, Politecnico di Milano, Italy (1992)
11. Reinelt, G.: TSPLIB - A Traveling Salesman Problem Library. ORSA Journal on Computing **3**(4), 376–384 (1991)
12. Chirico, U.: A java framework for ant colony systems, Technical report, Siemens Informatica S.p.A (2004)
13. Cochrane, E.M., Beasley, J.E.: The co-adaptive neural network approach to the Euclidean traveling salesman problem. Neural Networks **16**(10), 1499–1525 (2003)
14. Masutti, T.A.S., Castro, L.N.D.: A self-organizing neural network using ideas from the immune system to solve the traveling salesman problem. Information Sciences **179**(10), 1454–1468 (2009)
15. Somhom, S., Modares, A., Enkawa, T.: A self-organizing model for the traveling salesman problem, Journal of the Operational Research Society, 919–928 (1997)
16. Idoumghar, L., Chérin, N., Siarry, P., Roche, R., Miraoui, A.: Hybrid ICA-PSO algorithm for continuous optimization. Applied Mathematics and Computation **219**, 11149–11170 (2013)

Parallel and Distributed Implementation Models for Bio-inspired Optimization Algorithms

Hongjian Wang[✉] and Jean-Charles Créput

IRTES-SeT, Université de Technologie de Belfort-Montbéliard,
90010 Belfort, France
hongjian.wang@utbm.fr

Abstract. Bio-inspired optimization algorithms have natural parallelism but practical implementations in parallel and distributed computational systems are nontrivial. Gains from different parallelism philosophies and implementation strategies may vary widely. In this paper, we contribute with a new taxonomy for various parallel and distributed implementation models of metaheuristic optimization. This taxonomy is based on three factors that every parallel and distributed metaheuristic implementation needs to consider: *control*, *data*, and *memory*. According to our taxonomy, we categorize different parallel and distributed bio-inspired models as well as local search metaheuristic models. We also introduce a new designed GPU parallel model for the Kohonen's self-organizing map, as a representative example which belongs to a significant category in our taxonomy.

Keywords: Parallel and distributed computing · Metaheuristic · Genetic algorithm · Ant colony optimization · Self-organizing map

1 Introduction

In the combinatorial optimization community, there exist a number of different bio-inspired optimization metaheuristics, such as genetic algorithms (GA), ant colony optimization (ACO), and artificial neural networks (ANN). Inspired by natural systems and designed to mimic certain phenomena or behaviors of biology, these algorithms aim at finding, as optimally as possible, approximate solutions to real-life difficult problems which are usually not able to be solved by exact approaches in reasonable computing time. Biologic systems are usually made up of populations of simple individuals, ants, birds or neurons, interacting locally with one another and with their environment. This trait should imply some potential for parallel and distributed implementations of the derived bio-inspired optimization algorithms. However, the implantation, from nature to practical parallel and distributed computational systems, is not as smooth as it looks like, owing to various restrictions of the latter, coming from 1) resource sharing and competition, 2) communication and synchronization among computing nodes, 3) system robustness requirement. As a result, gains from different parallelism philosophies and implementation strategies may vary widely,

© Springer International Publishing Switzerland 2014
P. Siarry et al. (Eds.): ICSIBO 2014, LNCS 8472, pp. 68–79, 2014.
DOI: 10.1007/978-3-319-12970-9_8

and it is very tricky to come out with a consummate model. Trying to cast some interesting insights on this issue, this paper firstly contributes with a new taxonomy for various parallel and distributed implementation models of metaheuristic optimization, and then categorizes different bio-inspired models as well as local search metaheuristic models according to our taxonomy, including the introduction of a new designed GPU parallel model for the Kohonen's self-organizing map (SOM) [1], as a representative of "control distributed, data decomposition, shared memory" category.

The rest of this paper is organized as follows. Section 2 describes the proposed taxonomy with three factors. According to this new taxonomy, Section 3 categorizes some parallel and distributed implementation models of metaheuristic optimization algorithms, including GA, ACO, SOMANN, and local search. A new designed GPU parallel model for SOMANN is also introduced in Section 3. The partly distributed model and the fully distributed model are discussed in Section 4 before some conclusions of this work are drawn in Section 5.

2   Taxonomy for Parallel and Distributed Strategies

Generally, parallel computing speeds up computation by dividing the work load among a certain amount of processors. In the parallel computing community, two main sources of parallelism which are well accepted are *data parallelism* and *control parallelism* [2,3]. Data parallelism refers to the execution of the same operation or instruction on multiple large data subsets at the same time [2]. This is in contrast to control parallelism (or task parallelism, or function parallelism, or operation parallelism), which refers to the concurrent execution of different tasks allocated to different processors, possibly working on the "same" data and exchanging information [3]. Parallel computation based on these two parallelisms is particularly efficient when algorithms manipulate data structures that are strongly regular, such as matrices in matrix multiplications. Algorithms operating on irregular data structures or on data with strong dependencies among the different operations remain difficult to parallelize efficiently and to characterize comprehensively, using only data or control parallelism. Metaheuristics generally belong to this category, and parallelizing them offers opportunities to find new ways to use parallel and distributed computational systems and to design parallel algorithms [4]. In our opinion, the traditional dual classification for general parallel computing looks inadequate when dealing with the various parallel and distributed optimization metaheuristics. One important point that should be emphasized concerns the allocation of processors and memory according to the instance size of the problem. We think this point, specific to optimization, should be alighted in the taxonomies of parallel and distributed metaheuristic implementations, since it determines the maximum size of the input that could be solved in systems on hand *and* how the performance should grow according to the amount of physical cores and memory.

We propose a new taxonomy as shown in Fig. 1. It is based on the three factors that every parallel and distributed implementation model of metaheuristic

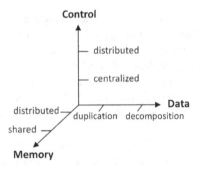

Fig. 1. Taxonomy based on *control, data, memory*

optimization needs to consider: *control, data,* and *memory.* Note that though the two terms of our taxonomy are literally similar to the traditional parallelism classification, they stand for very different considerations.

— *Control.* This term is about algorithmic organization and its corresponding execution pattern on parallel processors. Some parallel and distributed implementation models are based on centralized control on different levels. The most common case is the so called "master-slave" model, as shown in Fig. 2(a), in which a *master* process manages the population and hands out individuals to evaluate to a number of *slave* processes. After the evaluation, the master process iteratively collects the results and applies some global operations, such as selection, to produce the next generations. Ergo in this case, the master process plays a central role while the slave processes act as co-processors to accelerate computation. In out taxonomy, we call this kind of implementation model "control centralized". The opposite implementation model should be under a completely distributed control pattern, without depending on any central control that would break the entire computing network if it was suppressed from the computation implementation, as the cellular model shown in Fig. 2(b). Thus the robustness can be guaranteed because the computation can continue even when some computing units fall down. We call this kind of implementation model "control distributed".

— *Data.* This term denotes the input problem data, of size N, and the representation of the solution. The size of the solution could generally be $O(N)$ since it is in relation to the input. However, the size might depend on optimising operations and the implementation choices of designers. Some algorithms perform metaheuristic exploration and exploitation within a set of solutions (population), handling each solution in parallel, and then select the best-so-far solution iteratively. Implementation models of this kind are built upon "data duplication" and the required memory is with $O(NM)$ where M is the population size. Alternatively, other algorithms generate every part of the whole solution separately in parallel. The final solution can be then obtained by combining together partial results from all the processors. Hence implementation models of this kind are founded on "data decomposition" and their memory employment could remain

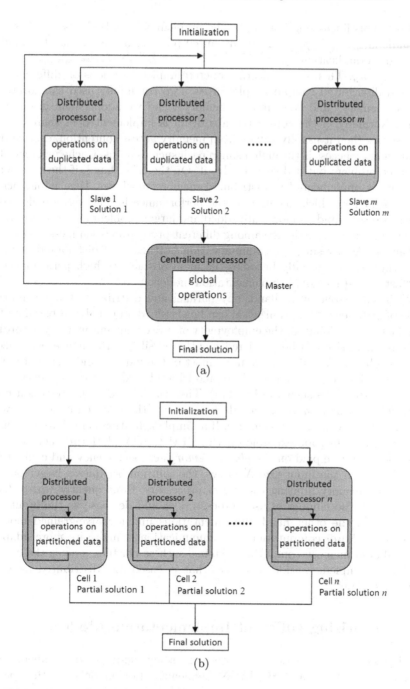

Fig. 2. Comparison between (a) "master-slave" model and (b) cellular model. The parallel "master-slave" model is under "control centralized, data duplication" pattern while the cellular model is under "control distributed, data decomposition" pattern.

in $O(N)$. This linear relationship to the problem size makes these models able to handle larger scale problems with limited physical memory, than the models under "data duplication" pattern.

— *Memory.* This term concerns concrete implementations on different parallel and distributed computing platforms. Two commonly used categories are "shared memory" and "distributed memory", and we adopt them in our taxonomy. Normally, if the considered algorithm is implemented in shared memory systems, then it usually suffers from memory access contention, especially if global memory access is through a single path such as a bus. Cache memory alleviates the problem but it does not solve it. On the other hand, if the considered algorithm is implemented in distributed memory machines, then it has better scaling behavior, which means that the performance is relatively unaffected if more processors (and memory) are added and larger problem instances are tackled. The information exchange among different processors is via message passing mechanism. As a result, the communication bottleneck of distributed memory computing systems usually becomes the main obstacle to high performance of the "distributed memory" implementation models.

With our taxonomy in hand, any parallel and distributed implementation model of metaheuristic optimization can be classified and analyzed based on the three factors. By doing so, the employment of processors and memory according to the problem size can be predicted *and* the possible performance bottlenecks could also be forecasted. For example, most of the parallel and distributed GA implementations under "master-slave" model are based on "control centralized, data duplication", as shown in Fig. 2(a). Then the amount of processors needed is with $O(M)$ where M is the population size *and* the required memory is with $O(NM)$ where N is the problem size. If an implementation is in shared memory computing systems, for example on the GPU CUDA platform, then a lot of attention should be paid on the *global memory* access efficiency and contention. Note that when the input size N grows, the solution occupies a larger part of the central memory limiting the use of processors. Consequently with a fixed memory size, the number of used processors should decrease as the input size increases. On the other hand, implementations under coarse-grained models, where the radio of computation to communication is high, are more adapted to distributed memory computing systems, such as clusters. This is the case of cellular GA implementation model [5] that is based on "distributed memory, data duplication".

3   Categorizing Different Implementation Models

In this section, we consider and categorize some bio-inspired metaheuristics, including GA, ACO, and SOMANN. Implementation models of other parallel metaheuristics, such as local search, are also classified and analyzed in our taxonomy.

3.1   Parallel Genetic Algorithms

GAs are search algorithms inspired by genetics and natural evolutionary principles. The most important operations in GAs are reproduction, mutation, fitness
evaluation and selection (competition). There are several possible levels at which
GAs can be parallelized: the fitness evaluation level, the individual level or the
population level [5]. Parallelization at the fitness evaluation level is usually implemented under "master-slave" model, in which each individual fitness is evaluated
simultaneously on a different processor. This architecture belongs to the "control
centralized, data duplication" category according to our taxonomy, and it can
be implemented on both shared memory multiprocessors as well as distributed
memory machines.

Individual or population-based parallel approaches for GAs introduce additional terms that should be considered, such as *deme*, *migration* and *topology*
[6]. These approaches are inspired by the observation that natural population
tends to possess a spatial structure. The two important spatial structure based
categories are the *island* and the *cellular* models. The island model [7] features
geographically separated subpopulations of relatively large size. Subpopulations
may exchange information from time to time by allowing some individuals to
migrate from one subpopulation to another according to various patterns. In
the cellular model [8], individuals are placed on a large toroidal one or two-
dimensional grid, one individual per grid location. Fitness evaluation is done
simultaneously for all individuals, and selection, reproduction and mating take
place locally within a small neighborhood. From an implementation point of
view, these two kinds of models are often adapted to distributed memory systems [9,10] and accordingly they are classified into the "control distributed, data
duplication, distributed memory" category according to our taxonomy.

3.2   Parallel Ant Colony Optimization

As early as when Dorigo [11] initially proposed ACO, he suggested the application of parallel computing techniques to enhance both the ACO search and
its computational efficiency. A comprehensive survey on parallel ACO can be
found in [12]. Among various parallel ACO implementations, the "master-slave"
model has been quite popular in the research community, mainly due to the
fact that this model is conceptually simple and easy to implement. According
to Pedemonte et al. [12], the "master-slave" model is further divided into three
distinguished subcategories regarding the *granularity*. The standard implementation of *coarse-grain master-slave* ACO assigns one ant to a slave that is executed
on an available processor. The master globally manages the global information
(i.e. the pheromone matrix, the best-so-far solution, etc.), and each slave builds
and evaluates a single solution. The communication between the master and
slaves usually follows a synchronous model. This kind of implementation model
is under "control centralized, data duplication" pattern. In the *medium-grain
master-slave* model, a domain decomposition of the problem is applied. The
slaves solve each subproblem independently, whereas the master manages the

overall problem information and constructs a complete solution from the partial solutions reported by the slaves. Furthermore, in the *fine-grain master-slave*, the slaves perform minimum granularity tasks, such as processing single components used to construct solutions, or parallel evaluation of solution elements. These two kinds of implementation models are under "control centralized, data decomposition" pattern and they can be implemented both in shared memory systems and in network of workstations or clusters, with each node having independent memory. Frequent communications between the master and slaves are usually required in these models, and this issue is more severe when they are implemented in distributed memory systems than shared memory systems.

There exist other parallel and distributed ACO implementation models that are under "control distributed" pattern. In the *cellular* model [12,13], a single colony is structured in small neighborhoods, each one with its own pheromone matrix. Each ant is placed in a cell in a toroidal grid, and the trail pheromone update in each matrix considers only the solutions constructed by the ants in its neighborhood. In the *multicolony* model [12,14], several colonies explore the search space using their own pheromone matrices. The cooperation is achieved by periodically exchanging information among the colonies. In the *parallel independent runs* model [12,15,16], several sequential ACOs, using identical or different parameters, are concurrently executed on a set of processors. The executions are completely independent, without communication among the ACOs, therefore the model does not consider cooperation between colonies. The latter two models have distributed controlling at colony level. These three models above are all under "data duplication" pattern and they can be implemented in both shared memory [16] and distributed memory [13] systems.

3.3   Parallel Self-Organizing Map Artificial Neural Networks

Partly motivated by how visual, auditory or other sensory information is handled in separate parts of the cerebral cortex in the human brain, the Kohonen's SOM [1] is a prominent unsupervised ANN model providing a topology-preserving mapping from a high-dimensional input space onto a two-dimensional map space. Some methods for computing SOM on GPU have been proposed [17,18]. These methods accelerate SOM process by parallelizing the inner steps at each basic iteration, firstly, to find out the winner neuron in parallel, secondly, to move the winner neuron and its neighbors in parallel. Consequently these kinds of implementation models fall into the "control centralized" category.

In our opinion, one interesting model for parallel SOM should be attributed to the "control distributed, data decomposition, shared memory" category, in that, firstly, distributed control guarantees the model's robustness, secondly, data decomposition eases the burden of massive memory usage when dealing with large-scale problems, and thirdly, shared memory reduces the communication costs among different processing units and allows easy implementation on Graphics Processing Unit (GPU) like systems. Given this ambition, we have designed a novel parallel SOM model and implemented it on GPU Compute Unified Device Architecture (CUDA) platform, trying to deal with large scale

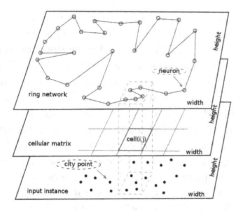

Fig. 3. Parallel cellular model: the input data density distribution, the cellular matrix and the neural network. To a given cell of the cellular matrix corresponds a constant part of the input data as well as a part of the neural network made up of SOM's topological grids/neurons.

travelling salesman problems (TSP) [19]. As illustrated in Fig. 3, three main data structures are used to implement the parallel model. Between the neural network and the input data, we add a uniform two-dimensional cellular matrix with linear relationship to the input size, as a level of decomposition of the plane and the input data. Its role is to memorize the neurons in a distributed fashion and authorize many parallel closest point searches in the plane by a spiral search algorithm [20,21], and then many parallel training procedures. Each uniformly sized cell in the cellular matrix is a basic training unit and will be handled by one parallel processor/GPU thread. Thus, the model proceeds from a cellular decomposition of the input data, in Euclidean space, such that each processor represents a constant and small part of data. Therefore, according to the increase of parallel processors in the future, this approach should be more and more competitive, while at the same time being able to deal with very large size inputs. This quintessential property holds because of the linear memory and processors needed according to the input size. More design details and experimental results of the parallel SOM model can be found in [19].

3.4 Parallel Local Search

Local search is a metaheuristic algorithm which could be viewed as "walks through neighborhoods". The walks are performed by iterative procedures that allow moving from one solution to another, through the solution domains of the problems at hand. Parallelism naturally arises when dealing with a neighborhood, since each of the solutions belonging to it is an independent unit. This kind of parallelization is called *iteration-level parallel model*, a low level "master-slave" model in which evaluation of the neighborhood is made in parallel [22,23]. At the beginning of each iteration, the master duplicates the current solution among parallel nodes. Each of them manages a number of candidates, and the results are returned to the master. This implementation model is obviously under "control centralized, data duplication" pattern. In [23], Luong et al. have re-designed the above model on GPU platform. Considering a neighbor as a slight variation of the candidate solution which generates the neighborhood, they only copy the representation of this candidate solution from CPU to GPU. Then N^2 threads are employed to carry out the parallel 2-opt moves and evaluations, where N is the TSP instance size. Each parallel evaluation only deals with the slight variation based on the candidate solution, with the help of a neighborhood mapping which locates each thread's corresponding variation position in the solution representation. Then the fitness results generated by parallel threads need to be gathered and selected for a best one, which will become the new starting solution, called "pivot", at the next local search iteration. The solution representation and the fitness structure are stored in the global memory of GPU. From the above, it can be concluded that this strategy is under "control centralized, data decomposition, shared memory" pattern.

Other two major parallel models for local search can be distinguished as *solution-level* and *algorithmic-level*. In the solution-level parallel model, the focus is on the parallel evaluation of a single solution *and* the function can be viewed as an aggregation of partial functions. Implementations based on this model are under "control centralized, data decomposition" pattern. In the algorithmic-level parallel model, several local search metaheuristics are simultaneously launched for computing robust solutions. The well-known multistart local search, in which different local search algorithms are launched using diverse initial solutions, is an instantiation of this model [22]. Implementations based on this model are under "control centralized, data duplication" pattern. In our opinion, centralized selection procedures among parallel processors are inevitable, as long as each processor deals with a whole solution. Differently, an interesting model should be fully distributed, where each processor carries out its own local search based on part of the input data, generating one part of the whole solution. Operations on different processors are completely independent with each other *and* no centralized selection procedure is needed. Eventually, a final solution can be obtained by combining all the partial results from different processors. Ergo this implementation model of local search is under "control distributed, data decomposition" pattern, as shown in Fig. 2(b), and it is supposed to be able to solve very large challenging problems, such as the World TSP Challenge, in distributed computing systems such as clusters.

4   Partly Distributed Model vs. Fully Distributed Model

In literature, many implementation models are labeled as "distributed model". Actually, some of them belong to the "control centralized, distributed memory" category according to our taxonomy while others belong to the "control distributed, shared memory" category. In our opinion, these two kinds of implementation models are only *partly distributed*, or distributed in a weak sense.

For example, even if the "master-slave" model is implemented in distributed memory systems with computing nodes communicating by message transfers, the master process necessarily deals with specific data structures different from the slave data structures. We think only the implementation model based on "control distributed, distributed memory" is *fully distributed*, or distributed in a strong sense. No component has special role in this kind of implementation and it could be carried out on networks of stations, or processors, communicating by message transfers, and with all processors executing the same code.

From our point of view, a very significant conceptual implementation model should be under "control distributed, data decomposition, distributed memory" pattern, because it is fully distributed and makes possible to solve very large problems in distributed computing networks. In literature, we found one example which belongs to this category and it was proposed by Nguyen et al. in [24]. They applied an effective implementation of hybrid GA incorporating Lin-Kernighan heuristic, to the 1,904,711-city World TSP Challenge. They divided the world instance into a number of smaller subinstances and then applied PHGA to these subinstances. Finally, they reconnected all the best segments of each subinstance to form a new best tour for the world instance. This example, however, has a high level of granularity since each processor deals with a significant part of the input data using a hybrid GA incorporating Lin-Kernighan heuristic. Based on the same requirement of data decomposition, we have also designed a cellular SOM model to the TSPs, as introduced in this paper. However, in our current work, we implement this model on GPU CUDA platform with global memory, which makes the implementation partly distributed and belong to the "control distributed, data decomposition, shared memory" category. This model however has very low level of granularity with few input data assigned to each processor. Executing low-level granularity models based on data decomposition in distributed memory systems means an important challenge.

5   Conclusion

Parallel and distributed metaheuristics offer the possibility to address large scale problems which are often intractable to traditional sequential algorithms. A good way of formulating, analyzing and classifying different parallel and distributed implementations will be very helpful in designing efficient, scalable, and robust algorithms in return. One important point that should be emphasized concerns the allocation of processors and memory according to the problem size. We think this point, specific to optimization, should be alighted in the taxonomies of parallel and distributed metaheuristic implementation models, since it determines the maximum size of the problem that could be solved in systems on hand *and* how the performance should grow according to the amount of physical cores and memory. With this in mind, we have proposed a new taxonomy and categorized different bio-inspired metaheuristic implementation models according to this taxonomy. Also we have contributed with a new designed GPU parallel model for SOMANN. Furthermore, we have discussed partly distributed models and fully distributed models, in weak and strong senses. We hope the efforts made in this paper will help others, particularly designers and engineers who want to use bio-inspired optimization algorithms for large scale complex problems, choose the right parallelization model for their applications.

References

1. Kohonen, T.: Self-organizing maps, vol. 30. Springer (2001)
2. Freitas, A.A., Lavington, S.H.: Data parallelism, control parallelism, and related issues. In: Mining Very Large Databases with Parallel Processing, pp. 71–78. Springer (2000)
3. Crainic, T.G., Toulouse, M.: Parallel meta-heuristics. In: Handbook of Metaheuristics, pp. 497–541. Springer (2010)
4. Crainic, T.G., Toulouse, M.: Parallel strategies for meta-heuristics. Springer (2003)
5. Tomassini, M.: Parallel and distributed evolutionary algorithms: A review (1999)
6. Konfrst, Z.: Parallel genetic algorithms: Advances, computing trends, applications and perspectives. In: Proceedings. 18th International Parallel and Distributed Processing Symposium, p. 162. IEEE (2004)
7. Cohoon, J.P., Hegde, S.U., Martin, W.N., Richards, D.: Punctuated equilibria: a parallel genetic algorithm. In: Genetic Algorithms and their Applications: Proceedings of the Second International Conference on Genetic Algorithms, July 28-31. Massachusetts Institute of Technology, L. Erlbaum Associates, Cambridge, Hillsdale (1987)
8. Manderick, B., Spiessens, P.: Fine-grained parallel genetic algorithms. In: Proceedings of the Third International Conference on Genetic Algorithms, pp. 428–433. Morgan Kaufmann Publishers Inc. (1989)
9. Andre, D., Koza, J.R.: Parallel genetic programming: A scalable implementation using the transputer network architecture. In: Advances in Genetic Programming, pp. 317–337. MIT Press (1996)
10. Folino, G., Pizzuti, C., Spezzano, G.: A scalable cellular implementation of parallel genetic programming. IEEE Transactions on Evolutionary Computation 7, 37–53 (2003)
11. Dorigo, M.: Optimization, Learning and Natural Algorithms. PhD thesis, Politecnico di Milano (1992)
12. Pedemonte, M., Nesmachnow, S., Cancela, H.: A survey on parallel ant colony optimization. Applied Soft Computing 11, 5181–5197 (2011)
13. Pedemonte, M., Cancela, H.: A cellular ant colony optimisation for the generalised steiner problem. International Journal of Innovative Computing and Applications 2, 188–201 (2010)
14. Randall, M., Lewis, A.: A parallel implementation of ant colony optimization. Journal of Parallel and Distributed Computing 62, 1421–1432 (2002)
15. Stützle, T.: Parallelization Strategies for Ant Colony Optimization. In: Eiben, A.E., Bäck, T., Schoenauer, M., Schwefel, H.-P. (eds.) PPSN 1998. LNCS, vol. 1498, pp. 722–731. Springer, Heidelberg (1998)
16. Bai, H., OuYang, D., Li, X., He, L., Yu, H.: Max-min ant system on gpu with cuda. In: 2009 Fourth International Conference on Innovative Computing, Information and Control (ICICIC), pp. 801–804. IEEE (2009)
17. McConnell, S., Sturgeon, R., Henry, G., Mayne, A., Hurley, R.: Scalability of self-organizing maps on a gpu cluster using opencl and cuda. Journal of Physics: Conference Series 341, 012018 (2012)

18. Yoshimi, M., Kuhara, T., Nishimoto, K., Miki, M., Hiroyasu, T.: Visualization of pareto solutions by spherical self-organizing map and its acceleration on a gpu. Journal of Software Engineering and Applications 5 (2012)
19. Wang, H., Zhang, N., Créput, J.-C.: A Massive Parallel Cellular GPU Implementation of Neural Network to Large Scale Euclidean TSP. In: Castro, F., Gelbukh, A., González, M. (eds.) MICAI 2013, Part II. LNCS, vol. 8266, pp. 118–129. Springer, Heidelberg (2013)
20. Bentley, J.L., Weide, B.W., Yao, A.C.: Optimal expected-time algorithms for closest point problems. ACM Transactions on Mathematical Software (TOMS) **6**, 563–580 (1980)
21. Créput, J.C., Koukam, A.: A memetic neural network for the euclidean traveling salesman problem. Neurocomputing **72**, 1250–1264 (2009)
22. Talbi, E.G.: Metaheuristics: from design to implementation, vol. 74. John Wiley & Sons (2009)
23. Van Luong, T., Melab, N., Talbi, E.G.: Gpu computing for parallel local search metaheuristic algorithms. IEEE Transactions on Computers **62**, 173–185 (2013)
24. Nguyen, H.D., Yoshihara, I., Yamamori, K., Yasunaga, M.: Implementation of an effective hybrid ga for large-scale traveling salesman problems. IEEE Transactions on Systems, Man, and Cybernetics, Part B: Cybernetics **37**, 92–99 (2007)

Using Bio-inspired Algorithm to Compensate Web Page Color Contrast for Dichromat Users

Alina Mereuta, Sébastien Aupetit[✉], Nicolas Monmarché,
and Mohamed Slimane

Laboratoire Informatique (EA6300), Université François Rabelais Tours,
France 64, avenue Jean Portalis, 37200 Tours, France
{alina.mereuta,aupetit,monmarche,slimane}@univ-tours.fr

Abstract. With this paper, we are focusing on improving web accessibility, more precisely on compensating the contrast loss for textual web content for dichromat users. A study over the entire sRGB color space showed that the loss experienced by a dichromat user may be significant. With the current approach, we assess the interest of using API for our problem. Several tests for different parameters settings were performed on both real and synthetic data in order to assess the algorithm efficiency.

Keywords: Dichromacy · Assistive technologies · API · Accessibility · Recoloring · Optimization · Swarm intelligence

1 Introduction

Accessibility concern is to ensure the same level of availability of resources for both standard and disabled people. Web accessibility, in particular, focuses on ensuring unlimited web access for users with disabilities. Towards improving web accessibility, several steps were made by developing standards and policies. Guidelines that may serve as references for developing accessible web sites are: Web Content Accessibility Guidelines (WCAG) 1.0[1] and 2.0, proposed by Web Accessibility Initiative (WAI), a World Web Consortium (W3C) working group. Web site compliance with such policies may increase the degree of accessibility of a web site. However, very few web designers check for accessibility issues their web sites. This results in web content that can be difficult to access by users having some form of disability. To address this, a series of transformation tools that attempt to correct these shortcomings were proposed [3,4,9].

A form of deficiency is Dichromacy. It is a color deficiency which makes difficult for a person to perceive the difference between certain colors. This is due to the lack of one of the three types of cone cells in eye's retina which constitute the photoreceptors in charge of color perception. Corresponding to the range of misperceived shades of colors, two main categories of dichromacy exist: (1) red-green deficiencies (protanope (missing L cones) and deuteranope (lack of M cone cells)) and (2) blue-yellow deficiency (tritanope (S cones are missing)). To

---

[1] http://www.w3.org/TR/WCAG10/

© Springer International Publishing Switzerland 2014
P. Siarry et al. (Eds.): ICSIBO 2014, LNCS 8472, pp. 80–88, 2014.
DOI: 10.1007/978-3-319-12970-9_9

address this issue a series of algorithms and tools were proposed. To simulate color deficiencies several algorithms [1,2,6,11] and tools[2] were developed. Many attempts to diminish the shortcomings induced by this type of deficiency exist [5,10,12].

In the following, we are focusing on compensating color contrast for web textual information for dichromats users.

2 The Problem

WCAG 1.0 structures accessibility standards into four main groups: understandable, perceivable, robust and operable. For all of them it introduces a three steps way to measure web page accessibility from Level A to AAA. Level A corresponds to the minimum of accessibility required for a web site. One requirement concerning the representation of textual information on the page and more precisely, concerning the color contrast, (Guideline 2) states the following "Ensure that foreground and background color combinations provide sufficient contrast when viewed by someone having color deficits or when viewed on a black and white screen".

WCAG provides ways to measure the contrast ratio for textual information on the web. Let $a, b [\in 0, 255]^3$ be two colors represented in the sRGB color space (known as the Internet standard color space). The luminance of $x \in [0, 255]^3$ is defined as:

$$L(x) = 0.2126 * h(x^r) + 0.7152 * h(x^g) + 0.0722 * h(x^b) \tag{1}$$

with

$$h(z) = \begin{cases} \frac{z/255}{12.92} & \text{if } z/255 \leq 0.03928 \\ \left(\frac{z/255+0.055}{1.055}\right)^{2.4} & \text{otherwise} \end{cases} \tag{2}$$

The contrast between a and b is given by:

$$\Gamma_{a,b} = \frac{\max(L(a), L(b)) + 0.05}{\min(L(a), L(b)) + 0.05} \in [1 : 21] . \tag{3}$$

We denote by $D(a) \in [0 : 255]^3$ the function used to obtain the corresponding color as perceived by a dichromat user and by $\Gamma_{a,b}^D = \Gamma_{D(a),D(b)}$ the simulated contrast for the colors a and b. The simulation algorithm used is the one proposed by [6].

A small study on contrast ratio revealed that the contrast loss experienced by a dichromat user may be significant. At its worst, it can reach a decrease of around 3.8 for protanope or deuteranope and 3.7 for tritanope, while the minimum level specified by the standards (WCAG 1.0) is 4.5:1.

In this work, we attempt to compensate the textual contrast loss that might be experience by a dichromat user.

---

[2] http://www.vischeck.com/

Let C be the set of colors that may be found on an arbitrary web page and $\mathcal{E} \subset C \times C$ the set of entities characterized by foreground and background colors. Let be $\Delta_i = |a_i - a_i^F|_{CIELab}$, $\forall a_i \in C$ the Euclidean distance between the original and the transformed color

The contrast compensation problem can be modeled as a mono-objective function given by:

$$F(a_1^F, a_2^F, \ldots, a_N^F) = (1 - \alpha) \sum_{(a_i, a_j) \in \mathcal{E}} \frac{1}{2} \left[\max(\Gamma_{a_i, a_j}^I - \Gamma_{a_i, a_j}^{F,D}, 0) \right]^2 + \alpha \sum_{c_i \in C} \frac{1}{2} \Delta_i^2$$

(4)

that aims:

1. to compensate the contrast loss by minimizing $\max(\Gamma_{a_i, a_j}^I - \Gamma_{a_i, a_j}^{F,D}, 0)$, $\forall (a_i, a_j) \in \mathcal{E}$
2. to reduce the change in the final transformed colors by minimizing (Δ_i)

We also use a constant α to weight between the amount of compensation needed and the change in colors. The compesation contrast problem may be reduced at minimizing (4).

In previous work, we have considered a mass-spring approach and the CMA-ES algorithm [7] to solve the problem. The results on both real and artificial data were encouraging. In the following, we are investigating the interest of using the API algorithm for solving our problem.

3   The Proposed Approach

For the experiments, we are using the proxy part of the SWAP (Smart Web Accessibility Platform)[3]. The platform has as main goal to improve web accessibility for disable users. In this work, we are only using the proxy part of SWAP which allows on-the-fly transformation of web pages when the user access Internet. SWAP handles colors extraction from the CSS of the page and the inclusion of the changes in the web page sent to the client browser.

The goal with this paper is to assess the efficiency of the API algorithm for our problem. The API algorithm [8] is based on the foraging strategy of the *Pachycondyla apicalis* ants. It allows to minimize a function f in a search space S. In the following, we recall its main principles. Let be $\{1, 2 \ldots, n\}$ an ant colony and $\{h_i\}_{\overline{1,n}}$ a set of hunting sites, associated to the ant colony (each ant has an hunting site). Two operators are fundamental to the algorithm behaviour:

1. $\mathcal{O}_i$ is used to initialize the colony nest ($\mathcal{N}$) (in our approach it will be given by the set of initial colors)
2. $\mathcal{O}_e(x, \mathcal{A})$ is used to generate a new color set $(y_i)_i$ from the color set $(x_i)_i, i \in [0 : 255]^3, i = \overline{1, |C|}$. The amount of change in colors' coordinates will be controlled by amplitude $\mathcal{A}_i \in (0, 1]$. The new colors y_i will be computed as $y_i = x_i + z$ where $z \in [-I : I]$ is uniformly generated and $I = \lfloor \mathcal{A}_i \cdot 255 \rfloor$.

---

[3] http://projectsforge.org/projects/swap

Two sets of amplitudes are needed: one for the hunting sites ($\{\mathcal{A}_i^h\}$) and one that gives the extend to which a hunting site will be explored($\{\mathcal{A}_i^l\}$). In the following we consider them to be given by: $\mathcal{A}_i^h = 1 + (0.01 - 1)\frac{i-n}{1-n}$ and $\mathcal{A}_i^l = \mathcal{A}_i^h/10$ as defined initially by N. Monmarche. To control the number of failures for a hunting site a counter and a maximum limit are defined.

The algorithm behaves as follows: A hunting site (h_i) is assigned to each ant from the colony if they don't have one using $\mathcal{O}_e(\mathcal{N}, \mathcal{A}_i^h)$. If they have one a search for a new solution is done with ($\mathcal{O}_e(h_i, \mathcal{A}_i^l)$). If the solution found is better than the current solution represented by the hunting site, the hunting site is moved to the new solution and the counter of failures is brought to zero. If the explored solutions are worst than the current one (the hunting site) the failure counter is increased. If the maximum number of failures (ϕ^M) is attained for a hunting site, the ant abandons it. Regularly at a τ_{max} frequency, the nest is moved in the best solution ever found and all the hunting sites are abandoned by all ants. The whole process is repeated for T times.

The algorithms main steps are presented in Algorithm 1.

Algorithm 1. API algorithm

1: $\mathcal{N} \leftarrow \mathcal{C}$
2: T, ϕ^M, τ_{max}
3: **for** $i = 1$ **to** T **do**
4:     **for** $i = 1$ **to** n **do**
5:         **if** $h_i = \emptyset$ **then**
6:             $h_i \leftarrow \mathcal{O}_e(\mathcal{N}, \mathcal{A}_i^h)$
7:             NoFailures$_i \leftarrow 0$
8:         **else**
9:             $c \leftarrow \mathcal{O}_e(h_i, \mathcal{A}_i^l)$
10:             **if** $F(c) < F(h_i)$ **then**
11:                 $h_i \leftarrow c$
12:                 NoFailures$_i \leftarrow 0$
13:             **else**
14:                 NoFailures$_i \leftarrow$ NoFailures$_i + 1$
15:                 **if** NoFailures$_i \geq \phi^M$ **then**
16:                     $h_i \leftarrow \emptyset$
17:                 **end if**
18:             **end if**
19:         **end if**
20:     **end for**
21:     **if** $t \bmod \tau_{max} = 0$ **then**
22:         move nest in the best solution ever recorded
23:         **for** $i = 1$ **to** n **do**
24:             $h_i \leftarrow \emptyset$
25:         **end for**
26:     **end if**
27: **end for**

In the following experiments were conducted in order to evaluate the interest of using it for solving our problem, on both real and synthetic data.

4   Results and Discussion

A set of experiments were conducted in order to assess the behaviour of the API algorithm on the given problem (color optimization for dichromat users). Tests were performed on two types and data: real and synthetic. Real data was obtained by from CSS analysis on over 170 pages using SWAP. Concerning the synthetic data, the colors were generated according to the given confusion range used in [2] (the pairs of colors that fall in that specific range are perceived similar by a dichromat user, so the contrast ratio perceived will be much smaller than the one perceived by a standard user). 170 synthetic data files were computed.

$\mathbb{P}$ represents the dataset considered, in our case, is either RD (real data) or SD (synthetic data).

For API, we have considered many parameters settings (PS), varying the maximal limit for the number of failures for a given hunting site $\phi^M \in \{5, 10, 15\}$, the number of explored solutions by iteration, number of ants $n \in \{5, 10, 15\}$ and the frequency with which the nest is moved $\tau_{max} \in \{10, 20, 30\}$. The same settings were maintained for both real and synthetic data.

For each web page, 10000 evalutions were perfomed using the API algorithm, for a number of 50 tries, for all types of parameter settings and all forms of dichromacy. We denote by $\bar{F}_{p,s}(t)$ the average fitness value over 50 tries at evaluation t, for the page p corresponding to the parameter setting s. In order to assess the parameter settings behaviour, we have normalized $\bar{F}_{p,s}(t)$ $\forall t$ as follows:

$$g_{p,s}(t) = \frac{1}{|\mathbb{P}|} \sum_{p \in \mathbb{P}} \frac{\bar{F}_{p,s}(t) - m_p}{M_p - m_p} \qquad (5)$$

with

$$m_p = \min_{s \wedge t = 1..10000} \bar{F}_{p,s}(t) \qquad (6)$$

and

$$M_p = \max_{s \wedge t = 1..10000} \bar{F}_{p,s}(t) \qquad (7)$$

where g is the normalized average fitness values for the page p and parameter setting s, m_p and M_p represent the minimum, and the maximum value for $\bar{F}_{p,s}$ for the entire set of parameter settings considered for the page p.

Experiments showed that the algorithm behaviour does vary with the change in the chosen parameters. The performance is better for the PS-1(5,5,10) compared to the others on real data. The last two perform similary on real data, slightly better for PS-2(10,10,20). On synthetic data the behaviour is very similar for all types of PS and all types of deficiencies.

The first parameter setting, PS-1 (5,5,10) gives the best results for both real and synthetic data as depicted by Figure 1 and 2. This may be due to the fact that by limiting the number of failures at hunting site level it has the oportunity

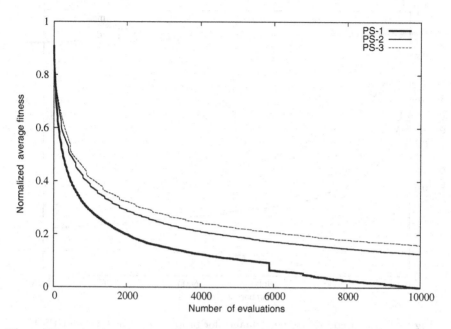

Fig. 1. Normalized average fitness for deuteranope on real data for PS-1, PS-2 and PS-3

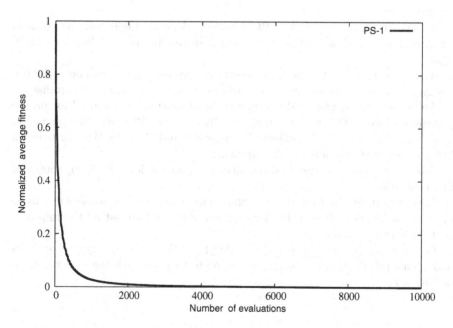

Fig. 2. Normalized average fitness for tritanope on synthetic data for PS-1

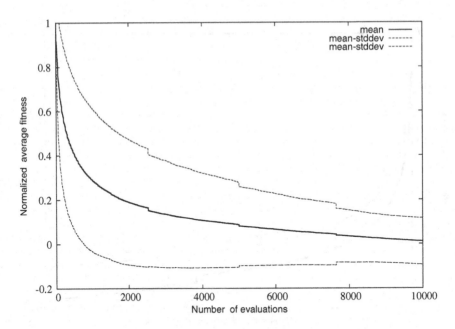

Fig. 3. Normalized average performance for protanope on real data for PS-1

to explore a larger area of the search space and that allows to find rapidly, better solutions.

It worth meantioning, that API behaviour depends highly on the dataset. It can produce good as well as poor results, depending on the data as seen in Figure 3.

We can notice that API performs better on synthetic data than on real data. The algorithm behaviour doesn't vary too much with the type of dichromacy.

We are interested also to determine if the algorithm can be used for on the fly page recoloring. This may be translated by the possibility of obtaining a good improvement over a small number of evaluation and that the time to perform that number of evaluations is not significant.

Table 1 shows the normalized average performance for 500, 1000, 1500 and 2000 evaluations.

As we can notice in Table 1, more than half of the total improvement can be achieved for less than 500 evaluations for real data and almost all the improvement for synthetic data.

The time to recolor a page varies with: (1) DOM retrieval, (2) CSS analysis , (3) color optimization and sending the modified page with the new colors to the browser).

Table 1. Normalized average fitness at 500, 1000, 1500 and 2000 evaluations for PS1 for protanope, deuteranope and tritanope on real (RD) and synthetic (SD) data

Type of deficiency	real data					synthetic data				
	500	1000	1500	2000	2500	500	1000	1500	2000	2500
Deuteranope	0.39	0.29	0.24	0.20	0.17	0.08	0.03	0.02	0.01	0.01
Protanope	0.41	0.29	0.23	0.19	0.17	0.08	0.03	0.02	0.01	0.01
Tritanope	0.42	0.32	0.26	0.22	0.20	0.07	0.03	0.01	0.01	0.01

5 Conclusion

With this paper, we have assessed the interest of using API algorithm for the problem of contrast compensation for dichromat user. We have obtained good results on both real and synthetic dataset for all three types of dichromacy considered. Several tests still need to be performed in order to determine if the algorithm is more suitable than our previous approaches to be used for on-the-fly recoloring of web pages.

References

1. Brettel, H., Vienot, F., Mollon, J.: Computerized simulation of color appearance or dichromats. Journal of Optical Society of America **14**(10), 2647–2655 (1997)
2. Brettel, H., Vienot, F., Mollon, J.: Digital video colourmaps for checking the legibility of displays by dichromats. Color Research and Application **24**(4), 243–251 (1999)
3. D. Lunn, S.H., Bechhofer, S.: Combining SADIe and AxsJAX to Improve the Accessibility of Web Content. In: Proceedings of W4A2009 Communication, Spain, Madrid, April 20-21, pp. 75–78 (2009)
4. Gupta, S., Kaiser, G.: Extracting Content from Accessible Web Pages. In: Proceedings of the 2005 International Cross-Disciplinary Workshop on Web Accessibility (W4A 2005), New York, USA, pp. 26–3 (2005)
5. Iaccarino, G., Malandrino, D., et al.: Efficient Edge-Services for Colorblind Users. In: WWW 2006 The 15th International Conference on World Wide Web, Edinburgh, Scotland, UK, May 22–26, pp. 919–920 (2006)
6. Kuhn, G.R., Oliveira, M.M., Fernandes, L.A.F.: Efficient Naturalness-Preserving Image-Recoloring Method for Dichromats. IEEE Visualization and Computer Graphics **6**(14), 1747–1754 (2008)
7. Mereuta, A., Aupetit, S., Monmarche, N., Slimane, M.: Web page textual color contrast compensation for CVD users using optimization methods. Journal of Mathematical Modelling and Algorithms in Operations Research (October 2013)
8. Monmarché, N., Venturini, G., Slimane, M.: On how it Pachycondyla apicalis ants suggest a new search algorithm. Future Generation Computer Systems **16**(8), 937–946 (2000)

9. Parmanto, B., Ferrydiansyah, R., Zeng, X., Saptono, A., Sugiantara, I.W.: Accessibility Transformation Gateway. In: HICSS: Proceedings of the 38th Annual Hawaii International Conference on System Sciences, Island of Hawaii, Hilton Waikoloa Village, pp. 3–6 (January 2005)
10. Rodriguez-Pardo, C.E., Sharma, G.: Adaptive color visualization for dichromats using a customized hierarchical palette, vol. 7866, pp. 786603–786603-9 (2011). http://proceedings.spiedigitallibrary.org/proceeding.aspx?articleid=1348327
11. Ruminski, J., Wtorek, J., Ruminska, J., Kaczmarek, M., Bujnowski, A., Kocejko, T., Polinski, A.: Color transformation methods for dichromats. In: 2010 3rd Conference on Human System Interactions (HSI), pp. 634–641 (May 2010)
12. Wakita, K., Shimamura, K.: SmartColor: Disambiguation Framework for the Colorblind. In: The sixth International ACM Access Conference on Assistive Technologies, ASSETS 2005, Baltimore, USA, October 9–12, pp. 158–165 (2005)

Comparison of Two Swarm Intelligence Optimization Algorithms on the Textual Color Problem for Web Accessibility

Sébastien Aupetit[(✉)], Nicolas Monmarché, and Mohamed Slimane

Laboratoire Informatique (EA6300), Université François Rabelais Tours,
64, avenue Jean Portalis, 37200 Tours, France
{aupetit,monmarche,slimane}@univ-tours.fr

Abstract. Currently, web accessibility is not a major concern of web-masters while creating web sites. For disabled people, it rapidly becomes an obstacle to inclusion in the society. Identifying and circumventing existing barriers constitute an important research topic. In this work, we are concerned with the problem of color accessibility of textual contents in web pages. In many cases, the textual colors of a web page do not respect the minimum constraints defined by recommendations like WCAG 2.0. For example, WCAG 2.0 requires that a minimum difference of brightness, tonality and contrast is ensured. Using the Smart Web Accessibility Platform, we try to transform the colors using a client-side HTTP proxy the best possible while retaining a reasonable access time for the web content. To solve the textual color problem for accessibility, we adapt two swarm intelligence based optimization methods (ABC and API) and we hybridize them with a line search.

Keywords: Accessibility · Assistive technology · Recoloring · Web · Swarm intelligence based optimization · ABC · API

1 Introduction

Web accessibility is a big concern for disabled people when accessing Internet. While Internet contributes to the insertion in the society, it can leads to exclusion when it is not accessible. To reduce exclusion, active or passive accessibility can be used. Active accessibility consists in a pro-active approach relying on norms, recommendations[1], laws [1], tools[2] and methodologies [2] to enforce a proper structuring and tagging of documents during their creation by webmasters. While it is the ideal way for achieving accessibility, in practice, a fully accessible web is not possible mainly due to limited implication of webmasters or external constraints (money, time...). Moreover, many web sites are unmaintained or ageing. Passive accessibility consists in using assistive technologies

---

[1] http://www.w3.org/TR/WCAG10/, http://www.w3.org/TR/WCAG20/
[2] http://achecker.ca/checker, http://www.binaryblue.com.au/access_wizard...

© Springer International Publishing Switzerland 2014
P. Siarry et al. (Eds.): ICSIBO 2014, LNCS 8472, pp. 89–97, 2014.
DOI: 10.1007/978-3-319-12970-9_10

and transformation tools to allow a better access to web contents. This form of accessibility is our concern in the project Smart Web Accessibility Platform (SWAP)[3] that we develop. It is a set of open source modular components and tools designed to facilitate content transformation (the proxy tool), to store and to share global knowledge and to create metadata (annotations...) on web pages. A more detailed description of the project can be found in [3]. In this work, we are concerned only by the proxy tool. It is located on the user computer and is used by the browser to access Internet. On request of the browser, the proxy fetches the content on Internet, applies transformations on the page and sends the modified page to the browser. It allows to transform any content passing by the proxy (even secured ones) and to preserve existing user assistive technologies (speech synthesis, zoom...) so increasing the adoption of our tool. The transformations do not aim to make the content accessible for the average disabled user but for specific user needs: we transform only what the user wants and needs. The transformations are done on the fly while the page passes by the proxy. For ergonomic reasons, the user can not wait too long. Moreover, a perfect improvement of the content is not possible due to the lack of information on the contents. Consequently, the transformation of the content using the proxy tool is a time limited and imperfect process. However, a partial improvement of the content is nevertheless a big improvement for the user.

In this work, we are focused on textual color improvement which can be formalized as an optimization problem. In previous works [4–7], we considered simple heuristics and metaheuristics to solve the problem and a fitness function prioritizing four measures and using an integral and a fractional parts formulation. This fitness function while allowing a huge improvement of the colors suffers a big practical defect. It introduces discontinuities leading to color schemes which are equally ranked but which can be very different. From a user perspective, the important changes on the color schemes, each time the user access the same web page, is an issue. From now, the fitness function is modified into a weighted function of the four measures on the color schemes. It produces more stable color schemes over time at the price of eventually reducing constraints satisfaction. In the following, we define the textual color problem, its specificities and how it can be solved with three swarm intelligence based optimization methods.

2   The Textual Color Problem for Accessibility

2.1   Textual Colors Accessibility

The accessibility definitions considered are defined by WCAG 1.0 and 2.0 (Web Content Accessibility Guidelines)[1]. In the following, colors are considered in the sRGB space. To be accessible, the foreground (f) and background (b) colors of any text must satisfy three constraints: a minimal brightness ($\Delta B(f,b) \geq \eta_B$), a minimal tonality difference ($\Delta T(f,b) \geq \eta_T$) and a minimal contrast ($\Delta C(f,b) \geq \eta_C$). η_B, η_T and η_C are the accessibility thresholds fixed at 125, 500 and 7 in

---

[3] https://projectsforge.org/projects/swap

the following. For any colors $x = (x_1, x_2, x_3)$ and $y = (y_1, y_2, y_3)$ defined on $[0 : 255]^3$, we have:

$$\Delta B(x, y) = |0.299(x_1 - y_1) + 0.587(x_2 - y_2) + 0.114(x_3 - y_3)| \tag{1}$$

$$\Delta T(x, y) = |x_1 - y_1| + |x_2 - y_2| + |x_3 - y_3| \tag{2}$$

$$\Delta C(x, y) = \frac{\max(L(x), L(y)) + 0.05}{\min(L(x), L(y)) + 0.05} \tag{3}$$

$$L(x) = 0.2126h(x_1) + 0.7152h(x_2) + 0.0722h(x_3) \tag{4}$$

$$h(v) = \begin{cases} \frac{v/255}{12.92} & \text{if } v/255 \leq 0.03928 \\ \left(\frac{v/255 + 0.055}{1.055}\right)^{2.4} \end{cases} \tag{5}$$

2.2 Distance Between Colors

We define $\Delta E(x, y)$ the classical perceptual distance in CIE L*a*b* divided by $100\sqrt{3}$. This distance is an euclidean distance in the CIE L*a*b* color space which measures the difference between two colors like what a human perceives it. To compute $\Delta E(x, y)$, the colors in the sRGB space must be transformed into colors in the CIE L*a*b* color space. For concision, details are not given here.

2.3 Objective Function

Colors of textual contents are extracted from web pages parsing CSS (Cascading Style Sheets) and HTML contents. Identical colors in foreground are merged and the same is done for the background colors. We do it in order to preserve the coloring intention of the webmaster (visual identification...). Let $\mathcal{C} = \{c_1, \ldots, c_{|\mathcal{C}|}\}$ be the set of colors used to represent the textual information of a web page. Let $\mathcal{E}$ be the set of couples (foreground, background) presented in our page and $w_{x,y} \in \mathbb{R}^+$ the associated weights. In our modeling, these weights are the number of characters in the web page that use the couple of colors (x, y). Let $c_x^I \in [0 : 255]^3$ be the initial color coordinates for $x \in \mathcal{C}$ and $c_x^F \in [0 : 255]^3$ the coordinates of the same color after the transformation. We define $S_w = \sum_{(x,y)\in\mathcal{E}} w_{x,y}$ the sum of the weights of the all couple of colors.

Interdependencies between colors can lead to unsatisfiable problems. To handle this issue, we relax the constraints using the Φ function as an evaluation of the constraint violation such that, for all $v \in [0 : M]$: $\Phi(v, T) = \max(0, (T - v)/T)$. If $v \geq T$ then $\Phi(v, T) = 0$. Otherwise, $\Phi(v, T)$ increases linearly until 1 when v decreases to 0 (the worst violation). We define :

$$S_B(c^F) = S_w^{-1} \sum_{(x,y)\in\mathcal{E}} w_{x,y}\Phi\left(\Delta B(c_x^F, c_y^F), \eta_B\right) \tag{6}$$

$$S_T(c^F) = S_w^{-1} \sum_{(x,y)\in\mathcal{E}} w_{x,y}\Phi\left(\Delta T(c_x^F, c_y^F), \eta_T\right) \tag{7}$$

$$S_C(c^F) = S_w^{-1} \sum_{(x,y)\in\mathcal{E}} w_{x,y}\Phi\left(\Delta C(c_x^F, c_y^F) - 1, \eta_C - 1\right) \tag{8}$$

$$S_E(c^F) = S_w^{-1} \sum_{(x,y)\in\mathcal{E}} w_{x,y}\left(\Delta E(c_x^I, c_x^F) + \Delta E(c_y^I, c_y^F)\right)/2 \tag{9}$$

S_B, S_T and S_C measure the constraints violation while S_E measures the color difference perceived by an human between the initial colors and the new colors. Let ϵ_B, ϵ_T and ϵ_C be three weights defined by the user to weight the constraints according to his needs. In ours experiments, we considered $\epsilon_B = \epsilon_T = \epsilon_C = 1$. Two color schemes can satisfy the constraints to the same level (for example, $S_B(c^F) = S_T(c^F) = S_C(c^F) = 0$). To differentiate the schemes, we use S_E to prefer the scheme which changes the less the perceived colors (for example, we prefer changing pink into red instead of green). Let $\alpha \in]0 : 1]$ be an user definable weight to balance between the satisfaction of the constraints and the minimization of the colors change. In experiments, we considered $\alpha = 0.8$. The objective function is defined by:

$$F(c^F) = \alpha * \frac{\epsilon_B S_B(c^F) + \epsilon_T S_T(c^F) + \epsilon_C S_C(c^F)}{\epsilon_B + \epsilon_T + \epsilon_C} + (1 - \alpha) * \Delta E(c^F) \qquad (10)$$

The textual color problem for web accessibility consists in minimizing $F(c^F)$. The computation must be accomplished on-the-fly while the content passes by the proxy. The available computation time depends on the user computer speed, on the running processes and on the other transformations applied to the content. We do not known *a priori* how much computation time is available so we consider that the minimization of F may be interrupted at any moment. The best found solution is used to recolor the page. Even if the recoloration is not optimal, it is nevertheless an improvement for the disabled user. The recoloring is done by inserting styles in the HTML document that overwrite the existing styles.

3   Swarm Intelligence Based Optimization for Solving the Problem

For the minimization of F, we considered two swarm based optimization methods: Artificial Bee Colony and the API metaheuristic. In the following, we denote by $\mathcal{U}(X)$ and $\mathcal{R}(X \sim P)$ a random value in X which is uniformly distributed in the first case or distributed according to the probability distribution P in the second case. In the following, a recoloring is represented as an integer vector of dimension $3|\mathcal{C}|$. The search space is $\mathcal{S} = [\![0 : 255]\!]^{3|\mathcal{C}|}$. The best solution is memorized when F is computed and stored in s^*. We suppose that values are truncated to $\mathcal{S}$ when it is appropriate.

3.1   Artificial Bee Colony

Bees inspired many optimization algorithms [8]. Artificial Bee Colony (ABC) [9] is one of the most popular. ABC principles are defined by the foraging behavior of onlooker bees, employed bees and scout bees. We denote by $\mathbb{S} = \{s_1, \ldots, s_S\}$ the food sources and by e_i the fail counter associated to s_i. e_{Max} is the maximum number of failure allowed for a food source before abandoning it. We denote by $\nu(x, y)$ the creation of a solution from the two food sources x and y. Let k be a random number in $[\![1 : 3|\mathcal{C}|]\!]$ then we have, for all $i \neq k$, $\nu(x, y)_i = x_i$ and

```
/* Choose initial food sources                                        */
for i = 1 to |S| do
 |  s_i ← U(S); e_i ← 0
while not done do
    /* Employed bees go out                                           */
    for i = 1 to |S| do
     |  v_i ← ν(s_i, U(S − {s_i}))
    for i = 1 to |S| do
     |  if F(s_i) > F(v_i) then s_i ← v_i; e_i = 0 else e_i ← e_i + 1
    /* Onlooker bees exploit food sources                             */
    for i = 1 to |S| do
     |  p_i = (1/(1 + F(s_i))/ ∑_{s∈S}(1/(1 + F(s)))
    for i = 1 to N_{onlooker} do
     |  x_i ← R([1 : |S|] ∼ P); w_i ← ν(s_{x_i}, U(S − {s_{x_i}}))
    for i = 1 to N_{onlooker} do
     |  if F(s_{x_i}) > F(w_i) then e_{x_i} = 0; s_{x_i} ← w_i else e_{x_i} ← e_{x_i} + 1
    /* Employed bees abandon useless sources and become scout bees */
    x = 1; C = {i ∈ 1..|S| | e_i >= e_Max}
    while x ≤ N_{scout} et C ≠ ∅ do
     |  i = arg max_{j∈C} e_j; s_i ← U(S) ; e_i ← 0; Update C; x ← x + 1;
```

Algorithm 1. The ABC algorithm for the textual color problem

$\nu(x, y)_k = x_k + U([-(x_k − y_k); (x_k − y_k)])$. Algorithm 1 proceeds in three steps. First, the employed bees go out of the colony toward their food sources and explore a new solution in its neighborhood. If the new solution is better then the food sources is replaced and the fail counter is reset. Otherwise, the fail counter is increased. Second, the onlooker bees spread over the food sources according to theirs qualities $(1/(1 + F(s_i)))$ and explore a new solution in the neighborhood of the chosen food source. The food source and the fail counter are updated as for the employed bees. Finally, the food sources whose fail counter exceeds e_{Max} are abandoned and replaced by a new random food source. The process is repeated as needed. More detailed presentations of ABC can be found in the literature.

3.2   The API Metaheuristic

The API metaheuristic [10] is inspired by the foraging strategy of primitive *Pachycondyla apicalis* ants [11,12] which do not use pheromones. In this paper, we introduce only a shorten description of the algorithm. More details can be found in [10,13]. We consider a colony of n ants. Each ant i has an associated hunting site denoted by $s_i \in S$. If a hunting site is not defined, we have $s_i = \emptyset$. The behaviour of the algorithm is completely defined by two operators: $\mathcal{O}_{init}$ and $\mathcal{O}_{explo}$. $\mathcal{O}_{init}$ defines the initial position of the nest ($\mathcal{N}$) of the colony and, in this work, it is set to c^I. $\mathcal{O}_{explo}$ defines the foraging strategy of ants. $\mathcal{O}_{explo}(x, \mathcal{A})$ generates a solution y in the neighborhood of a solution x such that $||x−y||_{max} \leq \lfloor \mathcal{A} * 255 \rfloor$. $\mathcal{A}$ is the neighborhood amplitude and takes its values in $[0 : 1]$. The

```
/* Choose initial nest position                                          */
𝒩 = c^I
for i = 1 to n do s_i ← ∅

while not done do
    for i = 1 to n do
        if s_i = ∅ then
            /* Create a hunting site                                     */
            s_i ← 𝒪_explo(𝒩, 𝒜_i^site) ; e_i ← 0
        else
            /* Explore the neighborhood of a hunting site                */
            p ← 𝒪_explo(s_i, 𝒜_i^local)
            if F(p) < F(s_i) then
                | s_i ← p ; e_i ← 0
            else
                e_i ← e_i + 1
                if e_i ≥ e_Max then s_i ← ∅
    /* Update nest if needed                                             */
    every 𝒯_move iterations do
        𝒩 ← s*
        for i = 1 to n do s_i ← ∅
```

Algorithm 2. The API metaheuristic for the textual color problem

operator is used to create hunting sites and to explore the neighborhood of hunting sites. The algorithm relies on two sets of amplitudes: $\{\mathcal{A}_i^{\text{site}}\}$ used for the hunting sites and $\{\mathcal{A}_i^{\text{local}}\}$ used for the exploration of hunting sites. In this work, we considered the classical definitions which are $\mathcal{A}_i^{\text{site}} = 1 + (0.01 - 1)\frac{i-n}{1-n}$ and $\mathcal{A}_i^{\text{local}} = \mathcal{A}_i^{\text{site}}/10$. We denote by e_i the counter for the number of failure of a hunting site s_i and e_{Max} the maximal number of failure allowed before a hunting is abandoned. Algorithm 2 proceeds in two steps. First, the ants go out of the nest. If the ant does not have a hunting site ($s_i = \emptyset$) then a new hunting site is chosen with $\mathcal{O}_{\text{explo}}(\mathcal{N}, \mathcal{A}_i^{\text{site}})$. If the ant already has a hunting site then it explores a new solution in the neighborhood of the hunting site using $\mathcal{O}_{\text{explo}}(s_i, \mathcal{A}_i^{\text{local}})$. When the new solution is better than the hunting site, the hunting site is replaced by the new solution and the fail counter is reset. Otherwise, the counter is increased and depending of its value, the hunting site is abandoned. When all ants have explored a new solution, the nest is tested. Every $\mathcal{T}_{\text{move}}$ iterations, the nest $\mathcal{N}$ is moved to the best known solution and the hunting sites of the ants are cleared. The whole process is repeated as needed.

3.3 Hybridization with a One Step Gradient Descent and a Descent Acceleration

For each solution $x \in \mathcal{S}$, we define $D(x)$ the set of solutions that have one and only one component varying of one unit ($+1$, -1) compared to x. The one step gradient descent is defined by:

$$g(x) = \arg \min_{y \in D(x)} F(y) \,.$$

An acceleration of the one step gradient descent can be achieved using a line search in the direction of the gradient $(g(x) - x)$. We define $(y_t)_{t \in \mathbb{N}^+}$ the sequence of solutions such that $y_t = g(x) + t * (g(x) - x)$. The gradient descent acceleration consists in computing y_T such that $\forall t = 1..T - 1$, $F(y_t) \geq F(y_{t+1})$ and $F(y_T) < F(y_{T+1})$. Hybridizing with the one step gradient descent consists in applying g, optionally with the acceleration, on any solution returned by $\nu(x, y)$ or $\mathcal{O}_{\text{explo}}(x, \mathcal{A})$.

4   Experimental Study and Comparison

To compare the two methods, we consider different parameter settings and a set of 196 real web pages chosen randomly on Internet verifying $F(c^I) > 0$. The algorithms are run 50 times and the averaged "best fitness ever found" curves are computed for each pages. To alleviate scaling issues, the curves are normalized for every page such that $F(c^I)$ is mapped to 1 and the best found solution by any algorithm/parameter setting is mapped to 0. The averaged curve for an algorithm/parameter setting is obtained using the normalized curves on each page. The normalization formulas are given in [5]. For ABC, we considered $|\mathbb{S}| = \mathcal{N}_{onlooker} = \mathcal{N}_{scout} \in \{5, 10, 15, 20\}$ and $e_{\text{Max}} \in \{5, 10\}$. The initials colors c^I are included or not in the initial food sources and the usefulness of the one step gradient descent and its acceleration is evaluated. From experiments, we noted that the inclusion of c^I in the initial food sources is very important. The convergence is accelerated and F converges toward its lowest values when the number of food sources decrease (5 is the best). The other parameters have low influence on first evaluations. When considering the behavior after 5000 evaluations, it appears that the one step gradient descent with the acceleration tends to provide best performance when $e_{\text{Max}} * \mathcal{N}_{onlooker} = 50$. The best parameters are $e_{\text{Max}} = 10$ and $\mathcal{N}_{onlooker} = 5$. For API, we considered setting the initial nest position to c^I or not, using the line search or not, setting $n \in \{5, 10, 15, 20\}$, $\mathcal{T}_{move} = 20$ and $e_{\text{Max}} \in \{5, 10\}$. Experiments showed that the nest must be set to the initial color scheme (c^I) for better results. Moreover, none of the remaining parameter showed a significant influence on the behavior of the algorithm for the considered instances of the color problem. The best fitness values at 10000 evaluations are obtained for $n = 10$, $e_{\text{Max}} = 5$ and when the one step gradient descent is not used. The comparison of the best ABC and API settings showed that on most web pages, API converges faster than ABC (see Fig. 1). However, API fails to improve the initial solution for 5 web pages and ABC fails for 1 web pages. Supposing a fair time sharing between the two algorithms, it is possible to run API and ABC in parallel in order to take the best of the two. To be fair, the same quantity of evaluated solutions (half, 5000 evaluations) are used. The averaged curves on all pages are given by Fig. 1. This parallel approach is the most efficient. It demonstrates an often faster convergence suitable for the interruption of the algorithm at any time and all web pages are improved (since the algorithm never failed).

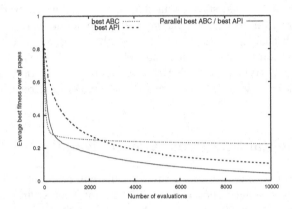

Fig. 1. Averaged curves on all pages for ABC, API and parallel ABC-API

5 Conclusion

In this paper, we studied two swarms algorithms (ABC and API) on the textual color problem for web accessibility. A parameter study was lead and best parameters are established against a set of web pages. We demonstrated that the two swarms algorithms can be combined in order to get the best features of both algorithms and to ensure an improvement of the color scheme in all cases. We also showed that this combined algorithm has the required features allowing to interrupt computation whenever it is needed to ensure a reduced waiting time for the user (ergonomic feature).

References

1. République Française: Loi n°2005-102 du 11 février 2005 pour l'égalité des droits et des chances, la participation et la citoyenneté des personnes handicapées. JO n° 36 du 12 février 2005, p. 2353 (2005)
2. Colas, S., Monmarché, N., Burger, D., Slimane, M.: A web site migration support tool to reach european accessibility standards. In: 9th European Conference for the Advancement of Assistive Technology in Europe, vol. 20 of Assistive Technology Research Series, San Sebastian (Spain), pp. 907–911 (october 2007)
3. Aupetit, Sébastien, Rouillé, Vincent: Annotation Tool for the Smart Web Accessibility Platform. In: Miesenberger, Klaus, Fels, Deborah, Archambault, Dominique, Peňáz, Petr, Zagler, Wolfgang (eds.) ICCHP 2014, Part I. LNCS, vol. 8547, pp. 93–100. Springer, Heidelberg (2014)

4. Mereuţă, Alina, Aupetit, Sébastien, Slimane, Mohamed: Improving Web Accessibility for Dichromat Users through Contrast Preservation. In: Miesenberger, Klaus, Karshmer, Arthur, Penaz, Petr, Zagler, Wolfgang (eds.) ICCHP 2012, Part I. LNCS, vol. 7382, pp. 363–370. Springer, Heidelberg (2012)

5. Aupetit, Sébastien, Mereuţă, Alina, Slimane, Mohamed: Automatic Color Improvement of Web Pages with Time Limited Operators. In: Miesenberger, Klaus, Karshmer, Arthur, Penaz, Petr, Zagler, Wolfgang (eds.) ICCHP 2012, Part I. LNCS, vol. 7382, pp. 355–362. Springer, Heidelberg (2012)

6. Mereuta, A., Aupetit, S., Monmarché, N., Slimane, M.: Web page textual color contrast compensation for CVD users using optimization methods. Journal of Mathematical Modelling and Algorithms in Operations Research (October 2013). http://link.springer.com/10.1007/s10852-013-9239-3

7. Mereuta, A., Aupetit, S., Monmarché, N., Slimane, M.: An evolutionary approach to contrast compensation for dichromat users. In: Legrand, P., Corsini, M.M., Hao, J.K., Monmarché, N., Lutton, E., Schoenauer, M., eds.: EA 2013. LNCS 8752. pp. 239–250. Springer, Heidelberg (2013)

8. Karaboga, D., Gorkemli, B., Ozturk, C., Karaboga, N.: A comprehensive survey: artificial bee colony (ABC) algorithm and applications. Artificial Intelligence Review (March 2012). http://link.springer.com/10.1007/s10462-012-9328-0

9. Karaboga, D.: An idea based on honey bee swarm for numerical optimization. Technical Report TR06, Erciyes University, Engineering Faculty Computer Engineering Department, Kayseri/Türkiye (October 2005)

10. Monmarché, N.: Algorithmes de fourmis artificielles : applications à la classification et à l'optimisation. Thèse de doctorat, Laboratoire d'Informatique de l'Université François Rabelais Tours (December 20, 2000)

11. Fresneau, D.: Individual foraging and path fidelity in a ponerine ant. Insectes Sociaux, Paris **32**(2), 109–116 (1985)

12. Fresneau, D.: Biologie et comportement social d'une fourmi ponérine néotropicale (Pachycondyla apicalis). Thèse d'état, Université de Paris XIII, Laboratoire d'Ethologie Expérimentale et Comparée, France (1994)

13. Aupetit, S., Monmarché, N., Slimane, M.: Training hidden Markov models using the API ant algorithm. In: Artificials ants: from Collective Intelligence to Real-Life Optimization and Beyond. ISTE, Wiley (2010) ISBN 9781848211940

How Much Forcing Is Necessary to Let the Results of Particle Swarms Converge?

Bernd Bassimir, Manuel Schmitt[(✉)], and Rolf Wanka

Department of Computer Science, University of Erlangen-Nuremberg,
Erlangen, Germany
bernd.bassimir@fau.de, {manuel.schmitt,rolf.wanka}@cs.fau.de

Abstract. In order to improve the behavior of Particle Swarm Optimization (PSO), the classical method is often extended by additional operations. Here, we are interested in how much "PSO" remains in this case, and how often the extension takes over the computation. We study the variant of PSO that applies random velocities (then called *forced moves*) as soon as the so-called *potential* of the swarm falls below a certain bound. We show experimentally that the number of iterations the swarm actually deviates from the classical PSO behavior is small as long as the particles are sufficiently far away from any local optimum. As soon as the swarm comes close to a local optimum, the number of forced moves increases significantly and approaches a value that depends on the swarm size and the problem dimension, but not on the actual fitness function, an observation that can be used as a stopping criterion. Additionally, we provide an explanation for the observed phenomenon in terms of the swarm's potential.

1 Introduction

In the past few years Particle Swarm Optimization (PSO) has received increased attention because it can be easily implemented and adapted to the users' applications. Unfortunately, the results are not always as good as wanted. Hence, many authors present changes in the original, "plain," or classical PSO scheme (for exact definitions, see Section 2) in order to improve the quality of the returned solution. In the following, some of these PSO variants are mentioned.

In [7], van den Bergh/Engelbrecht introduce a PSO variant where the particles are allowed to count the number of times they improve the global attractor and to use this information.

In [5], a discrete variant of PSO for the Traveling Salesperson Problem is presented, where the PSO mechanism is enhanced by additional k-OPT-based intermediate phases. However, as experiments turn out, the quality of the solutions this algorithm returns does not significantly change when the PSO is completely turned off.

The phenomenon of premature stagnation, i. e., the convergence of the swarm to a non-optimal solution, has been addressed by Lehre/Witt [2]. To overcome

© Springer International Publishing Switzerland 2014
P. Siarry et al. (Eds.): ICSIBO 2014, LNCS 8472, pp. 98–105, 2014.
DOI: 10.1007/978-3-319-12970-9_11

such stagnation, they propose *Noisy PSO* that adds a "noise" term to the velocity at every move. The authors prove that for the Noisy PSO started on a certain 1-dimensional function the first hitting time of the ε-neighborhood of the global optimum is finite.

As proved in [3], premature stagnation of classical PSO does not occur when the search space is 1-dimensional. I. e., in the 1-dimensional case, PSO provably finds a local optimum. Furthermore, [3] shows a similar result for a slightly modified PSO in the more general D-dimensional case. This modified PSO assigns a small random velocity only if the so-called *potential* of the swarm falls below a certain (small) bound. Such moves are called *forced*. This modified PSO provably finds a local optimum.

The goal of this paper is to determine, how much the modified algorithm relies on the forced moves, i. e., how often the modification actually is applied. We present experiments, implying that the forced moves will only have a small impact on the overall behavior of the swarm, as long as it is far away from any local optimum. Furthermore, our experiments show that the number of forced moves does not only increase significantly when the distance to the next local optimum falls below a certain bound, but that additionally the number of forced moves performed near a local optimum is independent of the fitness function. Therefore, the concentration of forced moves can act as a stopping criterion. Additionally, we give experiments that show the dependencies of this concentration, i. e., how it is influenced by the swarm size and the problem dimension.

2   Definitions

Definition 1 (Classical PSO Algorithm). *A swarm $\mathcal{S}$ of N particles moves through the D-dimensional search space $\mathbb{R}^D$. Each particle $n \in \mathcal{S}$ consists of a position $X^n \in \mathbb{R}^D$, a velocity $V^n \in \mathbb{R}^D$ and a local attractor $L^n \in \mathbb{R}^D$, storing the best position particle n has visited so far. Additionally, the swarm shares information via the* global attractor *$G \in \mathbb{R}^D$, describing the best point any particle has visited so far, i. e., as soon as a particle has performed its move[1], it possibly updates the global attractor immediately.*

The actual movement of the swarm is governed by the following movement equations where χ, c_1, $c_2 \in \mathbb{R}^+$ are some positive constants to be fixed later and r and s are drawn u. a. r. from $[0,1]^D$.

$$V^n := \chi \cdot V^n + c_1 \cdot r \odot (L^n - X^n) + c_2 \cdot s \odot (G - X^n)$$
$$X^n := X^n + V^n$$

Here, $\odot$ denotes entrywise multiplication (Hadamard product). The application of the equation on particle n is called the move *of n. When all particles have executed their moves, the swarm has executed one* iteration.

---

[1] The particles' moves are executed sequentially, so there is some arbitrary order of the particles.

Now we define a swarm's potential measuring how close it is to convergence, i. e., we describe a measure for its movement. A swarm with high potential should be more likely to reach search points far away from the current global attractor, while the potential of a converging swarm approaches 0. These considerations lead to the following definition [4]:

Definition 2 (Potential). *For $d \in \{1, \ldots, D\}$, the potential of swarm S in dimension d is Φ_d with $\Phi_d := \sum_{n=1}^{N}(|V_d^n| + |G_d - X_d^n|)$. The total potential of S is $\Phi = (\Phi_1, \ldots, \Phi_D)$.*

The current total potential of a swarm has a portion in every dimension. Between two different dimensions, the potential may differ much, and "moving" potential from one dimension to another is not possible. On the other hand, along the same dimension the particles influence each other and can transfer potential from one to the other. This is the reason why there is no potential of individual particles.

To address the phenomenon of stagnation, we modify the movement equations from Definition 1 as follows [3]:

Definition 3 (Modified PSO). *The modified movement of the swarm is governed by the following movement equations where χ, c_1, c_2, $\delta \in \mathbb{R}^+$ are some positive constants to be fixed later and r and s are drawn u. a. r. from $[0, 1]^D$.*

$$V^n := \begin{cases} (2 \cdot r - 1) \cdot \delta, & \text{if } \forall d \in \{1, \ldots, D\} : |V_d^n| + |G_d - X_d^n| < \delta \\ \chi \cdot V^n + c_1 \cdot r \odot (L^n - X^n) + c_2 \cdot s \odot (G - X^n), & \text{otherwise,} \end{cases} \quad (1)$$

$$X^n := X^n + V^n.$$

If the first case of (1) applies for a particle, we call its move forced. *An iteration of the swarm is called* forced *if at least one particle performs a forced move.*

Algorithm 1 below provides an overview over the modified PSO. The introduction of forced moves guarantees that the swarm does not converge to a non-optimal point, but finds a local optimum [3].

3   Number of Forced Iterations

In the following experiments, we tested the modified PSO algorithm with the fixed parameters $\chi = 0.729, c_1 = c_2 = 1.49$ as suggested in [1]. Additionally, we set the swarm size $N = 3$, the problem dimension $D = 30$ and the parameter $\delta = 10^{-6}$. The total number of iterations was set to 4.000.000 and for every period of 2.000 iterations, we counted the forced iterations. As fitness functions, we used selected benchmarks from [6], namely SPHERE (F_1), SCHWEFEL 1.2 (F_2), (unrotated) H. C. ELLIPTIC (F_3), ROSENBROCK (F_6), RASTRIGIN (F_9)

Algorithm 1. Modified PSO

---

output: $G \in \mathbb{R}^D$

1   **for** $n = 1 \rightarrow N$ **do**

2   Initialize X^n randomly;   Initialize V^n randomly;

3   Initialize $L^n := X^n$;

4   Initialize $G := \underset{\{L^n \mid n \in \{1,\ldots,N\}\}}{\mathrm{argmin}} f$;

5   **repeat**

6   **for** $n = 1 \rightarrow N$ **do**

7   **if** $\forall d \in \{1, \ldots, D\} : |V_d^n| + |G_d - X_d^n| < \delta$ **then**

8         $V^n := (2 \cdot r - 1) \cdot \delta$;

9   **else**

10         $V^n := \chi \cdot V^n + c_1 \cdot r \odot (L^n - X^n) + c_2 \cdot s \odot (G - X^n)$;

11   **if** $f(X^n) \leq f(L^n)$ **then** $L^n := X^n$;

12   **if** $f(X^n) \leq f(G)$ **then** $G := X^n$;

13   **until** *termination criterion met*;

---

and SCHWEFEL 2.13 (F_{12}). The results can be seen in Figure 1. Initially, the positions were uniformly and independently distributed over $[-100, 100]^D$ and the velocities were uniformly and independently distributed over $[0, 1]^D$. To measure the quality of the solution found at each time, the gradient is calculated at the end of each interval. In each run and for every examined fitness function, we can observe the following behavior. In the beginning of the optimization process, the number of forced iterations is low. When the swarm reaches (the neighborhood of) a local optimum, this number will rise and then begin to stagnate around a certain value. While the time when that happens may depend on the fitness function, one can clearly see that this value does not. Note that the point in time when the particles come close to a local optimum and the number of forced iterations increases is random. In case of SCHWEFEL 2.13, the point has a comparatively high variance, so the smaller increase of the respective curve in Figure 1 results from averaging over the 100 runs rather than generally smaller increases of the single runs on this function. As seen in Figure 1, the number of forced iterations is low in the beginning of the algorithm. This is due to the nature of the modification made. Whenever the swarm begins to converge to a point that is no local optimum the modification applies and enables the swarm to search for a new, promising direction. For that purpose only a few forced iterations are necessary. When the swarm reaches a local optimum, the modification is also applied and the swarm will again try to find a new direction. However, since every direction yields worsenings, the swarm will never switch back to standard swarm behavior for longer than a few iterations. From Figure 1, one can see that the number of forced moves at that point will stay around a certain and

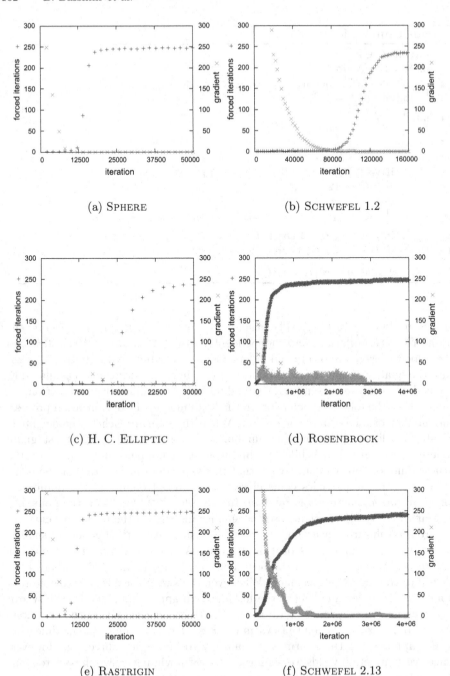

(a) SPHERE

(b) SCHWEFEL 1.2

(c) H. C. ELLIPTIC

(d) ROSENBROCK

(e) RASTRIGIN

(f) SCHWEFEL 2.13

Fig. 1. Forced iteration count and gradient for various fitness functions. Each point represents the average over 100 different runs. The forced iteration count is the sum over 2.000 iterations and the gradient is calculated at the global attractor every 2.000 iterations.

comparatively high value. An explanation is that the particles will now be gathered in a neighborhood with radius of about δ around the global attractor. At that point, the global attractor is very close to the local optimum, so the swarm's potential is small. As known from, e. g., [1], the unmodified PSO converges and therefore looses potential. It is now in a situation where its moves will be forced. These forced moves can lead to an increase in potential. Consequently, as soon as the modified PSO has enough potential to apply the classical movement equations, after some iterations it is again in a situation where its moves are forced. Therefore the stochastic process of the particle swarm becomes a stationary process. The number of forced iterations under this stationary distribution will in the following be called the *stagnation value*. The stagnation value is independent of the fitness function, because the changes of the attractors are the only influence the function has on the movement of the particles. So the smaller the attractors' movement gets, the less relevant is the actual function for the behavior of the swarm. Note that the time when the particles come close to a local optimum decreases when the swarm size is increased. In particular, with a larger swarm size, this time is less than 2000. Consequently, we chose a very low number of particles to highlight the difference between the optimization phase, when the behavior of the swarm is mostly governed by the standard movement equations, and the stagnation phase, when a large share of the iterations is forced.

4   Dependencies of the Stagnation Value

In Section 3 we have seen that the value at which the number of forced iterations stagnates is independent of the fitness function. In this section we will give a further insight into this phenomenon. We provide experimental results pointing out that there are two dependencies for this value, namely the search space dimension and the swarm size. Figure 2 shows how the stagnation value changes when these parameters are varied. Each point is the arithmetic mean over the last 50 values of the forced iteration number, i. e., the values are obtained from the last 100.000 iterations. Each run in Figure 2a consists of 500.000 iterations and each run in Figure 2b of 200.000 iterations. SPHERE is chosen as the fitness function.

In Figure 2a, one can see that the value at which the number of forced iterations stagnates decreases exponentially as the number of dimensions increases. To explain this behavior, we have to look at the probability of the occurance of a forced move. In Equation (1), one can see that a forced move will occure when the sum of the absolute value of the velocity and the distance of the particle to the global attractor fall below a certain bound in every dimension. As soon as the swarm is sufficiently close to a local optimum, such that updates of attractors are rare and the differences between the old values and the updated values are small, the dimensions are almost independent of each other. The probability of the necessary condition for a forced move, as specified in (1) of Definition 3, to be fulfilled in a given dimension does not depend on the actual dimension. This

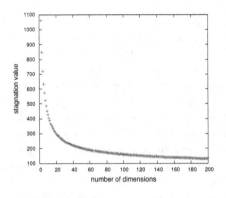
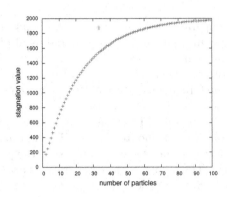

(a) Dependency of the stagnation value on the number of dimensions for SPHERE, with $\delta = 10^{-6}$ and a swarm-size of $N = 3$

(b) Dependency of the stagnation value on the swarm size for SPHERE, with $\delta = 10^{-6}$ and a number of dimensions of $D = 30$

Fig. 2. Influence of dimension number and swarm size on the stagnation value

leads to the following equation describing the probability of a forced move for a given particle n:

$$\Pr(\text{forced\_move}_n) \approx \Pr(|V_1^n| + |G_1 - X_1^n| < \delta)^D.$$

Additionally, the stagnation value depends on the swarm size. As specified before, we call an iteration forced if at least one particle performs a forced move, i. e., if the following equation holds:

$$\Pr(\text{forced\_iteration}) = \Pr\left(\bigcup_{n=1}^{N} \text{forced\_move}_n\right)$$

Figure 2b shows the obtained stagnation value for a fixed search space dimension of $D = 30$ and swarm sizes from 2 to 100. As one can see, the increase of the stagnation value is almost linear for small swarm sizes. An explanation for this phenomenon is the following: At the time of the stagnation, the global attractor will be almost constant. As a direct consequence of this, the particles are moving almost independent from all other particles. With a low number of particles used, the resulting value is nearly the sum of the probabilities that a particle performs a forced move, summed up over all particles. As this number rises, it can be observed that this value converges towards 2000. At this point, the probability of more than one forced move during the same iteration rises and has to be taken into account. This convergence to 2000 comes from the stagnation value being calculated as the sum over 2000 iterations. Given this two dependencies and the results shown in Section 3, we conclude that the stagnation value of the number of forced iterations is a function $F_{\max}(N, D)$ that is independent of the fitness function. To compute a result of this function given the two parameters, one can first run the PSO algorithm for a simple function like SPHERE. The obtained stagnation value can then be applied as a stopping criterion in the PSO algorithm that computes the desired fitness function with the same values for N and D.

5   Conclusion

This paper focused on a modified PSO variant, in which whenever the swarm reaches a state close to convergence the velocity update in each dimension is done uniformly over a small interval. We gave experiments suggesting that the influence of this modification is relatively small as long as the swarm is far away from any local optimum. Additionally, the experiments have clearly shown that the number of forced iterations reaches a stationary distribution when a local optimum is reached. Under that stationary distribution, the number of forced iterations is orders of magnitude higher than the number of forced iterations performed during the optimization process. Experiments have shown that the actual value of the forced iterations under the stationary distribution depends on the number of particles and the number of search space dimensions, but is independent of the fitness function. Therefore, this concentration of forced iterations can act as a stopping criterion for the PSO. For future work, the influence of other characteristics of the algorithm like the neighborhood topology will be studied.

References

1. Clerc, M., Kennedy, J.: The particle swarm - explosion, stability, and convergence in a multidimensional complex space. IEEE Transactions on Evolutionary Computation **6**, 58–73 (2002); doi:10.1109/4235.985692
2. Lehre, P.K., Witt, C.: Finite first hitting time versus stochastic convergence in particle swarm optimisation (2011). http://arxiv.org/abs/1105.5540
3. Schmitt, M., Wanka, R.: Particle swarm optimization almost surely finds local optima. In: Proc. 15th Genetic and Evolutionary Computation Conference (GECCO), pp. 1629–1636 (2013); doi:10.1145/2463372.2463563
4. Schmitt, M., Wanka, R.: Particles prefer walking along the axes: Experimental insights into the behavior of a particle swarm. In: Companion of Proc. 15th Genetic and Evolutionary Computation Conference (GECCO), pp. 17–18 (2013); doi:10.1145/2464576.2464583
5. Shi, X.H., Liang, Y.C., Leeb, H.P., Lu, C., Wang, Q.: Particle swarm optimization-based algorithms for TSP and generalized TSP. Information Processing Letters, (103), 169–176 (2007); doi:10.1016/j.ipl.2007.03.010
6. Suganthan, P.N., Hansen, N., Liang, J.J., Deb, K., Chen, Y.-P., Auger, A., Tiwari, S.: Problem definitions and evaluation criteria for the CEC 2005 special session on real-parameter optimization. Technical report, KanGAL Report Number 2005005 (Kanpur Genetic Algorithms Laboratory, IIT Kanpur) (2005)
7. van den Bergh, F., Engelbrecht, A.P.: A new locally convergent particle swarm optimiser. In: Proc. IEEE Int. Conf. on Systems, Man and Cybernetics (SMC) vol. 3, pp. 94–99 (2002); doi:10.1109/ICSMC.2002.1176018

The Use of Ontology in Semantic Analysis of the Published Learners Messages for Adaptability

Samia Ait Adda[✉] and Amar Balla

National High School for Computer Science (ESI), Ouad Smar, Algiers, Algeria
{s_ait_adda,a_balla}@esi.dz

Abstract. Communication tools for online learning environments are ways that let learners to exchange messages between them and with their teachers. It is also a way to interpret their social behavior patterns and their learning styles. In this paper, we are interested in the semantic analysis of the contents messages published by learners by use of domain ontology. The purpose of this analysis is to identify the domain concepts that are most published and shared by learners and to keep them into the leaners model as concepts not well mastered. We hypothesize that all concepts edited and exchanged over email, chat and especially in discussion forums can be considered as knowledge poorly or badly acquired by learners and deserve thus more attention and consideration both by the tutor for the pedagogical monitoring of learners on these concepts and from designer of course, to restructure and more enrich the educational content which articulates these concepts identified beforehand in this analysis.

Keywords: e-Learning · Communications tools · Domain ontology · Semantic indexing · Learner model · Adaptability

1 Introduction

Our work is placed in the field of the Interactive Educational System; we set us therefore in a context of an online learning. Hence, learners work remotely on platforms which allow them to attend course, make tests and exercises or discuss by means of communication tools that are always integrated on these platforms.

The progressive integration of these communication tools offers opportunities for learners geographically dispersed to exchange without any time constraint and allows considering a new forms of social interaction between learners and between learners and teachers [1]. With this simplified sharing of information, a new forms of interaction have emerged, and new skills have been developed both in social, cognitive, or meta-cognitive [2].

These communication tools are generally places of meetings and discussing for learners who are often in difficulties on some concepts of the taught domain,

© Springer International Publishing Switzerland 2014
P. Siarry et al. (Eds.): ICSIBO 2014, LNCS 8472, pp. 106–114, 2014.
DOI: 10.1007/978-3-319-12970-9_12

which may be weakly assimilated. If we take the example of a learner who publishes a question on a forum, this fact can interpret an obstacle of this learner on the concepts contained in the content of this question. As well as the messages exchanged between learners by email or chat.

We aim in this article to analyze the content of messages discussed by the learners to identify the most exchanged concepts and be able to help learners with their needs. We introduce among other things, to do this, ontology of teaching domain to correlate information between the different contents of messages published by the learner and those of the studied course. The goal that we want to achieve through this study is essentially enriching and updating the learner profile, by marking the domain concepts that pose a problem for him and that are detected due to its posted messages. Recognize the problematic concepts, of the learners participating in the learning process, can help the designer of the course to review the course content on these concepts and adapt it to the learners' level, and the tutor to assist and support learners who are already published these concepts. Hence, here we are talking about the adaptability of learning.

The paper will be structured as follows, in the first section we present some research that are carried on the analysis of communication tools and their users, then we are interested in some semantic web tools, such as ontologies and the possibility, thanks to these tools to exploit the contents of messages to detect concepts badly acquired by the learner, further we detail and explain our approach. Finally we present some results which we have achieved through an implementation of our approach on a considered domain.

2 Related Work

In several studies, the analysis of the content and the structure of the written exchanges may offer an interesting educational trail for helping learners to succeed, we have thus identified two kinds of these analysis. Some works [3] analyze the external factors of messages, these analyzes attempt to account for what is played on forums from readily observable indicators such as the number of posts by each user or group, the number of responses, the length of discussions, the number of learners participating in discussion, the average duration of a session on the forum . . . etc.

While others were focused to analyze the internal ones. Indeed various researches [4,5] have conducted a study to evaluate the use of data and text mining to analyze the learners' discussions, they propose systems for classifying textual contribution, such as: topics that come up in the debates, announcements, questions, students? initiatives or answers, conflicts . . . etc. Another type of frameworks [6,7] have been proposed for characterizing and analyzing discussions for the classification and structuring, based on the Semantic Analysis which includes the tools of Web Semantic, like ontology, to organize the vocabulary and refine the analysis.

These studied works aim to show the cognitive, social and semantic advantage of published messages. Our approach is inscribed in the same perspective. On the other hand, we propose a method which gives a semantic meaning to learners? messages with an ultimate goal of detecting concepts of the studied domain that are poorly or badly learned by the learner and keep them into his profile for adaptability. To do this, the concepts of the studied domain are modeled through ontology of the taught course, as we describe it below.

3   Domain Ontology

The Semantic Web [8] is an understandable and navigable space by both human and software agents. It introduces an additional meaning to the navigational data of the classical web, based on a formal ontology and controlled vocabularies through semantic links. In standpoint of e-learning, it can help learners to locate, access, querying, processing and evaluating learning resources across distributed heterogeneous network, or assist teachers in creating, using, locating, or the sharing and exchanging learning objects. Ontology [9] includes a set of terms, knowledge, including vocabulary, semantic relations, and a number of logic-inference rules for some particular domain. The ontology applied to Web creates thus the Semantic Web [10]. Ontologies [11] facilitate the sharing and reuse of knowledge, i.e. a common understanding of diverse content by persons and machines.

The use of ontology in our case consists in the conceptual indexing of the edited messages to facilitate their identification and semantic search by the learner since they become learning knowledge?s basis available for consulting [12]. On top of that indexing, the most edited domain concepts will thus detected. This ontology also represents the structure of the learner?s model, since it is part of the domain model, i.e. the domain ontology in our case.

In our case of study, we consider that ontology is composed of a set of concepts and relations between these concepts. A unique identifier is assigned for each concept, these concepts are labeled with one or several terms. Expressly an ontology O is defined as follows: $O=\{C, R, Vo\}$

- C : set of domain ontology concepts
- R: set of relations between the ontology concepts,
- Vo: is the ontology vocabulary which is composed with terms (mono or composed words) corresponding to the domain ontology concept.

4   The Proposed Approach

To detect knowledge of domain supposed poorly assimilated by learners, we propose an approach that consists in constructing a text document relative to the messages published by the learners in their email, chat and discussion forums.

These documents are taken from the database of the platform and then indexed according to the concepts of the taught course through the domain ontology (semantic indexing). The most edited concepts by a learner or group of learners are then highlighted. Our goal is threefold. On the one hand we try to index the messages to facilitate their research and consultation, on the other hand to detect the most edited concepts of domain by learners, and finally we want to identify learners who have used these concepts via the communication tools to make inquiries about some domain concepts.

The approach that we propose is divided into three basic processes: (1) Building of the messages corpus, (2) Semantic Indexing and (3) the management and processing of results, this is what will be detailed in the following of this paper.

4.1   Building of the Edited Messages Corpus

To perform indexing, we need textual content messages. It just consists to access to the database of the platform to get messages exchanged by all learners from the corresponding tables. The result will be in the form of text documents, thus closing the content of message, paths to the attachments if exists, information about the sender and receivers of the message and the time of dispatching. These documents will be saved in a repository to constitute a local corpus of documents.

Below, a diagram summarizes the structure of the message in learning platform, that we will indexed with the concept of the studied domain via an ontology of domain, which is the purpose of this work.

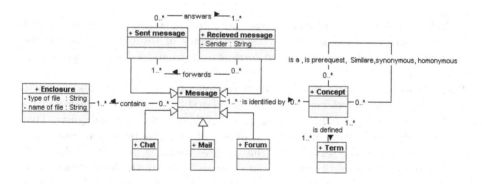

Fig. 1. The ontology model of message

4.2   The Semantic Indexing

We propose to use domain ontology to build the semantic index of documents. The process of document indexing is handled through three main steps: (1) Identifying ontology concepts, (2) Assigning concepts to document terms and (3) Weighting concepts. In the following, we present these steps.

Concept Identification. The purpose of this step is to identify ontology concepts that correspond to document words. Concept identification [13] is based on the overlap of the local context of the analyzed word with every corresponding domain ontology entry. Concepts are referred in the text documents with

---

Input: document D.
Output: Vector of all ontology concepts belonging to terms in document *D*.
Procedure
Let *wi* be the next word to analyze in the document *d*. We define the *context sent_i which is the sentence in document D that contains the word occurrence wi being analyzed.*
Compute $Vi = \{C1, C2, ..., Cn\}$ the of ontology entries containing *wi*.
Each $Cj \in Vi$ is represented by a multiword or mono-word term.
Rank concepts Cj in set *Vi* in where: $| C(1) | > | C(2)| > | | ... > | C(n) | // |$ | *denotes the concept length, in terms of the number of words in the corresponding terms.*
For each *element* Cj in *Vi* do
  Get common words between *senti* and representative term of Cj , which is the intersection
$N = \cap(sent_i, Cj)$
    If $|N| < | Cj |$ **then** The concept-sense is not within the context.
EndIf
If $|N| = | Cj |$ **then** The concept-sense Cj is within the context *senti.*
Add Cj to the set of vectors' element (index) associated to the document D.
EndIf
EndFor

Fig. 2. The algorithm of terms Mapping into Concepts

simple or compound words (term). The concept identification algorithm is given in figure 2.

In the ontology, a set of terms is used for labeling concepts and relationships between concepts. That set forms the vocabulary of the ontology.To respond nevertheless in case if the processed term is ambiguous, a disambiguation step is so necessary.

Term Disambiguation. Each term *ti* (simple or compound words) in document may be associated with a number of related possible ontology concepts.

Thus we distinguish the situation of semantic or polysemy ambiguity. That set forms the vocabulary of the the situation of semantic or polysemous ambiguity.For example, the term "*table*" has a three meaning in PHP ontology: (1) table of data structure, (2) table in database and table in the html structure. It can refer to three different concepts. In this case we proceed as follows, for an ambiguous term *ti* in the document, we seek a label of a concept *Ck* linked in the ontology with a concept *Ci* which is indicated by the ambiguous term *ti*. If *Ck* exists, *Ci* is taken as the concept designated by the term *ti*.

Concept Weighting. The extracted concepts are weighted according to a method more general than tf *idf named Cfc * idf (concept-frequency-inversed document frequency). In this method each extracted term represents necessarily a concept of the ontology since we used ontology to identify them. For a concept C its frequency in a document depends on the frequency of the term itself [14]. It is calculated as follows:

$$idfc = \log \frac{n}{fc} + 1 \tag{1}$$

$$Cfc = \sum_{tm \in t(c)} tf_{tm} \tag{2}$$

Where: t(c) is the set of terms corresponding to different concept C and tftm is the frequency of term t(c) in document i. The weight of each concept in a document d is so calculated as follows:

$$CfIdf = Cfc \times idfc \qquad (3)$$

5   Semantic Representation of Learner Knowledge

Each indexed document is represented by a vector of weighted key concepts. For this purpose, all documents that constitute the corpus C will be represented by an occurrence matrix of document and concept. We will distinguish two kinds of corpus, a first corpus C*learner* consists of each message published by a learner, and a second C*Grp* represents the sum of all messages edited by all learners who participated in the learning process.

Thanks to the first corpus, we can specify the knowledge which poses a problem to the learner. Since the occurrence matrix, we naturally recognize the most published concepts by the learner through adding instances of the same matrix row; the result is a vector V*learner* containing the concepts occurrences in the corpus Clearner. V*learner* = *(Wc1, Wc2 .... Wcn)* Concepts with a high weight by estimating a threshold α, that we will fixed by experimentation, will be reviewed as problematic domain concepts for a learner. There-fore, the tutor may intervene to help the learner on these concepts.

In fact, we distinguish several ways to represent the learner?s knowledge; the largest used method is *the Overlay model* [15]. This model represents the learner?s knowledge as a subset of the domain model, which reflects the expert-level knowledge of the subject. The domain model is presented in our case of study as domain ontology.

Hence, we propose an overlay knowledge model with *two layers* (2 levels). The first layer concerns *assessment* and contains the mark obtained by the learner in the test on the concept. As for the second layer, it stores the weight of the edited concept on *the communication tools* using the equation(3).Consequently, the learning model in the proposed system has been shown in an ontological form since using the domain ontology to represent the domain model.

For the general corpus C*Grp* we proceed with the same process as a learner, so the result will be a general vector of concepts occurrence in the corpus C*Grp*. Similarly, the concepts greater than a threshold β, which we also determine the value by evaluation, will be considered as wrong developed concepts in the course. To this end, the designer of course can review the content of resources that explain these identified concepts, and further enrich its course on these concepts.

6   Experimentation

6.1   The Test Collection

For our experiments, we have proceeded to test on group of computer science students in the second years, with the number of 27. We have proposed to them PHP course, shown in *eFAD* (www.ufc.efad.dz) platform and modeled with the ontology of SKOS format[1] (Simple Knowledge Organization System). The experiments were established in three sessions of one hour. The *PHP* course is mainly composed of 8 top concepts and 49 sub-concepts. To consolidate our experiment, we have conceived a questionary paper which we have distributed to students, asking them to place concepts which pose problem to them. At the end of the test, a written assessment was performed for all learners.

6.2   Evaluation of Results

The result of the experimentation consists of 27 corpus of each learner plus the general corpus. Therefore, we constituted a number of 105 textual documents of the messages extracted from the platform database. The following diagram shows the score characterizing the main domain concepts for each learner : The challenge of this test was to

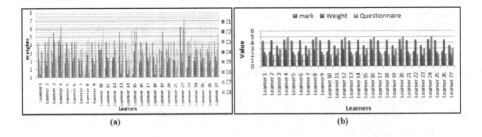

(a)   (b)

Fig. 3. The editing weights of the main domain concepts

find the concepts insufficiently mastered by each learner. That is to say; the threshold α, that we set to evaluate the most concepts which posed a problem for student j, is estimated by the median of the weights of concepts edited by this learner. This threshold is different from learner to learner; accordingly we have counted 27 values of this threshold (figure 3.a). Indeed, we found that the concepts C4 and C6 have posed a problem for some students who are recognized by the following process.

As that is signaled, a written assessment was performed for each learner on each concept of the domain as well as a questionnaire which we have asked them to indicate the concepts not mastered. Therefore, the diagram in the figure 3.b shows a comparison of different results obtained from the assessment, the weight of edited concepts and questionnaire responses.As for the threshold β, which we considered to estimate the concepts which are badly defined in course, it is determined by comparing the result with that obtained through the written assessment and questionary responses, the value is fixed at 0.24. As a result, we detect that 5 learners have problems with some concepts of the domain (learners 2, 10, 14, 18, 22).

7   Conclusion

The adaptability educational systems provide good support for learners on their individual characteristics. It can also provide information on the needs and deficiencies of

---

[1] http://www.w3.org/2006/07/SWD/SKOS/reference/20090315/implementation. html

these learners, either for the tutor or designer of the course, even for evaluation, monitoring and customizing the process and strategy of learning. In fact, the learner model must be developed for each student, containing information about the history of social interactions, objectives and knowledge badly acquired. In this article, we have highlighted the need to analyze the messages edited by learners during the learning sessions and we have proposed an approach for semantic analysis that we have presented and explained which permits to detect domain concepts that were difficult for learners, by comparing the content of their messages with a domain ontology of the studied course. An experiment was carried out on a group of students taking a PHP course, and has enabled us to validate the proposed approach and to set some parameters.

This result needs to be further refined by additional tests, which we are currently conducting. Moreover, it should however be raised that we have considered here only the internal discussions, so one of our prospects would be to take into account the external discussions by use of log file to identify them.

References

1. Develotte, C., Mangenot, F., Nissen, E.: Actes du colloque Epal 2009 Echanger pour apprendre en ligne : conception, instrumentation, interactions, multimodalit, universit Stendhal- Grenoble 3, 5–7 (Juin 2009)
2. Baker, M.: Forms of cooperation in dyadic problem-solving. Revue d'Intelligence Artificielle **16**(4), 587–620 (2002)
3. Huynh Kim Bang, B., Bruillard, E.: Vers une nouvelle interface de lecture pour des forums de discussion ddis des laborations collectives. In: actes de H2PTM 2005, pp. 43–56. Lavoisier, Paris (2005)
4. Azevedo, B.F.T., Reategui, E.B., Behar, P.A.: Qualitative Analysis of Discussion Forums. In: IADIS International Conference on e-Learning, Freiburg, Alemanha, pp. 251–258 (2010)
5. Breno, F., Terra, A.P., Alejandra, B., Eliseo, B.R.: Automatic analysis of messages in discussion forums. In: 14th International Conference on Interactive Collaborative Learning (ICL 2011), Piesany, Slovakia, 21–23 (2011)
6. Gloor, P.A., Zhao, Y.: Analyzing actors and their discussion topics by semantic social network analysis. In: Conference on Information Visualization, pp. 130–135 (2006)
7. Leprovost, D., Abrouk, L., Gross-Amblard, D.: Discovering implicit communities in web forums through ontologies. Web Intelligence and Agent Systems: An International Journal 10, 93–103 (2011)
8. Dicheva, D.: Ontologies and Semantic Web for E-Learning. In: Handbook on Information Technologies for Education and Training, Springer, Heidelberg (2008) 978-3-540-74155-8
9. Siti, U., Rohiza, A., Shakirah, M.: Ontology of Programming Resources for Semantic Searching of Programming Related Materials on the Web. IEEE (2010) 978-1-4244-6716-7110
10. Berners-Lee, T., Hendler, J., Lassila, O.: The semantic web, A new form of web content that is meaningful to computers will unleash a revolution of new possibilities. Scientific American, 35–43 (2001)
11. Zschocke, T., de León, J.C.V.: Towards an Ontology for the Description of Learning Resources on Disaster Risk Reduction. In: Lytras, M.D., Ordonez De Pablos, P., Ziderman, A., Roulstone, A., Maurer, H., Imber, J.B. (eds.) WSKS 2010. CCIS, vol. 111, pp. 60–74. Springer, Heidelberg (2010)

12. Reffay, C., Greffier, F.: Les chos du forum de discussion en FAD. In: JOCAIR : Premires journes Communication et Apprentissage instruments en rseau, Amiens. France, pp. 130–144 (2006)
13. Salah, T.B., Khaled, M.F., Naveed, A.: Personalized Semantic Retrieval and Summarization of Web Based Documents. In: (IJACSA) International Journal of Advanced Computer Science and Applications, vol. 4(1) (2013)
14. Dragoni, M., Da Costa Pereira, C., Tettamanzi, A.G.B.: An Ontological Representation of Documents and Queries for Information Retrieval Systems. In: García-Pedrajas, N., Herrera, F., Fyfe, C., Benítez, J.M., Ali, M. (eds.) IEA/AIE 2010, Part II. LNCS, vol. 6097, pp. 555–564. Springer, Heidelberg (2010)
15. Carr, B., Goldstein, I.: Overlays: A theory of modeling for computer-aided Instruction. Massachusetts Institute of Technology, Cambridge, Massachusetts (1977)

A Hybrid PSO Applied to the Flexible Job Shop with Transport

Laurent Deroussi [(✉)]

Université Blaise Pascal, LIMOS UMR CNRS 6158, Avenue des Landais,
63173 Aubière Cedex, France
deroussi@moniut.univ-bpclermont.fr

Abstract. In this paper, we study the hybridization of particle swarm optimization (PSO) with stochastic local search. This hybrid metaheuristic is applied to a difficult scheduling problem, recently appeared in the literature, the flexible job shop problem with transport. The objective is to determine experimentally the best balance between the exploration ability of PSO and the exploitation ability of the local search. The obtained results show that local search is effectively an important component which permits to significantly improve the basic PSO algorithm.

1 Introduction

The hybridization between a population-based metaheuristic (genetic algorithm, particle swarm optimization, ant colony system, ...) and a local search technique (local search, simulated annealing, tabu search, ...) permits to develop powerfur hybrid metaheuristics, because a such approach combines the exploration ability of the former with the exploitation ability of the latter. More specifically, this paper is devoted to the hybridization of particle swarm optimization (PSO) with stochastic local search (SLS).

In SLS, the stopping criterion is often defined as the maximal number of consecutive attempts without improvement of the current solution. This parameter offers a very simple and intuitive way for tuning the exploitation ability of SLS. Higher this number is, and better the exploitation of the search space is. Our objective is to study the effect of this parameter on the performance of the hybrid PSO.

We propose to study this hybrid metaheuristic on a difficult scheduling problem recently appeared in the literature: the flexible job shop problem with transport. This problem arises in Flexible Manufacturing Systems environment.

The paper is organized as follows. Section 2 describes the scheduling problem under consideration. Section 3 presents a general framework of the hybridization PSO - SLS. In section 4, we detail how PSO - SLS is implemented. Section 5 gives the obtained results. We conclude by indicating some directions for further research.

2 The Flexible Job Shop Problem with Transport

The problem under consideration consists in the simultaneous solution of the scheduling of AGVs and the scheduling of machines in an FMS environment.

© Springer International Publishing Switzerland 2014
P. Siarry et al. (Eds.): ICSIBO 2014, LNCS 8472, pp. 115–122, 2014.
DOI: 10.1007/978-3-319-12970-9_13

The scheduling problem under study is a combination of two problems well referenced in the literature: the flexible job-shop problem [1] and the job-shop with transport [2].

2.1   The Job Shop Scheduling Problem

The Job Shop (JSP) Scheduling Problem $(J||C_{max})$ is one of the oldest scheduling problem. The $J2||C_{max}$ problem has been proved to be NP-hard [3]. This problem can be described by a set $J = \{J_1, \ldots, J_n\}$ of n jobs which must be processed on a set $M = \{M_1, \ldots, M_m\}$ of m machines subject to the constraint that each machine can handle at most one job at a time. Each job must follow a specified sequence of machines. Assuming that α_j is the number of operations of job J_j, let us note by $O^j = \{o_{j,i}, i \in [\![1, \alpha_j]\!]\}$ the set of operations of J_j, and by $O = \bigcup_{J_j \in J} O^j$ the set of all the operations. Each operation $o_{j,i}$ must be processed on a given machine $M_{j,i} \in M$ during a specified processing time $p_{j,i}$.

2.2   The Flexible Job Shop Problem

The Flexible Job Shop (FJSP) scheduling problem $(FJ||C_{max})$ is a generalization of the JSP, in which each operation $o_{j,i}$ can be performed by a subset $T_{j,i} \subset M$ of machines. For each machine $M_l \in T_{j,i}$, a processing time $p_{j,i,l}$ is given (the notation $p_{j,i}$ can be kept in the case of identical machines).

According to [1], this problem consists of a routing subproblem and a scheduling subproblem. The former is assigning each operation $o_{j,i}$ to a machine $M_l \in T_{j,i}$. The latter is sequencing the assigned operations on each machine. Two kinds of approximated approaches have been proposed in the literature: hierarchical approaches and integrated approaches. In hierarchical approaches, the two subproblems are treated separately. On the contrary, the integrated approaches consider them simultaneously. Many metaheuristics have been developed for tackling the FJSP. We can suggest the following references for a first introduction to this problem: [1], [4], [5] who have proposed a Tabu search and [6], [7] who have proposed a genetic algorithm.

2.3   The Job Shop Problem with Transport

The Job Shop problem with Transport (JSP-T) is another extension of the JSP. This problem occurs in a Flexible Manufacturing System (FMS) environment. A FMS consists of a set of machines performing production tasks and a set $V = \{V_1, \ldots, V_k\}$ of k automated guided vehicles (AGVs) performing the transportation tasks between the machines. Hence, we consider that the travel times of jobs between two consecutive machines cannot be neglected at all.

This problem is noted $(JR|t_{k,l}, t'_{k,l}|C_{max})$ according to the $\alpha|\beta|\gamma$ notation, extended by [8] for transportation problems. R indicates that we have a limited number of identical vehicles. $t_{k,l}$ indicates that we have job-independent, but machine-dependent loaded travel times. $t'_{k,l}$ indicates that we have machine-dependent empty travel times.

Like the FJSP, the JSP-T is more complex than the JSP. It is the combination of two NP-hard subproblems: the Vehicle Scheduling Problem (VSP) and the Job Shop Problem. [2] used a hierarchical approach with a heuristic that generates some machine schedules and a sliding time window technique that build a feasible vehicle assignment. [9] proposed an integrated approach with a genetic algorithm , [10] have developed a hierarchical approach with a genetic algorithm for the scheduling of vehicles and a greedy algorithm for the scheduling of the machines; [11] described an integrated hybrid metaheuristic (iterative local search / simulated annealing) and [12] also proposed an integrated metaheuristic based on memetic algorithms.

2.4   The Flexible Job Shop Problem with Transport

The Flexible Job Shop Problem with transport (FJSP-T) is the combination of the two extensions we have presented just above. This problem can be noted $(FJR|t_{k,l}, t'_{k,l}|C_{max})$. Solution approaches for this problems must integrate three subproblems. **the routing subproblem**: each operation $o_{j,i}$ must be assigned to a machine $M_l \subset T_{j,i}$. **The scheduling subproblem**: for each machine M_l, the sequence of operations that are assigned to it must be scheduled. **The transport subproblem**: the jobs must be carried between two consecutive machines defined by their routing.

Few works have been devoted to this problem. [13] extend their previous work on the JSP-T and propose a first integrated approach with an iterated local search. [14], [15] describe an extension in which the processing times are bounded on the machines. They propose a hierarchical approach based on a genetic algorithm with tabu search hybrid metaheuristic . The genetic algorithm tries to improve the routing and transport subproblems while the tabu search is dedicated to the scheduling subproblem. [16] use the FJSP-T as scheduling problem for improving the rearrangement of the machines in the system.

3   Description of the Hybrid PSO

The hybridization of a population-based method with a local search is a classical approach. We present in this section a general framework of this hybrid metaheuristic.

3.1   The PSO Framework

Particle Swarm Optimization (PSO) is a nature inspired metaheuristic developed by [17] for continuous optimization problems. The framework of PSO can be described as follows:

- At iteration k, each particle i has a position that represents a solution $x_{i,k}$ of the optimization problem. The objective function gives the cost of this solution and defines the fitness of the particle.
- Each particle i remembers the best solution $pbest_i$ it has encountered in its past (local memory).
- Each particle knows the best solution $gbest_i$ encountered either by the whole swarm, or by a subset of it (global memory).
- Each particle flies in the solution space with a given velocity $v_{i,k}$.

Starting from a swarm of random particles (position and velocity), each of them will move in the solution space using the two following equations where c_1 and c_2 are cognitive coefficients and ω is a constriction factor:

$$v_{i,k+1} = \omega \times v_{i,k} + c_1 * rand()(pbest_i - x_{i,k}) + c_2 * rand()(gbest_i - x_{i,k}) \quad (1)$$

$$x_{i,k+1} = x_{i,k} + v_{i,k+1} \quad (2)$$

3.2 Discrete PSO

Many works have been related in the literature about the adaptation of PSO for solving combinatorial optimization problems. Indeed, we can distinguish three classes of approaches, based on:

- **a stochastic velocity model.**[18] propose a of binary PSO algorithm. The velocity is a vector of probability $v^{(k)} = [p_1, \ldots, p_n]$ which determines how the position evolves in the search space.
- **a discrete definition for vector operations.** [19] proposes a general framework, illustrated by the Traveling Salesman Problem, in which vector operations are redefined in order to work on a discrete space.
- **a discrete definition for the search space.** The particles fly in a continuous space, exactly like a classical PSO. Each (continuous) position is transformed into a discrete solution by the application of a given rule (for instance, the SPV (Smallest Position Value) rule ([20])

The hybrid PSO described in this paper belongs to the second class. In section 4, we will show how the framework proposed by [19] is implemented to work on the FJSP-T.

3.3 Local Search

The general framework of local search is to improve a solution x by searching into a subset of solutions denoted $N(x)$ and called the neighborhood of x.

In the determinist case, a local search consists in enumerating the neighborhood $N(x)$ and in choosing either the first improving neighbor encountered (incomplete enumeration), or the best improving neighbor (complete enumeration). The stopping criterion is typically when the current solution x has reached a local minimum.

On the contrary, the stochastic local search consists in computing a sampling enumeration of the neighborhood. At each iteration, a neighbor $y \in N(x)$ is drawing at random. The stopping criterion if generally defined by a maximum number of successive failures ($MaxFailures$). The formula (3), where $|N|$ designs the number of elements of the set N, gives the number of trials that are necessary to obtain a local minimum with a given probability p.

3.4 The Hybrid PSO

Several authors attempt to specify some hybridization features ([21], [22], [23]). They are all agree to recognize that the hybridization of a population-based method (evolution algorithms, particle swarm, ant colony, ...) with a local search procedure (local search, tabu search, simulated annealing, ...) is of the best interest. Population-based metaheuristics are powerful in terms of exploration. The main idea of this kind of hybridization is to combine them with a local search procedure which is powerful in terms of exploitation. Each time a particle moves, its position is improved by the local search.

4   Implementation Details

In this section, we describe how the general algorithms presented in the previous section are implemented for the FJSP-T.

4.1 Solution Encoding and Solution Evaluation

We propose a solution encoding based on vehicles rather than machines. Obviously, each operation $o_{j,i} \in O$ requires a transportation task of the job J_j from its previous machine (if $i > 1$ then $M_{origin} \in T_{j,i-1}$ else $M_{origin} = LU$) to the assigned machine ($M_{dest} \in T_{j,i}$). Let us note this transportation task $\hat{o}_{j,i}$.

For each vehicle, we give the sequence of transportation tasks it must perform. Additionally, Some rules are defined for solving other subproblems. For the routing subproblem, we apply the first available machine rule. For the scheduling subproblem, we apply the FIFO rule in the input buffer of the machines.

4.2 The Local Search Procedure

This neighborhood integrates two basic moves, the exchange move and the insertion move, and a neighborhood reduction. The exchange move consists in exchanging two beforehand selected tasks. The insertion move consists in removing a randomly chosen task, and then to insert it elsewhere. We can notice that exchange moves preserve the number of tasks assigned to each vehicle. On the contrary, insertion moves modify the number os tasks of the vehicles. Their complementarity is a reason why we have considered these two moves simultaneously inside our neighborhood structure.

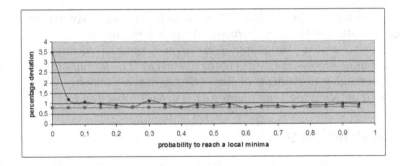

Fig. 1. The obtained results

The basic idea behing the neighborhood reduction is that it is probably bad to exchange two tasks which are completed at a very different time. The proposed reduction is the following: we only accept to exchange (or to insert) a task $\tilde{o}_{j,i}$ with a task $\tilde{o}_{j',i'}$ if $\tilde{o}_{j',i'}$ is in a time windows which depends on $\tilde{o}_{j,i}$. More precisely, this time window is defined by the formula (3).

$$CT(\tilde{o}_{j,i-1}) \leq CT(\tilde{o}_{j',i'}) \leq CT(\tilde{o}_{j,i+1}) \tag{3}$$

4.3 Discrete PSO

We describe here how the vector operations have been defined in order to adapt the movement equations (1) and (2) to discrete space.

We propose to define the velocity as a sequence of insertion moves. The operation "position plus velocity" simply consists to apply the moves from the position in the given order. The arrival position is then obtained. Moreover, it is always possible to compute a sequence of moves (and so a velocity) for transforming a given position into another one. Lastly, the operation "coefficient times velocity" ($\alpha * v$) is obtained by applying a part of the sequence $\alpha < 1$ or by repeating the sequence $\alpha > 1$.

5   Experimental Results

We consider a benchmark of ten instances used in [13], [14], [15]. It derives from the work of [2] for the JSP-T problem. 10 runs have been done for each of the 10 instances. The obtained results are given in figure 1. The curves give the percentage deviation as a function of the probability to obtain a local minimum. The percentage deviation is the average relative gap $\frac{(H(x)-H(x^*))}{H(x^*)}$ between the cost of the obtained solution $H(x)$ and the cost of the best known solution $H(x*)$.

The curve with square marks represents the results obtained by the hybridization of DPSO with a determinist local search. As it is independant of the probability p, the values are constant. We can notice several points:

- if $p = 0$, we have $MaxFailures = 0$. The resuting method is the DPSO without local search. The average performance is around 3.5
- if $p \neq 0$, the average performance is between 0.7
- The comparison between the two curves shows that there is not a significant difference between the stochastic and the determinist local search.

6 Conclusions and Further Work

In this paper, we study the hybridization between Particle Swarm Optimization (PSO) and Stochastic Local Search (SLS). This metaheuristic is applied on the Flexible Job Shop Problem with Transport (FJSP-T). We describe how the PSO is adapted to the studied problem and we study more specifically the balance between the exploration ability of PSO and the exploitation ability of SLS. The obtained results show that the hybridization is important and permits to improve significantly the basic PSO. However, the rate of hybridization doesn't seem to be a discriminent factor.

This work can be continued in different ways. The library of instances could be completed, for instance by extending the library of the flexible job shop problem. This will permit to consider large-size instances. Other metaheuristic approaches (memetic algorithm, iterated local search) could also be developed. This will permit to compare these metaheuristics and to provide first reference results for the FJSP-T.

References

1. Brandimarte, P.: Routing and scheduling in a flexible job shop by tabu search. Annals of Operations Research **41**, 157–183 (1993)
2. Bilge, U., Ulusoy, G.: A time window approach to simultaneous scheduling of machines and material handling system in an fms. Operations Research **43**, 1058–1070 (1995)
3. Lenstra, J., Rinnooy Kan, A.: Computational complexity of discrete optimization problems. Annals of Discrete Mathematics **4**, 281–300 (1979)
4. Gambardella, L., Mastrolilli, M.: Effective neighborhood functions for the flexible job shop problem. Journal of Scheduling 3 (1996)
5. Dauzère-Pérès, S., Paulli, J.: An integrated approach for modeling and solving the general multiprocessor job-shop scheduling problem using tabu search. Annals of Operations Research **70**, 281–306 (1997)
6. Pezzella, F., Morganti, G., Ciaschetti, G.: A genetic algorithm for the flexible job-shop scheduling problem. Computers & Operations Research **35**, 3202–3212 (2008)
7. Gen, M., Gao, J., Lin, L.: Multistage-based genetic algorithm for flexible job-shop scheduling problem. In: Gen, M., Green, D., Katai, O., McKay, B., Namatame, A., Sarker, R.A., Zhang, B.-T. (eds.) Intelligent and Evolutionary Systems. SCI, vol. 187, pp. 183–196. Springer, Heidelberg (2009)
8. Knust, S.: Shop-scheduling problem with transportation (ph d thesis). Universität Osnabrück, Fachbereich Mathematik/Informatik (1999)

9. Ulusoy, G., Sivrikaya-Şerifoglu, F., Bilge, Ü.: A genetic algorithm approach to the simultaneous scheduling of machines and automated guided vehicles. Computers & Operations Research **24**, 335–351 (1997)

10. Abdelmaguid, T.F., Nassef, A.O., Kamal, B.A., Hassan, M.F.: A hybrid ga/heuristic approach to the simultaneous scheduling of machines and automated guided vehicles. International Journal of Production Research **42**, 267–281 (2004)

11. Deroussi, L., Gourgand, M., Tchernev, N.: A simple metaheuristic approach to the simultaneous scheduling of machines and automated guided vehicles. International Journal of Production Research **46**, 2143–2164 (2008)

12. Lacomme, P., Larabi, M., Tchernev, N.: Job-shop based framework for simultaneous scheduling of machines and automated guided vehicles. International Journal of Production Economics **143**, 24–34 (2013)

13. Deroussi, L., Norre, S.: Simultaneous scheduling of machines and vehicles for the flexible job shop problem. In: International Conference on Metaheuristics and Nature Inspired Computing (2010)

14. Zhang, Q., Manier, H., Manier, M.A.: A hybrid metaheuristic algorithm for flexible job-shop scheduling problems with transportation constraints. In: Proceedings of the Fourteenth International Conference on Genetic and Evolutionary Computation Conference, pp. 441–448. ACM (2012)

15. Zhang, Q., Manier, H., Manier, M.A.: A genetic algorithm with tabu search procedure for flexible job shop scheduling with transportation constraints and bounded processing times. Computers & Operations Research **39**, 1713–1723 (2012)

16. Deroussi, L., Gourgand, M.: A scheduling approach for the design of flexible manufacturing systems. In: Siarry, P. (ed.) Heuristics: Theory and Applications. NOVA Publishers, pp. 161–222 (2013)

17. Eberhart, R., Kennedy, J.: A new optimizer using particle swarm theory. In: Proceedings of the 6th International Symposium on Micromachine and Human Science, Nagoya, Japan, pp. 39–43 (1995)

18. Kennedy, J., Eberhart, R.C.: A discrete binary version of the particle swarm algorithm. In: 1997 IEEE International Conference on Systems, Man, and Cybernetics, Computational Cybernetics and Simulation, vol. 5, pp. 4104–4108. IEEE (1997)

19. Clerc, M.: Discrete particle swarm optimization, illustrated by the traveling salesman problem. In: Clerc, M. (ed.) New Optimization Techniques in Engineering. STUDFUZZ, vol. 141, pp. 219–239. Springer, Heidelberg (2004)

20. Tasgetiren, M.F., Sevkli, M., Liang, Y.-C., Gencyilmaz, G.: Particle swarm optimization algorithm for permutation flowshop sequencing problem. In: Dorigo, M., Birattari, M., Blum, C., Gambardella, L.M., Mondada, F., Stützle, T. (eds.) ANTS 2004. LNCS, vol. 3172, pp. 382–389. Springer, Heidelberg (2004)

21. Talbi, E.G.: A taxonomy of hybrid metaheuristics. Journal of Heuristics **8**, 541–564 (2002)

22. Raidl, G.R.: A Unified View on Hybrid Metaheuristics. In: Almeida, F., Blesa Aguilera, M.J., Blum, C., Moreno Vega, J.M., Pérez Pérez, M., Roli, A., Sampels, M. (eds.) HM 2006. LNCS, vol. 4030, pp. 1–12. Springer, Heidelberg (2006)

23. Blum, C., Puchinger, J., Raidl, G.R., Roli, A.: Hybrid metaheuristics in combinatorial optimization: A survey. Applied Soft Computing **11**, 4135–4151 (2011)

Multiple Mobile Target Tracking in Wireless Sensor Networks

Charly Lersteau[(⊠)], Marc Sevaux[(⊠)], and André Rossi[(⊠)]

Lab-STICC Centre de recherche, Université de Bretagne-Sud,
92116 56321 Lorient cedex, BP, France
{charly.lersteau,marc.sevaux,andre.rossi}@univ-ubs.fr

Abstract. An *object tracking sensor network* (OTSN) is made of m *static* wireless *sensors* scattered throughout a geographical area for tracking n *mobile targets*. Assuming that sensors have non-rechargeable batteries, one of the most critical aspects of OTSN is energy consumption. In this paper, we propose linear programming models which handle two missions : *monitoring* and *reporting* data to a *base station*, and two distinct problems : *minimize energy consumption* and *maximize network lifetime*. We suppose that trajectories of targets are known and targets should be monitored by sensors. To reach our goals, we *schedule* the *active* and *sleep* states of the sensors and *route* the data to a base station while keeping track of the targets. To solve our problems, we process a *temporal discretization* according to the intersection points between the trajectories and the sensing ranges of the sensors. The obtained sets of sensors for each time window help us to create *linear programming* models. These basic problems offer perspectives in performance evaluation of energy-conservation protocols and distributed algorithms in wireless sensor networks.

Keywords: Multiple target tracking · Wireless sensor networks · Lifetime maximization · Energy consumption minimization

1 Introduction

During the last decade, Wireless Sensor Networks (WSN) have become more and more affordable and the number of application areas has increased. Sensor networks find their applications in battlefield or trafic surveillance, wildlife studies or healthcare [5, 7]. This paper focuses on target tracking using WSNs. Our problem is to cover *moving targets* using randomly deployed sensors. As the sensors used are often low-cost, a critical aspect of their deployment is battery limitation.

Two scenarios might occur: 1. battery capacity of sensors is large enough to ensure monitoring of all the targets during the whole time horizon ; 2. the targets cannot be monitored until the end of the time horizon. In the first case, our goal is to minimize the energy consumption, whereas in the second case, it

© Springer International Publishing Switzerland 2014
P. Siarry et al. (Eds.): ICSIBO 2014, LNCS 8472, pp. 123–130, 2014.
DOI: 10.1007/978-3-319-12970-9_14

is to maximize the network lifetime, i.e. the time during which all targets are monitored.

In this section, we describe existing works and details of our problem. In section 2, we reformulate the problem so as to solve it with the methods proposed in sections 3 (allocation) and 4 (scheduling). Finally, the proposed contribution is discussed before concluding the paper.

1.1   Related Work

Many protocols with energy-conservation in mind have been proposed [5,7]. Until 2012, a few methods relying on optimization techniques were reported [5]. Rossi et al. [8] proposed a column generation-based algorithm boosted by a genetic algorithm to solve the *maximum network lifetime under bandwidth constraints* (MNLB). However, this method is only suitable for missions involving static targets. To minimize the communication costs due to data reporting, Lin and Lee [2] proposed an algorithm applied to bi-directional moving objects. The authors formulate the problem as a 0-1 integer programming problem and apply a Lagrangean relaxation-based heuristic to solve it. Naderan et al. [6] solved the problem of multiple target coverage by determining the sensing range of each sensor using primal and dual-based algorithms. In [4], a continuous linear programming model which handles both monitoring and reporting is proposed. The model maximizes network lifetime but assumes that targets are static.

1.2   Problem Description

In a region, m sensors are randomly deployed to track n mobile targets as points and to report sensing data to a *base station*. A sensor $i \in \{1, \ldots, m\}$ is static and has its own sensing range R_i^S, communication range R_i^C and its own initial battery capacity E_i. Each sensor can be in *active* state, during which it can cover targets and consumes e_i^S units of energy per target and per unit of time, or in *sleep* state, in which the energy consumption is zero. Transmitting data to other sensors costs e_i^T and receiving data e_i^R per unit of data. For each target $j \in \{1, \ldots, n\}$, we know the position $T_j(t)$ at each instant t. We require that each target is covered by at least one sensor at any time.

Our method is composed of three steps : discretization, allocation and scheduling. In the first step, we reformulate the problem in terms of sets by splitting the time horizon into time windows and grouping candidate sensors for watching targets in a sequence of sets. Then from this reformulation we deduce two linear programming models to allocate monitoring time and reporting data amount to sensors. Finally we schedule the sensing tasks and the routing plan by solving a sequence of matching problems.

2   Discretization

To solve our problem, it is convenient to divide the total time into time windows for which we can deduce a static subset of candidate sensors covering the moving targets.

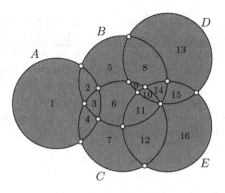

Fig. 1. A planar graph example with $m = 5$ sensors, resulting in 16 faces

In this paper, it is assumed that sensing area of every sensor $i \in \{1, \ldots, n\}$ is a disk of radius R_i^S. The monitored area can be seen as a *planar graph* [1,9] (Figure 1). Vertices are the points of intersections of boundaries of all sensor's disks. Edges connect vertices along the boundaries. The surfaces bounded by edges are called *faces*. In fact, all points inside a face are covered by the same set of sensors.

A circle can intersect at most two times any other circle. Suppose that every circle intersects exactly two times each other, then the number of vertices $|V|$ is at most $m(m-1)$ and the number of edges $|E|$ at most $2m(m-1)$. Thus using the Euler formula $|V| - |E| + |F| = 2$ with $|F|$ the number of faces, $|F|$ is at most $m(m-1) + 2$ (including the outer, infinitely large face) [1].

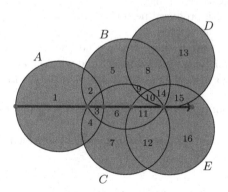

Fig. 2. Temporal discretization in 5 time windows (6 ticks)

We perform a temporal discretization by computing the intersections between each target's trajectory $T_j(t)$ and the boundaries of the faces (Figure 2). A convenient way to model the trajectories is to use piecewise linear curves, as it can be used to model any trajectory. Computing the intersections in this case is also equivalent to solve quadratic equations. This computation results to a set of *ticks*, i.e. the values of t for which a target goes from one face to another. Once all targets have been processed, we use all the ticks to split the time, producing p intervals called *time windows*. To each time window $k \in \{1, \ldots, p\}$ and each target $j \in \{1, \ldots, n\}$ is associated a set $S^k(j)$ of candidate sensors. $S^k(j)$ defines the set of sensors that are able to cover the target j during time window k. To cover the target j during the time window k, at least one sensor has to be activated from $S^k(j)$. Each time window k (defined by $[t_k, t_{k+1}]$) has a duration $\Delta^k = t_{k+1} - t_k$.

3   Allocation

In this section, we propose two models to solve the allocation problem. Precisely, the purpose of these models is to decide how long each sensor monitors which target, and the amount of data sent or received by each sensor. After processing the discretization, we can provide the following data:

I	Set of sensors $\{1, \ldots, m\}$.
J	Set of targets $\{1, \ldots, n\}$.
K	Set of time windows $\{1, \ldots, p\}$.
$S^k(j)$	Set of sensors covering target j during time window k.
$T^k(i)$	Set of targets covered by sensor i during time window k.
$N^T(i)$	Set of sensors that are able to receive data from sensor i (inc. BS).
$N^R(i)$	Set of sensors that are able to send data to sensor i.
e_i^S	Amount of energy spent by sensor i for sensing task per one unit of time.
e_i^T	Amount of energy spent by sensor i for transmitting one unit of data.
e_i^R	Amount of energy spent by sensor i for receiving one unit of data.
E_i	Battery capacity of sensor i.
β	Amount of data produced per unit of time for sensing.
Δ^k	Duration of time window k.

It can be observed that if there exists a couple (k, j) such that $S^k(j) = \emptyset$, then target j will never be covered during time window k.

We present the two essential sets of decision variables for our models.

- $d_{ij}^k \geq 0$ is the amount of time during which sensor i monitors target j during time window k.
- $f_{ii'}^k \geq 0$ is the amount of data transmitted by sensor i to sensor i' during time window k.

3.1   Energy Consumption Minimization

The following model assumes that sensors have enough energy to monitor all the targets during the whole time horizon, otherwise it becomes infeasible.

$$\min E = \sum_{i \in I} \sum_{k \in K} \left(\sum_{j \in T^k(i)} e_i^S d_{ij}^k + \sum_{i' \in N^T(i)} e_i^T f_{ii'}^k + \sum_{i' \in N^R(i)} e_i^R f_{i'i}^k \right) \quad (1)$$

$$\text{s.t.} \sum_{k \in K} \left(\sum_{j \in T^k(i)} e_i^S d_{ij}^k + \sum_{i' \in N^T(i)} e_i^T f_{ii'}^k + \sum_{i' \in N^R(i)} e_i^R f_{i'i}^k \right) \leq E_i \, , \forall i \in I \quad (2)$$

$$\beta \sum_{j \in T^k(i)} d_{ij}^k + \sum_{i' \in N^R(i)} f_{i'i}^k = \sum_{i' \in N^T(i)} f_{ii'}^k \, , \forall k \in K, i \in I \quad (3)$$

$$\sum_{i \in S^k(j)} d_{ij}^k = \Delta^k \, , \qquad \forall k \in K, j \in J \quad (4)$$

$$d_{ij}^k \geq 0 \, , \qquad \forall k \in K \, , i \in I \, , j \in T^k(i) \quad (5)$$

$$f_{ii'}^k \geq 0 \, , \qquad \forall k \in K \, , i \in I \, , i' \in N^T(i) \quad (6)$$

We want to minimize the total energy spent by all the sensors (1). Sensors can consume energy for three distinct tasks: sensing, transmitting and receiving data. Constraint (2) ensures that energy spent by each sensor does not exceed its battery capacity. Sensing task produces input data that needs to be transmitted to the base station. Constraint (3) enforces the connectivity and the data transmission to the base station. This constraint is a data flow conservation constraint, i.e. it implies that the amount of sensed and received data is equal to the amount of transmitted data. Constraint (4) ensures that each target is covered by at least one sensor for every time window.

3.2   Network Lifetime Maximization

When the network has not enough energy to track all the targets during the time horizon, we would like to maximize the network lifetime. We introduce two additional variables y^k and δ^k.

- $y^k \in \{0,1\}$ is equal to 1 if all targets are monitored during the whole time window k.
- $\delta^k \geq 0$ is a helper fractional variable in order to take into account the tracking duration in the last (incomplete) time window for expressing the network lifetime.

$$\max L = \sum_{k \in K} \Delta^k \left(y^k + \delta^k \right) \quad (7)$$

$$\text{s.t. } (2) - (3)$$

$$\sum_{i \in S^k(j)} d_{ij}^k = \Delta^k \left(y^k + \delta^k \right) \, , \qquad \forall k \in K, j \in J \quad (8)$$

$$\delta^k \leq y^{k-1} - y^k \, , \qquad \forall k \in K \, (y^0 = 1) \quad (9)$$

$$y^{k-1} \geq y^k \, , \qquad \forall k \in K \setminus \{1\} \quad (10)$$

$$y^k \in \{0,1\} \, , \qquad \forall k \in K \quad (11)$$

$$\delta^k \geq 0 \, , \qquad \forall k \in K \quad (12)$$

$$d_{ij}^k \geq 0 \, , \qquad \forall k \in K \, , i \in I \, , j \in T^k(i) \quad (13)$$

$$f_{ii'}^k \geq 0 \, , \qquad \forall k \in K \, , i \in I \, , i' \in N^T(i) \quad (14)$$

The problem objective is to maximize the time during which all the targets are covered by at least one sensor (7). We consider that the network lifetime is defined by the moment where some target is no longer covered by a sensor. Constraint (8) links the d_{ij}^k variables to the y^k and δ^k variables to ensure that all targets are covered during all the network lifetime L. Only one of the δ^k variables is allowed to be strictly positive (9), in particular in the last time window of the tracking lifetime. Constraint (10) enforces tracking continuity by setting the first consecutive y^k variables to 1 and all the following ones to zero.

One of the advantages of our models is their linearity which makes them suitable for solving in LP/MIP solvers to get an optimal solution. An important remark is that our models don't take into account the case when a sensor watching several targets consumes the same amount of energy as watching one target. The two models complement one another, i.e. the second model can be used as a fallback of the first in case the latter is infeasible. In the case that sensors have enough energy to watch all the targets at any time, the second model becomes irrelevant because it would give the time horizon as an optimal objective value, without considering the energy consumption.

4   Scheduling

4.1   Sensing Tasks

The previous step helps us to know which amount of time each sensor should watch targets, but does not say when the sensing tasks should start and stop.

The values of d_{ij}^k obtained in the optimal solution of the LPs, can be casted into a series of matrices called *workload matrices*. The basic idea to determine a schedule is to decompose each of these matrices as a sequence of q *schedule matrices* [3]:

$$D^k = \begin{bmatrix} d_{1,1}^k & d_{1,2}^k & \cdots & d_{1,n}^k \\ d_{2,1}^k & d_{2,2}^k & \cdots & d_{2,n}^k \\ \vdots & \vdots & \ddots & \vdots \\ d_{m,1}^k & d_{m,2}^k & \cdots & d_{m,n}^k \end{bmatrix} = \begin{bmatrix} 0c_10\ldots0 \\ c_100\ldots0 \\ 000\ldots c_1 \\ \ldots \\ 00c_1\ldots0 \end{bmatrix} + \begin{bmatrix} 000\ldots0 \\ 000\ldots c_2 \\ 0c_20\ldots0 \\ \ldots \\ c_20c_2\ldots0 \end{bmatrix} + \cdots + \begin{bmatrix} c_q00\ldots0 \\ 00c_q\ldots c_q \\ 000\ldots0 \\ \ldots \\ 0c_q0\ldots0 \end{bmatrix}$$

$$= P_1 + P_2 + \cdots + P_q$$

Each entry in *schedule matrix* P_i is either c_i or 0. Each column has exactly one c_i element (i.e. a target is watched by exactly one sensor).

To do the decomposition, we express the matrix D^k as a bipartite graph connecting sensors i (in one side) to targets j (in the other side). For each non-zero d_{ij}^k, there is an edge connecting i to j of weight d_{ij}^k.

The problem of finding a schedule matrix is equivalent to finding a n-matching in the bipartite graph. As long as the right hand side value is strictly positive, constraints (4) and (8) guarantee that such a matching exists, i.e. that each target is connected to at least one sensor in the bipartite graph. We find a matching by selecting one adjacent edge per target j, denoted by sel(j).

Let c be the minimum weight over all selected edges, then we subtract c to the weight of these selected edges. Let $\mathfrak{L}$ be the right hand side value of the equations (4) or (8). After this subtraction, the following equations:

$$\sum_{i \in S^k(j)} d_{ij}^k = \mathfrak{L}, \forall j \in J \tag{15}$$

become:

$$\sum_{i \in S^k(j) \setminus \{\text{sel}(j)\}} d_{ij}^k + \left(d_{\text{sel}(j),j}^k - c \right) = \mathfrak{L} - c \implies \sum_{i \in S^k(j)} d_{ij}^{k\,'} = \mathfrak{L}', \forall j \in J \tag{16}$$

Thus the underlying equations keep their original structure with the same right hand side value for all $j \in J$. The edge with the minimal weight c is then removed from the bipartite graph. Matchings can be found until the right hand side $\mathfrak{L}$ is zero. The sequence of matrices can be scheduled using any ordering during the time window.

4.2   Data Routing

As a result of our LPs, we obtain a sequence of flow matrices $F^k = \left(f_{ii'}^k \right)_{m \times (m+1)}$ that express a sequence of trees where the root is the base station. Each active sensor needs to forward its sensed data to the base station. The method proposed in [3] is to forward the data through non-zero edges (i, i') (i.e. such that $f_{ii'}^k > 0$) to the the base station. A sensor i sends its outgoing data to its first available neighbor i' until the edge is saturated (amout of data $f_{ii'}^k$ reached), then switches to another neighbor i'' until the value $f_{ii''}^k$ is met, etc. There is no specific ordering to follow to build an optimal routing plan.

5   Conclusion

We provide reformulations as a linear model to solve multiple mobile target tracking problems in WSNs. The basic problems considered are energy consumption minimization and network lifetime maximization. Our formulations can be used to evaluate the results of scheduling-based protocols using the optimal solution. Further research may focus on the following perspectives : decentralize the algorithm (swarm intelligence), deal with uncertainty (stochastic optimization) or improve the centralized algorithm. This work is sponsored by the *Direction Générale de l'Armement* (General Directorate for Armament of France).

References

1. Berman, P., Calinescu, G., Shah, C., Zelikovsky, A.: Power efficient monitoring management in sensor networks. In: 2004 IEEE Wireless Communications and Networking Conference, WCNC, vol. 4, pp. 2329–2334. IEEE (2004)
2. Lin, F.Y.-S., Lee, C.-T.: An efficient lagrangean relaxation-based object tracking algorithm in wireless sensor networks. Sensors **10**(9), 8101–8118 (2010)
3. Liu, H., Chu, X., Leung, Y.-W., Jia, X., Wan, P.-J.: Maximizing lifetime of sensor-target surveillance in wireless sensor networks. In: IEEE Global Telecommunications Conference, GLOBECOM 2009, pp. 1–6. IEEE (2009)
4. Liu, H., Chu, X., Leung, Y.-W., Jia, X., Wan, P.-J.: General maximal lifetime sensor-target surveillance problem and its solution. IEEE Transactions on Parallel and Distributed Systems **22**(10), 1757–1765 (2011)
5. Naderan, M., Dehghan, M., Pedram, H., Hakami, V.: Survey of mobile object tracking protocols in wireless sensor networks: a network-centric perspective. International Journal of Ad Hoc and Ubiquitous Computing **11**(1), 34–63 (2012)
6. Naderan, M., Dehghan, M., Pedram, H.: Primal and dual-based algorithms for sensing range adjustment in wsns. The Journal of Supercomputing, 1–21 (2013)
7. Ramya, K., Praveen Kumar, K., Srinivas Rao, V.: A survey on target tracking techniques in wireless sensor networks. International Journal of Computer Science and Engineering Survey 3(4) (2012)
8. Rossi, A., Singh, A., Sevaux, M.: Column generation algorithm for sensor coverage scheduling under bandwidth constraints. Networks **60**(3), 141–154 (2012)
9. Slijepcevic, S., Potkonjak, M.: Power efficient organization of wireless sensor networks. In: IEEE International Conference on Communications, ICC 2001, vol. 2, pp. 472–476. IEEE (2001)

Swarm Projects: Beyond the Metaphor

Pierre Parrend[1(✉),2,4], Pierre Masai[3,4], Cecilia Zanni-Merk[1,4],
and Pierre Collet[1,4]

[1] ICube Laboratory, Université de Strasbourg, Strasbourg, France
{pierre.collet,cecilia.zanni-merk}@unistra.fr
[2] ECAM Strasbourg-Europe, Schiltigheim, France
pierre.parrend@ecam-strasbourg.eu
[3] Toyota Motor Europe, Bruxelles, Belgium
[4] Complex System Digital Campus (UNESCO Unitwin), Da Nang City, Viet Nam
http://unitwin-cs.org/

Abstract. Swarming has become a management tool for letting individuals cooperate in order to generate emergent solutions to difficult issues in organizations. Beyond the buzzword, we claim that swarming actually matches specific project management practices having a great potential for improving project success. Swarming project management is defined, and the way it complements traditional and agile project management schemes is analysed. Metrics for evaluation of management practices are defined: required practices - practices that lead to failure if not implemented - success practices - practices that good teams put in place - and silver bullets - practices having a measurably significant impact on success. The analysis is performed through a controlled experiment involving 52 computer science students at the bachelor level, in the context of a 4 month development project involving 8 parallel teams working on the same software project.

Keywords: Swarm intelligence · Agile · SCRUM framework · Stigmergy · Emergent cognition

1 Introduction

IT project management is known for its huge rate of challenged or failed projects: the Standish Group chaos report from 2013 [cha13] evaluates to 24% the rate of endangered projects for small projects (< 1 million \$), and up to 90% for big projects ($>= 1$ million \$). A structured, emergent method for enabling teams to systematically discover, explore and evaluate project tasks, which makes a heavy use of message-based communication and visualisation (*ie.* stygmergy), has been proposed to address this challenge: agility [TN86]. It provides a first solution for leading IT projects to the success [cha12], and has also proved to be an efficient catalyst of the community of software developpers, like the success of the Agile Tour[1], which is now a global event, shows. However, the systematic adoption of agility and of its various flavours, like SCRUM[SB07, Ver13] or

---

[1] http://agiletour.org/

© Springer International Publishing Switzerland 2014
P. Siarry et al. (Eds.): ICSIBO 2014, LNCS 8472, pp. 131–138, 2014.
DOI: 10.1007/978-3-319-12970-9_15

Crystal Clear[Coc04] is far from being a reality. We believe that understanding the fundamental mechanisms behind agility, in particular dynamics of swarming in project teams, will enable to define an actionnable model of IT project management, to better evaluate success markers of IT projects, and to brush up the metaphor of swarm projects.

This paper is organised as follows: section 2 presents the state of the art. Section 3 gives the experimental setup and details the way project management practices are quantified through specific metrics. Section 4 gives and analyses the output of the experiment. Section 5 concludes the study.

2   State of the Art

It has been shown that human communities can behave like swarm, using stigmergy to communicate through simple signs deposited in the environement [Par06] and to discover optimal paths, as in online learning environments [VBJ+05]. To the best of our knowledge, swarm-base analysis has only be applied in the context of project to scheduling problems so far [JDSR08]. Analysis of project dynamics as a swarming phenomenon has not been addressed in the literature.

2.1   Swarm Principles

The swarming mechanism has first been formalised in [KE+95]. It is based on following principles [Mil94]:

1. **proximity principle**: ability to perform a behavioral response to the result of elementary utility functions
2. **quality principle**: response to quality factors; the group should be able to respond not only to time and space parameters, but also to quantitative parameters; in animal swarm, this is for instance food quality or safety of location
3. **diverse response principle**: the group should seek to distribute its resources against sudden changes in the environment
4. **stability principle**: the group should not switch its behavior from one mode to another upon every fluctuation of the environment
5. **adaptability principle**: when the reward for changing a behavioral mode is likely to be worth the investment in energy, the group should be able to switch.

Swarming processes are in particular characterized by the communication schemes between their agents [CRP03]. They alternate exploration phases, where the agents perform their own analysis, and communication phases, where information is exchanged between the agents. Several works explicit the ability of swarms to set up cognition models based on simple interactions [RFR05, Par06] [PSV08, Tur11, TT11]. However, parting cognition emerging from swarm interaction and cognition of humans would require a detailed analysis of each of these cognition types, which is beyond the scope of this paper. In our work, we therefore focus on the mechanical aspects of swarms.

2.2   The SCRUM Framework as a Swarm Phenomenon

Swarming is used in the context of agile project management as a buzzword for the *act of coming together to solve a problem or get something done quickly*[2]. However, it can be used as a conceptual framework to analyse whole agile processes, here with the example of the SCRUM framework.

SCRUM [SB07,Ver13] parts the project in sprints, which last from one to 4 weeks. The SCRUM process is maintained by the Scrum Master, who is responsible for it. The Product Owner has the ability to redefine the priority and scope of the project.

Figure 2.2 shows the chronology of a SCRUM project.

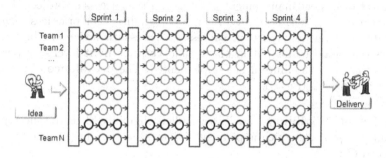

1. **proximity principle**: based on quantitative information displayed in the environment, the agile team is able to autonomously take decisions relative to planning and technical choices. This information is built in particular by the *backlog*, *ie.* the prioritized list of tasks (stories) to be done, and the velocity, *ie.* the progress rate of the project.
2. **quality principle**: quality of project practices is evaluated in a regular basis, at the end of each sprint, to identify suboptimal team behaviour and take corrective measures.
3. **principle of diverse response**: each member takes responsability for some of the tasks to be done, at the very moment they are to be handled. This is enabled by the principle of non-specialisation of team members.
4. **principle of stability**: inside a sprint, the team is not allowed to change the focus of the work. Moreover, it should be protected from external disturbance by the Scrum Master.
5. **principle of adaptability**: At the start of each sprint, the whole project objective and scope can be redefined according to business or technical needs. The way the team is organised and interacts is also subject to modification.

3   The Experiment

3.1   Experiment Setup

So as to characterize actual impact of swarming processes on IT project success, a controlled experiment it conducted. It involves 52 computer science students

---

[2] http://brainslink.com/2013/01/agile-teams-swarm-to-greatness/

at the bachelor level (CDED diploma, IUT Robert Schuman, Ilkirch, France), in the context of a 4 month development project. 8 parallel teams are competing by developing the same software project. The SCRUM framework is used for project management and implemented in a manner which can be considered as canonical: one training session, 4 sprints, each sprint begins with a sprint planning session and ends with a demonstration and a retrospective session. Teams elect a scrum master. The client of the project is available for providing feedback to the teams.

3.2 Metrics

The impact of project management practices on the success of projects is evaluated according to 3 criteria: **silver bullet** eligibility - for practices having a measurably significant impact on success - **success practice** eligibility - for practices that good teams put in place - and **requirement** level - property of practices that lead to failure if not implemented. The **prevalence** of the management practices is tracked.

'Silver Bullet' Eligibility SB. 'Silver bullet' eligibility SB is the success rate probability of projects which implement a given management practice (or criterion, noted C):

$$\forall C > \frac{3}{4} * C_{max} : SB = P_{S|C} = \frac{1}{N * S_{max}} \sum_{i=1}^{N} S \tag{1}$$

with S a quantified evaluation of success. We use a 0..5 scale to grade project success.

'Success Practice' Eligibility SP. 'Success practice' eligibility SP characterizes the practices used by successful teams. It is the probability of use of a given management practice for successful projects:

$$\forall S > \frac{3}{4} * S_{max} : SP = P_{C|S} = \frac{1}{N * C_{max}} \sum_{i=1}^{N} C \tag{2}$$

with C a quantified evaluation of compliance to the criterion. We use a 0..5 scale to grade criterion compliance.

A practice with high SP is only significant if it has a low prevalence, ie. if the practice is not a widespread one.

'Requirement Level' R. 'Requirement level' R is the project failure rate if a given management practice is not implemented:

$$\forall C < \frac{1}{4} * C_{max} : R = P_{F|\cancel{C}} = \frac{1}{N * S_{max}} \sum_{i=1}^{N} F = \frac{1}{N * S_{max}} \sum_{i=1}^{N} (S_{max} - S) \tag{3}$$

with $F = S_{max} - S$ a quantified evaluation of failure.

Prevalence P. P is the prevalence rate of a given management practice among all teams:

$$P = \frac{N_C}{N} \tag{4}$$

with N_C the number of teams matching the criterion and N the total number of teams.

We consider in this study that the quality of implementation of a given management practice (or criterion C) is defined by:

$$C > \frac{3}{4} * C_{max} \tag{5}$$

with C a quantified evaluation of the rigor of the implementation of this criterion, $0 < C1$, and $C_{max} = 1$ the measure for a perfect implementation of the criterion. One can note that for university project marks can simply be used as a criterion, whereas finer quantification must be chosen for production projects.

4   Success Markers of Observed Project Teams

This section details the results of the study. Quantified evaluations are given for the two first sprints of the project. Project success is simply set by the mark for this student development project. When no data is available in the context of our study, we indicate 'Case not present'. In a professional project, the achievement of expected budget, delivery time, scope and quality of the development should be considered instead [AG10].

4.1   The Chaos Criteria

The IT project success criteria elicited by the Chaos reports [cha12,cha13] are quantified as follows: executive management support quantifies the satisfaction of the client with regard to technical deliveries (NOT the overall satisfaction); optimisation quantifies the rigor in process optimisation, here agile retrospective; tools and infrastructure, the systematics of using tools for communication, tickets and bug tracking; execution, the quality of project deliverables (here the project mark); agile process, the rigor in implementing the SCRUM framework; emotional maturity, the ability to deal with conflicts in the team. In this study, management practices: user involvement, clear business objectives, PM expertise, skilled resources, are not considered, since objective quantified data are not available.

The importance of chaos report criteria are confirmed by our study, which is an argument for considering its results are representative in spite of the relatively small size of the experiment. **Execution management support** is a success practice: the metric is clearly biased since clients tend to spend more time for successful projects. Nonetheless, the fact that a client spends this time indicates here that he is confident the expected result for the team is worth it.

Study Rank	Rank (Standish)	Designation	SP	SB	R	Prevalence
1	1	Executive Management Support	83,30%	70,00%	Case not present	25%
2	5	Optimization	80,00%	77,50%	55,00%	25%
3	10	Tools and Infrastructure	78,75%	77,50%	70,00%	25%
4	9	Execution	77,50%	77,50%	Case not present	25%
5	6	Agile Process	72,78%	80,00%	70,00%	12,5%
6	4	Emotional Maturity	40,00%	62,50%	47,50%	75%

Fig. 1. Chaos report success markers

Optimisation is a practice which is clearly set up in a more rigorous manner by successful teams, and which is this another success practice, or symptom for likely success. The importance of good **tools and infrastructure**, as well as of a high-quality **execution**, is confirmed by the study. The fact that **agile process** is rated as a silver bullet for teams working using SCRUM simply states that a correct implementation of agility is a positive marker. This underlies again the consistency of the results of the study without enabling further statement about the method itself. Interestingly enough, student teams are very resilient to lack of **emotional maturity**, which should not be the case in professional teams.

4.2 SCRUM Principles

The IT project success criteria derived from SCRUM principles are quantified as follows: inspection rates the ability to perform rigorous restrospectives, transparency rates the systematic use of stigmergetic mechanisms materialized by the rigour of backlog use, and adaptation quantifies the subjective, perceived readiness of teams to implement changes. **Inspection** uses same data as chaos report optimisation, ie. the rigor in agile retrospective. Identification as a success practice is thus preserved. **Transparency** is another success practice, but its use is less discriminating and therefore a bit less meaningful. Figures for **adaptation** are weaker and should thus be considered with care.

Study Rank	Designation	SP	SB	R	Prevalence
1	Inspection	80,00%	77,50%	70,00%	25%
2	Transparency	77,50%	66,25%	70,00%	50%
3	Adaptation	72,00%	63,33%	Case not present	37,5%

Fig. 2. Scrum success markers

Study Rank	Designation	SP	SB	R	Prevalence
1	Stability	91,31%	68,00%	Case not present	50%
2	Quality	80,00%	77,50%	70,00%	25%
3	Proximity	77,50%	66,25%	70,00%	50%
4	Adaptability	72,00%	63,33%	Case not present	37,5%

Fig. 3. Swarm success markers

4.3 Swarm Success Markers

The IT project success criteria derived from swarm properties are: stability, *ie.* quantified as the ability to actually implement features selected for a given sprint in the time frame of this sprint; quality, as the ability to react to qualitative data, exploits the same data than SCRUM inspection ; proximity, as the ability to react to quantitative data, exploit the same data as transparency and includes the ability to track project velocity. Adaptability is identical to what was defined for SCRUM principles. The ability to set up diverse response is not considered here, because extracting factual data would require a high level of individual tracking which is contrary to SCRUM philosophy and would become an actual impediment in the experiment project. Swarm properties actually extend SCRUM principles without altering existing evaluation. It underlines that the ability to enforce project **stability** inside the sprint is a high-fidelity marker for success practice: it is not sufficient for ensuring success, but it is a practice to be promoted to help teams become better ones.

5 Conclusions and Perspectives

The results of this study are aligned with the results of the chaos report study, which claim for the representativity of the presented conclusions. They underline the importance of SCRUM principles as success practices. Moreover, they confirm that swarming properties are relevant success practices for IT project management. Note that they do not claim to be silver bullets, but that they behave like a symptom of performant management. Moreover, swarming teaches us that stability is a strong success marker for emergent, dynamic processes like SCRUM.

This study, conducted on more than 50 students working in parallel on the same development project for 4 months, offers an optimal experimental setup, in the sense one could hardly imagine having better conditions for team evaluation and comparison. However, it is clear that 8 teams is not a suitable quantity for performing statistics and drawing large scale conclusions. We therefore plan to extend this experiment using real SCRUM projects from industry partners. A dedicated evaluation process will be needed for gathering relevant data as well as for quantifing the evaluation of project practice quality.

Based on the results of this study, we advocate that swarming project management practice are powerful tools both for fostering emergent team behavior, and for supporting rigorous assessment of IT projects status.

References

[AG10] Ahsan, K., Gunawan, I.: Analysis of cost and schedule performance of international development projects. International Journal of Project Management **28**(1), 68–78 (2010)

[cha12] Chaos manifesto 2012 - the year of the executive sponsor. The Standish Group (2012)

[cha13] Chaos manifesto 2013 - think big, act small. The Standish Group (2013)

[Coc04] Cockburn, A.: Crystal Clear: A Human-Powered Methodology for Small Teams: A Human-Powered Methodology for Small Teams (2004)

[CRP03] Chu, S.-C., Roddick, J.F., Pan, J.-S.: Parallel particle swarm optimization algorithm with communication strategies. submitted to IEEE Transactions on Evolutionary Computation (2003)

[JDSR08] Jarboui, B., Damak, N., Siarry, P., Rebai, A.: A combinatorial particle swarm optimization for solving multi-mode resource-constrained project scheduling problems. Applied Mathematics and Computation **195**(1), 299–308 (2008)

[KE+95] Kennedy, J., Eberhart, R., et al.: Particle swarm optimization. In: Proceedings of IEEE International Conference on Neural Networks, vol. 4(2), pp. 1942–1948. Perth, Australia (1995)

[Mil94] Millonas, M.M.: Swarms, phase transitions, and collective intelligence. In: Santa Fe Institute Studies in the Sciences of Complexity-Proceedings, vol. 17, pp. 417–417. ADDISON-WESLEY PUBLISHING CO (1994)

[Par06] Van Dyke Parunak, H.: A Survey of Environments and Mechanisms for Human-Human Stigmergy. In: Weyns, D., Van Dyke Parunak, H., Michel, F. (eds.) E4MAS 2005. LNCS (LNAI), vol. 3830, pp. 163–186. Springer, Heidelberg (2006)

[PSV08] Passino, K.M., Seeley, T.D., Visscher, P.K.: Swarm cognition in honey bees. Behavioral Ecology and Sociobiology **62**(3), 401–414 (2008)

[RFR05] Ramos, V., Fernandes, C., Rosa, A.C.: Social cognitive maps, swarm perception and distributed search on dynamic landscapes. arXiv preprint nlin/0502057 (2005)

[SB07] Snowden, D.J., Boone, M.E.: A leader's framework for decision making. Harvard Business Review **85**(11), 68 (2007)

[TN86] Takeuchi, H., Nonaka, I.: The new new product development game. Harvard Business Review **64**(1), 137–146 (1986)

[TT11] Trianni, Vito, Tuci, Elio: Swarm Cognition and Artificial Life. In: Kampis, George, Karsai, István, Szathmáry, Eörs (eds.) ECAL 2009, Part II. LNCS, vol. 5778, pp. 270–277. Springer, Heidelberg (2011)

[Tur11] Turner, S.J.: Termites as models of swarm cognition. Swarm Intelligence **5**(1), 19–43 (2011)

[VBJ+05] Valigiani, G., Biojout, R., Jamont, Y., Lutton, E., Collet, P., et al.: Experimenting with a real-size man-hill to optimize pedagogical paths. In: Proceedings of the 2005 ACM Symposium on Applied Computing, pp. 4–8. ACM (2005)

[Ver13] Verheyen, G.: SCRUM a Pocket guide. Best Practice. Van Haren Publishing (April 2013)

An Enhanced Particle Swarm Optimisation Algorithm Combined with Neural Networks to Decrease Computational Time

Cédric Leboucher[1](✉), Patrick Siarry[2], Stéphane Le Ménec[1], Hyo-Sang Shin[3], Rachid Chelouah[4], and Antonios Tsourdos[3]

[1] MBDA France, 1, avenue Réaumur, 92350 Le Plessis Robinson, France
Leboucher.cedric@gmail.com
[2] Univ. de Paris-Est Créteil, Laboratoire Images, Signaux et Systèmes Intelligents,
LiSSi (E.A. 3956), 122 rue Paul Armangot, 94400 Vitry sur Seine, France
[3] Cranfield University,
College Road, Cranfield, Bedfordshire MK43 0AL, United Kingdom
[4] EISTI, Avenue du Parc, 95000 Cergy, France

Abstract. This paper proposes to reduce the computational time of an algorithm based on the combination of the Evolutionary Game Theory (EGT) and the Particle Swarm Optimisation (PSO), named C-EGPSO, by using Neural Networks (NN) in order to lighten the computation of the identified heavy part of the C-EGPSO. This computationally burdensome task is the resolution of the EGT part that consists in solving iteratively a differential equation in order to optimally adapt the direction search and the size step of the PSO at each iteration. Therefore, it is proposed to use NN to learn the solution of this differential equation according to the initial conditions in order to gain a precious time.

Keywords: Particle Swarm Optimisation · Swarm Intelligence · Evolutionary Game Theory · Neural Networks

1 Introduction

Over the last few decades, numerous scientists have been inspired by the modelling of social interactions of animals to solve NP-hard optimisation problems. Although the communication among the different agents is limited to an exchange of basic information, it results in a very effective team work. Particle Swarm Optimisation (PSO) is one of most well-known and established approaches using this concept. The aim of the original PSO method proposed by Kennedy and Eberhart was to reproduce this social interaction among agents in order to solve non-linear continuous optimisation problems [1], [2]. PSO not only provides efficient and satisfactory solutions like other meta-heuristic methods [3], [4], [5], but also achieves more accurate results than traditional methods, as Genetic Algorithms (GA) [6], [7], [8], for the problems involving unconstrained continuous functions and also more complex and highly constrained problems [9].

© Springer International Publishing Switzerland 2014
P. Siarry et al. (Eds.): ICSIBO 2014, LNCS 8472, pp. 139–156, 2014.
DOI: 10.1007/978-3-319-12970-9_16

The PSO principle is based on sharing simple information such as current fitness, best obtained fitness and the best global fitness among neighbouring particles in order to determine moving rules of a swarm of candidate solutions, named particles. The movements of the particles are based on a random linear combination of their own current velocity, and the relative position vectors of their own best position and the best known position of the neighbouring particles with respect to their current position. Random choice of the three weighting parameters of the linear combination keeps diversification of the particles' search.

Based on the principle that these directions could be identified as strategies of exploration, the PSO was combined with Evolutionary Game Theory (EGT) in order to improve the convergence speed as well as the efficiency of the proposed method to solve complex optimisation problems. This method was named C-EGPSO and outperformed the Standard PSO 2011 [10] in terms of capacity to solve complex and various kinds of problems as well as the number of iterations required to converge to the optimal solution [11].

From this observation, it was devised to adapt the proposed C-EGPSO to real-time oriented applications. Since the EGT part consists in determining an Evolutionary Stable Strategy (ESS) iteratively by solving a system of Ordinary Differential Equations, the process was identified as a computationally heavy part of the method. Thus, this paper proposes the use of Neural Networks to learn the output of the EGT process and predict the optimal strategy that optimises the exploration of the solution space.

The validation of the proposed approach will be done in two stages. First the validity of the NN will be verified by analysing the accuracy of the obtained results in the learning of the resolution of the Replicator equation, then the gain of computational time using NN will be quantified. Second, the proposed app-roach will be applied to a set of benchmarked continuous optimisation problems issued from [12] in order to confirm that the proposed algorithm obtains as good results as the original algorithm (C-EGPSO) in terms of precision of the final solution, as well as decreases the computation time for solving these problems. The second stage of the numerical validation will be done with a selection of benchmark functions issued from the CEC'2005 congress [12]. The benchmark definition is available in [13]. The efficiency of the proposed method was already tested in one of our previous studies[1].

The proposed paper is organised as follows: first, the essential notions to understand the global approach is provided to the reader, then the proposed method is described, before giving details on the experimental procedure used in order to validate the approach. Finally, the obtained results are presented and discussed. This ends with a conclusion and the perspectives of the presented approach.

---

[1] C. Leboucher, H-S. Shin, S. Le Ménec, P. Siarry, R. Chelouah, A. Tsourdos and A. Kotenkoff, *An Enhanced Particle Swarm Optimisation Method Integrated with Evolutionary Game Theory*, Submission in progress

2 Background

The herein Section proposes to describe all the necessary background to understand the foundations of the proposed method. First, the enhanced Particle Swarm optimiser that combines the SPSO 2011 proposed by Clerc [10] and Evolutionary Game Theory will be introduced. Then, a brief overview on Neural Networks will be given.

2.1 The Proposed C-EGPSO

The herein subsection describes the optimisation algorithm that will be used as basis. This algorithm is named C-EGPSO and comes from one of the previous authors' study in [11]. The aforementioned approach is based on the combination of Particle Swarm Optimisation (PSO) with Evolutionary Game Theory (EGT). Thus, the particles are following the classical PSO motion equations as defined by Clerc in [10] and named SPSO 2011, except that instead of using the coefficients defined by Clerc in [10], the search direction is updated at each iteration using EGT. This method was proved to be efficient in many different applications: logistic [14], task assignment [15], weapon target assignment problem [11].

Description of the SPSO. Let $X_i(t) = [x_{i1}(t), x_{i2}(t), \ldots, x_{iD}(t)]$, $x_{id}(t) \in \mathbb{R}$ be a particle in a population of N particles in a solution space S of dimension D. The velocity of this particle is denoted as $V_i(t) = [v_{i1}(t), v_{i2}(t), \ldots, v_{iD}(t)]$, $v_{id}(t) \in \mathbb{R}$. Each particle is communicating with its neighbourhood according to a communication network named topology. This network (or topology) plays an important role in the convergence speed and the exploration. For more details about the role of topology, the studies done by R. Mendes in [16] and M. Clerc in [17] well describe the influence of the topology over the ability of the algorithm to explore a solution space. From this topology, the best position $X_g(t) = [x_{g1}(t), x_{g2}(t), \ldots, x_{gD}(t)]$, among the informants is defined. Each particle has a memory in which it saves the best explored solution by itself. The vector $X_p(t) = [x_{p1}(t), x_{p2}(t), \ldots, x_{pD}(t)]$, denotes this position.

The state of one particle at the time $t+1$ is obtained from the three previously described components: the current velocity $V_i(t)$, its own memory $X_p(t)$ and the best position $X_g(t)$ among the informants of the particles. Let G denote the isobarycentre of the particles $X_i(t)$, $\phi_1 X_p(t)$ and $\phi_2 X_g(t)$, where ϕ_1 and ϕ_2 denote two positive real coefficients. Thus, the coordinates of the barycentre G can be obtained by computing:

$$G = \frac{X_i(t) + (X_i(t) + \phi_1(X_p(t) - X_i(t)) + \phi_2(X_p(t) - X_i(t)))}{3} \tag{1}$$

Then, a point X_i' is randomly drawn in the Hypersphere:

$$H(G, \|G - X_i\|)$$

centred on G with a radius equal to $\|G - X_i\|$. It results in the velocity update equation:

$$V_i(t+1) = wV_i(t) + X_i'(t) - X_i(t) \tag{2}$$

where w denotes a real coefficient representing the inertia of the particle. $X_i'(t)$ represents the randomly drawn point in the Hypersphere $H(G, \|G - X_i\|)$ at the instant t.

The position update equation is given by:

$$X_i(t+1) = \omega V_i(t) + X_i'(t) \tag{3}$$

Note that in the case where a particle is the best of the neighbourhood, its motion equation is slightly modified. Since the particle positions $X_p(t)$ and $X_g(t)$ are the same, indifferently one of them can be ignored. Then G becomes:

$$G = \frac{X_i(t) + (X_i(t) + \phi_2(X_g(t) - X_i(t)))}{2} \tag{4}$$

Figure 1 shows the moving rules for the particle $X_i(t)$.

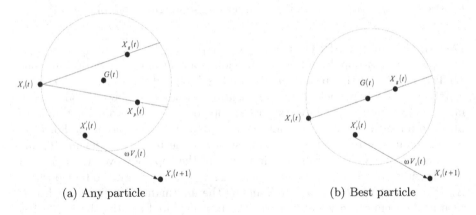

(a) Any particle   (b) Best particle

Fig. 1. Moving rule of the particles. Subfigure 1(a) shows an example of possible sampling for a particle of the swarm that is not the best of its neighbourhood. On the other hand, Subfigure 1(b) shows a possible sampling of a particle that is the best of its neighbourhood. Note that in this second case, the position $X_p(t)$ is ignored and the computation of $G(t)$ only depends on $X_i(t)$ and $X_g(t)$.

Determination of the Coefficients. In order to determine in one optimal way the parameters ω, ϕ_1 and ϕ_2 of SPSO 2011, the authors proposed to use the Evolutionary Game Theory. The herein section describes the integration of the EGT within SPSO.

The EGT has been designed to explain some animal behaviours when they are competing for some food resources for example. The example of the Hawk and Dove game is among the most famous in EGT and enables to understand the basement of the principle of an individual adapting his strategy according to the rewards that he previously got. Note that for more details the reader can refer to [11] where all the required background and details about the proposed method were given.

Based on this principle, the analogy is made:

EGT	Analogy in our method
Population	$\longrightarrow$ Swarm
Individual	$\longrightarrow$ Particle
Strategies	$\longrightarrow$ Follow X_p, X_g, V
Payoff matrix	$\longrightarrow$ Mean of the performance obtained by following a specific strategy

Then, each particle is a player having three available strategies (follow his memory, the best neighbour, or moving using only the inertia).

In order to optimise the coefficients ω, ϕ_1 and ϕ_2, the proposed approach is based on the use of EGT to determine the optimal ratio of each strategy to use to optimise the fitness of the particle. Each particle is using its own previous experience to fill the payoff matrix, then the ESS provides the optimal ratios that a particle must follow to optimise its exploration and improve the convergence [18].

Computation of the Evolutionary Stable Strategy. An Evolutionary Stable Strategy (ESS) is a strategy such that, if all members of a population adopt it, then no mutant strategy could invade the population under the influence of natural selection [19] [20]. Based on this principle, the natural selection is described using a dynamic that is usually an equation that takes into account the current state of the population and where each individual can change its strategy according to the outcome it got from previous challenge.

For the proposed method, the chosen dynamics is called replicator dynamics. The Replicator Equation (RE) is an Ordinary Differential Equation expressing the difference between the fitness of a strategy and the average fitness in the population. Thus, lower payoffs (agents are minimizers) bring faster reproduction in accordance with Darwinian natural selection process.

If the payoff matrix is denoted by A, the following replicator equation can be defined:

$$\dot{p}_i = -p_i(e_i \cdot Ap^T - p \cdot Ap^T) \tag{5}$$

RE for $i = 1, ..., m$ describes the evolution of strategy frequencies p_i. Moreover, for every initial strategy distribution $p(0)$, there is an unique solution $p(t)$ for all $t \geq 0$ that satisfies the replicator equation.

Based on the uniqueness of the solution to a given equation, it is proposed to train a NN to solve the replicator equation for a given input matrix and a predefined initial state of the population.

The subsequent section will briefly introduce the NN.

2.2 Neural Networks

The Neural Network (NN) model is inspired from the concept of how the human brain works. NN are composed of neurons and synapses that link the neurons between them. All the synapses are weighted in order to establish a relation between the input neurons and output neurons. These neurons are represented by state variables that are functions of the weighted sum of input neurons. Thus, for one input, all the neurons perform a simple transformation in parallel. This activation might take many different shapes and the most usual are linear, threshold function and sigmoid function [21]. The first use of this modelling appeared in [22] and was initially named *threshold logic*. In its recent use, three main categories emerge: the use of NN for task modelling [23], [24], [25]; the NN for solving optimisation problems [26], [27], [25]; and advent as promising for real-time applications for solving large scale optimisation problems [28], [29].

NN have been suggested to solve combinatorial optimisation problems where the key point is to map the optimisation problem to the NN for which the stable state represents the optimal solution [21]. Usually two approaches are identified [21]. The first is to minimise an energy function [28]. The second one is to design competition between neurons that become active under certain conditions [30]. The main advantage of NN is that they can be easily parallelised due to their natural architecture. Thus, many investigations were led to solve large scale optimisation problems [28] [29]. The first study that showed the efficiency of NN was led by Hopfield and Tank in [31] where the NN was used to solve the Traveller Salesman Problem for a number of cities of 10 and 30. It is reported in this study that a local optimum was always reached. Later numerous combinations of the NN with simulated annealing were proposed [32]. The study led by Abe *et al.* in [33] proposed to include inequality constraints within the NN. A more detailed analysis is given in [24] about the NN competition based.

3 Description of the Proposed Method

This section will describe how NN and C-EGPSO are combined in order to provide an algorithm that can maintain the performances of the original C-EGPSO, while using the ability of NN to learn to solve the replicator dynamics Differential Equation. Thus, an important gain of time computation could be obtained and thus allow to extend the current algorithm to real-time oriented applications.

This section is organised as follows: first the general principle of the proposed algorithm is introduced, then the training and validation of the NN are presented.

3.1 The Proposed Method

The introduced algorithm was devised with the idea that the promising obtained results of C-EGPSO [11] could be adapted for real-time applications. Since the method is based on the computation of optimal search direction using EGT, this computationally heavy process that consists in iteratively solving the replicator equation was identified as a lever to decrease the computational time. Thus, from the ability of Neural Networks to learn to solve problems, it was natural to combine the current C-EGPSO with NN, so the replicator equation can be solved within couple of milliseconds, leading to an important gain of time when solving a global optimisation problem. This approach will be named Combined-Evolutionary Game based Particle Swarm Optimisation using Neural Networks (C-EGPSO-NN).

The designed algorithm is described Figure 2. The only change compared to the original version of C-EGPSO stands in the computation of the ESS as highlighted by the bold box.

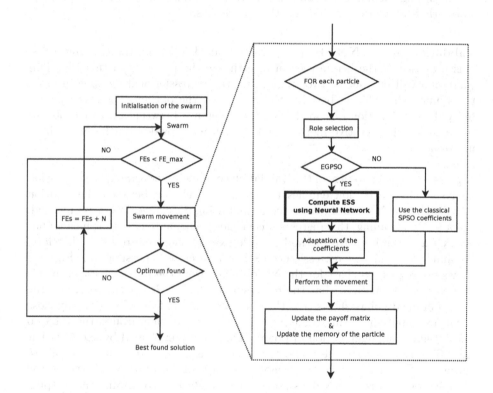

Fig. 2. Flowchart of the proposed C-EGPSO-NN

3.2   Training and Validation of the Neural Network

In this subsection, the training then the validation of the NN to learn the solution of the replicator equation will be described. Note that this training as well as the validation was performed using the MATLAB Toolbox Neural Network [34].

Training of the NN. Since the replicator equation is a deterministic process and is based on the principle that the payoff matrix depends on the three diagonal values only, it is proposed to use as input data the diagonal of the payoff matrix. The outputs will be the obtained ESS using the classical iterative resolution of the replicator equation as described by Equation (5). Thus, to each vector of 3 input data corresponds a vector of 3 numerical outputs that denotes the ESS (See Section 2.1 for details).

In order to train the NN, 15000 normalised payoff matrices were randomly drawn and for each payoff matrix the replicator equation was run in order to obtain the ESS. Then, based on that sample of 15000 instances, 70% were used for the training, 15 % for the validation and 15% for the testing.

Regarding the number of hidden neurons, the proposed approach empirically stated that 30 neurons provided satisfying results.

Validation of the NN. Based on the obtained NN from the training stage, it is proposed in the herein section to estimate the precision of this NN. This validation will be done in two stages: first the regression will be done in order to estimate the relation between the input and the output. Then, the probability density function obtained from the difference between a set of problems solved using the iterative method and the output provided by the NN will be investigated.

Regression. The first stage of this validation consists in performing the regression analysis. This regression enables to obtain the relation between the solution provided by the NN and the expected output using the classical iterative method. For a perfect training, this regression coefficient is equal to one, that means that the NN and the iterative method provide exactly the same results. Therefore, the aim is to obtain the regression coefficient R as close as possible to 1. Figure 3 shows the regression chart for the NN obtained from the previous stage. In this figure, it can be noticed that the regression coefficient R is close to 1, and the set of obtained points shows that the obtained outputs from NN are really close to the expected ones using the iterative method. Note that around the values 0 and 1 there is an aggregation of points. This can be explained by the fact that the ESS obtained from the replicator equation is composed by positive values, subject to $\sum_{i=1}^{S} p_i = 1$, where p_i denotes the ratio of the strategy i. However, the obtained output using NN does not always satisfy this constraint and outputs either negative or greater than 1 are possible.

Repartition error. Based on the obtained results from the difference between the NN training and the expected values using the iterative method, the quantification of the error repartition will be investigated. This analysis will be done by approaching the obtained empirical results by a Gaussian distribution.

$$\begin{cases} \mu = 1.5592 10^{-9} \\ \sigma = 0.022103 \end{cases} \tag{6}$$

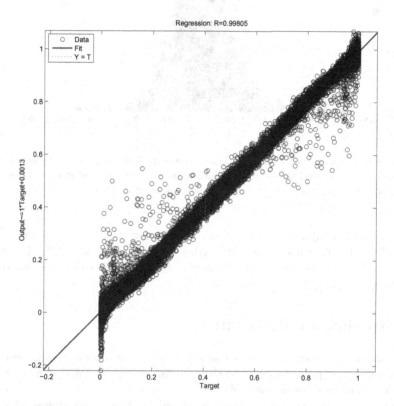

Fig. 3. Regression between the obtained value using NN and the expected value using the iterative approach

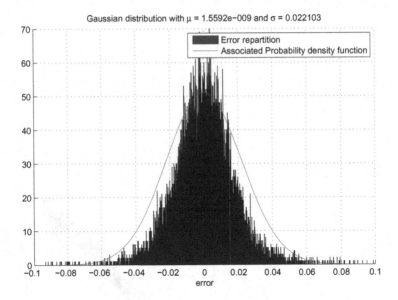

Fig. 4. Error repartition. This figure shows the empirical obtained distribution of the error and the associated Gaussian distribution using the mean and standard deviation of the difference between targeted and output values of the NN.

Based on this approached Gaussian distribution, there is an approximative probability of 0.95 to sample a point with an error lower than 4.42%. Therefore, based on this observation the precision of the trained NN can be considered as satisfying.

4   Experimental Procedure

In the previous section a NN was trained to solve the replicator equation. The herein section proposes to describe the experimental protocol that will be used to validate the introduced method.

The validation of the proposed approach will be done in two stages. First, the proposed approach will be applied to a set of benchmarked continuous optimisation problems issued from [12] in order to confirm that the proposed algorithm obtains as good result as the original algorithm (C-EGPSO) in terms of precision of the final solution. Then, the effective gain of time obtained using NN will be analysed using the previous experiences.

4.1   Description of the Benchmark Functions

To proceed this validation it is proposed in this paper to compare the NN based EGPSO to the original C-EGPSO. The aim of this investigation is to verify that the enhanced method can obtain as good results as the initial one. Thus, by running both methods on a set of benchmark problems it will be proved that the targeted improvement in terms of computational time won't affect the performances of the original algorithm. The chosen benchmark functions are issued from the Congress on Evolutionary Competition 2005 [12]. All the details on this benchmark are available in [13]. In order to test the designed method, the chosen benchmarked problems are:

- F_1, Sphere Function:

$$F_1(x) = \sum_{k=1}^{D} z_i^2 + f_b$$

with $z = x - x^*$, $x = [x_1, x_2, ..., x_D]$. D denotes the dimension of the problem and x^* the optimal solution. Finally, f_b denotes a bias. This classic test function is a convex problem usually used to test the convergence speed of local exploration.

- F_2, Shifted Schwefel's Function:

$$F_2(x) = \sum_{k=1}^{D} \left(\sum_{j=1}^{i} z_j \right)^2 + f_b$$

with $z = x - x^*$, $x = [x_1, x_2, ..., x_D]$. D denotes the dimension of the problem and x^* the optimal solution. Finally, f_b denotes a bias. This problem 2 is a non separable version of the first problem, so it prevents the method to use the symmetries of the solution space.

- F_5, Schwefel's Function:

$$F_5(x) = \max\left(A_i x - B_i\right) + f_b; i = 1 \ldots D$$

with $z = x - x^*$, $x = [x_1, x_2, ..., x_D]$. D denotes the dimension of the problem and x^* the optimal solution. A is a $D \times D$ matrix composed of random numbers in $[500, 500]$, and $det(A) \neq 0$. Finally, A_i denotes the ith row of A. The second matrix B_i is obtained as follows: $B_i = A_i * o$, where o is a random vector of dimension D composed of random values in $[-100, 100]$. Finally, f_b denotes a bias. The problem 5 is a problem that tests the ability of a method to find an optimal solution that is located on the bounds of the solution space.

- F_{12} Schwefel's Function:

$$F_{12}(x) = \sum_{i=1}^{D} (A_i - B_i(x)) + f_b$$

with,

$$\begin{cases} A_i = \sum_{j=1}^{D} a_{ij} \sin(\alpha_j) + b_{ij} \cos(\alpha_j) \\ B_i = \sum_{j=1}^{D} a_{ij} \sin(x_j) + b_{ij} \cos(x_j) \end{cases}$$

with $z = x - x^*$, $x = [x_1, x_2, ..., x_D]$. D denotes the dimension of the problem and x^* the optimal solution. The matrices A and B are of dimension $D \times D$, and the inner coefficients of these matrices a_{ij} and b_{ij} are randomly drawn in $[-100, 100]$. The bias is denoted by f_b. Finally, $\alpha = [\alpha_1, \ldots, \alpha_D]$, where the α_j are random numbers in $[-\pi, \pi]$. This function is a multi-modal and non-separable problem. It enables to test the capacity of the proposed method to escape from local minima.

4.2   Experimental Protocol

Based on the aforementioned benchmarked problems, SPSO 2011, C-EGPSO, C-EGPSO and M-C-EGPSO will be tested 25 times for each problem for a dimension $D = 10$. At reach run the initial conditions are randomly drawn and the swarm parameters that are the size, the topology and the motion equation were equally set for all the algorithms. The only difference between these methods is the way the coefficients ω, ϕ_1 and ϕ_2 are computed.

5   Simulation Results and Discussion

The herein section presents the obtained results following the experiment protocol described in Section 4. First, the ability of the proposed method to maintain the same performances as the original C-EGPSO will be described, then the effective gain of time using the proposed Mixed-C-EGPSO will be investigated.

5.1   Ability to Maintain C-EGPSO Performances

The purpose of this section is to check if the proposed C-EGPSO-NN can maintain the performances of the original method while significantly decreasing the computation time. Based on the described protocol Section 4, the initial SPSO 2011, C-EGPSO and C-EGPSO-NN are compared in terms of performances as shown in Figure 5. On these graphics, SPSO 2011 is represented by the blue line with circle markers, C-EGPSO with the dot markers and C-EGPSO-NN is represented using the cross markers.

From the analysis of the graphs Figure 5, it appears that both C-EGPSO and C-EGPSO-NN obtained similar performances while they outperform SPSO 2011. If for "simple" problems it can be identified that C-EGPSO and C-EGPSO-NN obtained almost exactly the same results, it can be noticed that for problems F_5 and F_{12} there is a slight difference between two algorithms. Indeed, C-EGPSO performs slightly better than C-EGPSO-NN, but this difference can be easily explained by the obtained difference between the solution provided by the iterative method and the one computed by the NN.

The upper left graph of Figure 5 shows the obtained results for the problem F_1. This problem is usually considered as the easiest one and is designed in order to evaluate the local convergence speed of algorithms. On the graph it can be seen that C-EGPSO and C-EGPSO-NN obtained nearly the same results and from almost the first iteration it seems that the particles following EGPSO are capable of quickly optimise their search directions.

On the upper right graph, the obtained results for the problem F_2 are close to the ones obtained for the problem F_1. Indeed, the two problems are similar, since both are unimodals. It can be concluded that both methods the C-EGPSO and the C-EGPSO-NN obtained same results, while outperforming the SPSO 2011.

Regarding problems F_5, it can be noticed that there exists a slight difference between the convergence speed of the C-EGPSO and the C-EGPSO-NN. The investigated problem can also stands as a sensitivity analysis and shows that the slight deviation between the obtained ESS using the iterative method and the obtained ESS using NN leads to different convergence speed. However, it can be also noticed that this difference does not compromise the algorithm precision performance, since the SPSO 2011 keeps being outperformed by the introduced methods.

Finally, the last problem F_{12} shows a similar phenomena as the previous problem F_5. The C-EGPSO and the C-EGPSO-NN are outperforming the SPSO 2011 in terms of convergence speed, but they also are slightly different. This experiment highlights an interesting point: there is a first phase where the C-EGPSO and the C-EGPSO-NN obtain similar convergence speed, but after 3000 iterations, the precision of the iterative method get the upper hand on the NN approach and allows for a better choice of the PSO parameters. Therefore, it can be interpreted that when approaching the optimal solution, the required precision to optimise the search direction becomes very sensitive. The same behaviour was also represented for the problem F_5 and happened around 2000 iterations.

Note that an extensive benchmarking was done in a previous authors' study[2] in order to prove the ability of C-EGPSO to solve highly complex problems. The aforementioned method was also compared to other kinds of algorithms, like Covariance Matrix Adaptation Evolution Strategy algorithm (G-CMA-ES) developed in [35] and K-PCX based on parent-centric recombination [36], and obtained in most of the investigated problems better results in terms of precision and success rate. Therefore, the choice of these benchmark problems was not done in order to prove the efficiency of the designed C-EGPSO, but the possible gain of time by replacing the iterative resolution of the replicator equation by a NN approach.

The subsequent section will focus on this objective to gain computational time by comparing both methods.

5.2   Gain of Time to Solve the Replicator Equation

The initial idea to design a NN capable of solving the replicator equation was to significantly decrease the computation time of C-EGPSO. In this section it is proposed to quantify this gain of time using numerical simulations. Based on the introduced simulation protocol, a timer is triggered before the resolution of

---

[2] C. Leboucher, H-S. Shin, S. Le Ménec, P. Siarry, R. Chelouah, A. Tsourdos and A. Kotenkoff, *An Enhanced Particle Swarm Optimisation Method Integrated with Evolutionary Game Theory*, Submission in progress

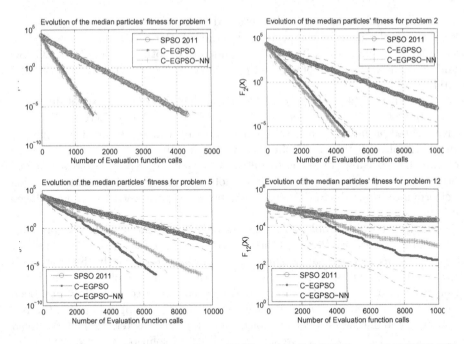

Fig. 5. Performance comparison. Here, SPSO 2011, C-EGPSO and C-EGPSO-NN are compared in terms of performances on the four previously described benchmarked problems.

the problem, then stopped when the exit conditions are satisfied. This process is repeated at each run in order to provide a global overview of the performances over the time.

The obtained results are compared in Figure 6 and show as expected that there is an important gain of time using the NN approach rather than the classical iterative method to solve the replicator equation. For the problem F_1, based on the obtained median result the gain can be estimated to $\sim 40\%$. Regarding the problem F_2 this gain can be estimated to $\sim 25\%$. For the problem F_5 the gain is $\sim 35\%$. Finally, for the problem F_{12}, the obtained gain is $\sim 33\%$.

5.3   Discussion

From the obtained numerical results in Section 5, it appears that the proposed method using the NN to solve the replicator equation obtained slightly worse results than the classical C-EGPSO in terms of precision of the optimal solution. However, the gain of time allowed by replacing the iterative resolution of the replicator equation by the trained NN shows that it is worth to extend initial C-EGPSO to real-time applications. Indeed, the qualities of the obtained solution using C-EGPSO-NN and C-EGPSO are nearly the same, while the computational time is dramatically decreased. Hence, these results lead to the trade-off

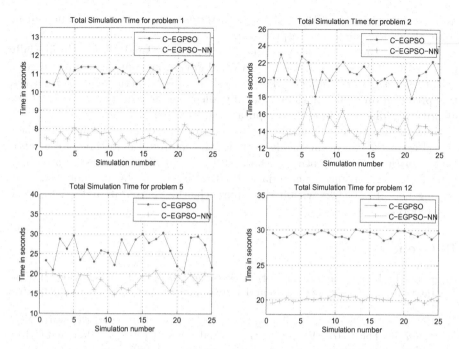

Fig. 6. Computational time comparison. These graphs compare the required computational time to solve the four benchmarked problems. The dotted line represents the C-EGPSO, while C-EGPSO-NN is denoted by the crossed markers. In ordinates, the computational time is given in seconds. The abscissa represents the number of ran simulations.

that the slight loss of precision using C-EGPSO-NN is worth by comparison to the obtained gain of time.

6   Conclusion and Perspectives

In this paper it was proposed to improve the computational time performance of an algorithm based on the combination of the SPSO 2011 proposed by Clerc in [10] and the Evolutionary Game Theory in order to optimise the search direction of the particles. This method was named C-EGPSO (Combined-Evolutionary Game based Particle Swarm Optimisation). The particles' search direction was obtained from the iterative resolution of the replicator equation. This part of the algorithm was identified as computationally intensive and it was natural to use this fragment as a lever to decrease the computation time. Therefore, it was proposed to replace the iterative resolution of the replicator equation, by a trained neural network to solve this equation. Thus, the resolution of this part was reduced to a couple of milliseconds. After training a NN and validating its learning phase, the NN was integrated within the C-EGPSO and tested on a set of benchmarked problems. The results proved that despite obtaining slightly worse results than C-EGPSO, the gain in terms of computational time can be trade-off for this slight loss of precision.

Note also that this study stands as a sensitivity analysis for the initially proposed C-EGPSO and proves that a small deviation from the computed coefficient using the iterative method leads to slightly worse performances. However, this precision difference does not globally affect the general performance of the algorithm while improving its computational time performance.

In a future study it would be interesting to pursue the investigation of how neural networks can dramatically decrease the computational time of optimisation algorithms. From another authors' study [3], the EGT was used as a lever to identify the importance of criteria in multi-objective problems. Thus, by integrating neural networks within this approach, the computational time can be also reduced.

References

1. Kennedy, J., Eberhart, R.C.: Particle swarm optimization. In: Proceedings of IEEE International Conference on Neural Networks, Piscataway, USA, pp. 1942–1948 (1995)
2. Kennedy, J., Eberhart, R.: A discrete binary version of the particle swarm algorithm. In: The 1997 IEEE International Conference on Systems, Man, and Cybernetics, vol. 5, Orlando, USA, pp. 4104–4108, October 1997
3. Hu, W., Song, J., Li, W.: A new PSO scheduling simulation algorithm based on an intelligent compensation particle position rounding off. In: ICNC '08 Proceedings of the 2008 Fourth International Conference on Natural Computation, vol. 1, Jinan, China, pp. 145–149, October 2008
4. Junker, U.: Air traffic flow management with heuristic repair. The Knowledge Engineering Review, vol. 0, pp. 1–24 (2004)
5. Shaa, D., H.H., L.: A multi-objective PSO for job-shop scheduling problems. Expert Systems with Applications, vol. 37, pp. 1065–1070 (2010)
6. Badamchizadeh, M., Madani, K.: Applying modified discrete particle swarm optimization algorithm and genetic algorithm for system identification. In: Computer and Automation Engineering (ICCAE), 2010, vol. 5, Singapore, Republic of Singapore, pp. 354–358, February 2010
7. Eberhart, R., Shi, Y.: Comparison between genetic algorithms and particle swarm optimization. In: Proceedings of the 7th International Conference on Evolutionary Programming, San Diego, USA, pp. 611–616, March 1998
8. Liaoa, C., Tsengb, C., Luarnb, P.: A discrete version of particle swarm optimization for flowshop scheduling problems. Computers & Operations Research **34**, 3099–3111 (2007)
9. Hassan, R., Cohanim, B., de Weck, O., Venter, G.: A comparison of particle swarm optimization and the genetic algorithm. Tech. rep., Massachusetts Institute of Technology, Cambridge, MA, 02139 (2004)
10. Clerc, M.: Standard particle swarm optimisation, Tech. rep., maurice.clerc@Writeme.com (2012)

---

[3] C. Leboucher, H-S. Shin, S. Le Ménec, A. Tsourdos, A. Kotenkoff, P. Siarry and R. Chelouah; *Novel Evolutionary Game Based Multi-Objective Optimisation for Dynamic Weapon Target Assignment*, Accepted for IFAC WC 2014 Conference

11. Leboucher, C., Shin, H.-S., Siarry, P., Chelouah, R., Ménec, S.L., Tsourdos, A.: A Two-Step Optimisation Method for Dynamic Weapon Target Assignment Problem. Recent Advances on Meta-Heuristics and Their Application to Real Scenarios, InTech (2013)
12. Congress on Evolutionary Computation, Edinburgh, UK, September 2005
13. Suganthan, P.N., Hansen, N., Liang, J.J., Deb, K., Chen, Y.P., Auger, A., Tiwari, S.: Problem definitions and evaluation criteria for the CEC 2005 special session on real-parameter optimization. Tech. rep., Technical Report, Nanyang Technological University, Singapore and KanGAL Report Number 2005005 (Kanpur Genetic Algorithms Laboratory, IIT Kanpur) (2005)
14. Leboucher, C., Chelouah, R., Siarry, P., Ménec, S.L.: A swarm intelligence method combined to evolutionary game theory applied to resource allocation problem. In: International conference on swarm intelligence, Cergy, France, June 2011
15. Leboucher, C., Chelouah, R., Siarry, P., Le Ménec, S.: A swarm intelligence method combined to evolutionary game theory applied to the resources allocation problem. International Journal of Swarm Intelligence Research (IJSIR) 3(2), 20–38 (2012)
16. Mendes, R.: Population topologies and their influence in particle swarm performance. PhD thesis, University Minho (2004)
17. Clerc, M.: Back to random topology. Tech. rep., maurice.clerc@Writeme.com (2007)
18. Taylor, P., Jonker, L.: Evolutionary stable strategies and game dynamics. Mathematical Bioscience 40, 145–156 (1978)
19. Cressman, R.: Evolutionary Dynamics and Extensive Form Games. MIT Press (2003)
20. Sandholm, W.: Population Games and Evolutionary Dynamics. MIT Press (2010)
21. Floudas, C.A., Pardalos, P.M.: Encyclopedia of Optimization. Springer (2009)
22. McCulloch, W.S., Pitts, W.: A logical calculus of the ideas immanent in nervous activity. The bulletin of mathematical biophysics 5(4), 115–133 (1943)
23. Ackley, D.H., Hinton, G.E., Sejnowski, T.J.: A learning algorithm for Boltzman machines. Cognitive Sciences 9, 147–169 (1985)
24. Fausett, L.: Fundamentals of neural networks: Architectures, algorithms, and applications. Prentice Hall (1994)
25. Haykin, S.: Neural Networks: A comprehensive foundation. MacMillan College (1994)
26. Cichocki, A., Unbehauen, R.: Neural networks for optimization and signal processing. Wiley (1993)
27. Looi, C.-K.: Neural network methods in combinatorial optimization. Computational Operations Research 19(3–4), 191–208 (1992)
28. Ansari, N., Hou, E.S.H., Yu, Y.: A new method to optimize the satellite broadcasting schedules using the mean field annealing of a Hopfield neural network. IEEE Transactions on Neural Networks 6(2), 470–482 (1995)
29. Lagerholm, M., Peterson, C., Soderberg, B.: Airline crew scheduling with Potts neurons. Neural Computation 9, 1589–1599 (1997)
30. Fang, L., Li, T.: Design of competition-based neural networks for combinatorial optimization. International Journal of Neural Systems 1(3), 221–235 (1990)
31. Hopfield, J., Tank, D.W.: Neural computation of decisions in optimization problems. Biological Cybernetics 52(3), 141–152 (1985)

32. Levy, B.C., Adam, M.B.: Global optimization with stochastic neural networks. In: First International Conference on Neural networks for Optimization and signal processing, San Diego, USA, pp. 681–690 (1987)
33. Abe, S., Kawakami, J., Hirasawa, K.: Solving inequality constrained combinatorial optimization problems by the Hopfield neural networks. Neural Networks **5**, 663–670 (1992)
34. MATLAB, Neural Networks Toolbox
35. Auger, A., Hansen, N.: A restart CMA evolution strategy with increasing population size. In: Proceedings of the IEEE Congress on Evolutionary Computation, pp. 1769–1776 (2005)
36. Sinha, A., Tiwari, S., Deb, K.: A population-based, steady-state procedure for real-parameter optimization. In: Proceedings of the IEEE Congress on Evolutionary Computation, vol. 1, pp. 514–521 (2005)

Robust Multi-agent Patrolling Strategies Using Reinforcement Learning

Fabrice Lauri[(✉)] and Abderrafiaa Koukam

IRTES-SeT, Rue Thiery-Mieg, 90010 Belfort, France
{fabrice.lauri,abder.koukam}@utbm.fr

Abstract. Patrolling an environment involves a team of agents whose goal usually consists in continuously visiting the most relevant areas as fast as possible. In this paper, we follow up on the work by Santana *et al.* who formulated this problem in terms of a reinforcement learning problem, where agents individually learn an MDP using Q-Learning to patrol their environment. We propose another definition of the state space and of the reward function associated with the MDP of an agent. Experimental evaluation shows that our approach substantially improves the previous RL method in several instances (graph topology and number of agents). Moreover, it is observed that such an RL approach is robust as it can efficiently cope with most of the situations caused by the removal of agents during a patrolling simulation.

Keywords: Multi-agent patrolling · Reinforcement Learning · Extended-GBLA · Robustness

1 Introduction

The multi-agent patrolling problem has been rigourously addressed only recently [1–7]. In these works, many patrolling strategies have been devised and experimentally validated using common evaluation criteria [1]. They are based on different approaches, ranging from heuristic laws enabling agents to better choose the next node to visit [1], negotiation mechanisms [2], reinforcement learning techniques [3], techniques based on graph theory [4] to techniques based on ACO [5–7]. Most of these solutions yield good empirical results on different graphs constituted from less than fifty nodes and one hundred edges. Nevertheless, none of these solutions have been evaluated in terms of robustness. In some applications though, one might also want to know how the performances of one of these solutions are influenced by an *online* change in the size of the population of the individuals (or agents) involved in a patrol.

In this paper, we first propose an improvement of the learning agents' architecture presented in [3], by characterizing more precisely the MDP employed by an agent. Moreover, we experimentally show that a reinforcement learning based approach can be efficiently applied to the multi-agent patrolling problem for dealing with both an increase in the graph complexity and removals of agents.

© Springer International Publishing Switzerland 2014
P. Siarry et al. (Eds.): ICSIBO 2014, LNCS 8472, pp. 157–165, 2014.
DOI: 10.1007/978-3-319-12970-9_17

We chose the reinforcement learning framework for studying the robustness of the patrolling problem for two main reasons. On the one hand, a machine learning approach can theoretically cope with any graph topology and any agents' set, so that a larger range of situations can be considered. On the other hand, we assume that all the agents are located at the same node at the initial time. Under this condition, the patrolling task starts with a preliminary phase where agents spread out in the graph. This step cannot be handled by the most efficient techniques based on Single Cycle [2,4], which limits agents to be located at different nodes.

The remainder of this paper is organized as follows. Section 2 describes the commonly used framework of a patrolling problem and gives an overview of the related works. Section 3 reviews the fundamental concepts of a reinforcement learner. Section 4 proposes a formulation of the patrolling problem as a reinforcement learning problem. Experimental results are shown in section 5. Finally, concluding remarks and future research works are given in section 6.

2   Problem Definition

The patrolling problem is usually specified formally as follows [1,3,4]. The environment to patrol is reduced to a graph $G = (V, E)$, V representing the strategically relevant areas and E the safe ways of movement or communication between them. A cost c_{ij}, associated with each edge (i, j), measures the time required to go from node i to node j. Let be r agents bound to visit at regular intervals the areas defined in the graph G. Each agent is located at one of the nodes of V at the initial time. Solving the patrolling problem consists of elaborating a multi-agent graph coverage strategy π. Such a strategy must optimize a given quality criterion. $\pi = \{\pi_1 \cdots \pi_r\}$ is made up of the r individual strategies π_i of each agent i. An individual strategy π_i is defined such that $\pi_i : \mathbb{N} \to V$, $\pi_i(j)$ denoting the j-th node visited by the agent i.

Intuitively, a relevant patrolling strategy is one that minimizes, for each node, the time span between two visits to the same node. Several criteria have been devised in [1] in order to evaluate the quality of a multi-agent patrolling strategy after T time steps (or *cycles*) of simulation. All of them are based on the notion of *instantaneous node idleness* (INI). The INI $I_t(i)$ of a node i at time t is the number of time steps this node remained unvisited. By convention, at the initial instant, $I_0(i) = 0$, $\forall i = 1, 2, \cdots, |\mathcal{V}|$. At a given instant t, GI_t is the *instantaneous average graph idleness* (IGI). Similarly the *instantaneous worst graph idleness* WI_t is the highest INI encountered since t time steps of simulation. A multi-agent patrolling strategy π can be evaluated after T cycles of simulation using either the *average idleness* criterion AI_π or the *worst idleness* WI_π. The average idleness denotes the mean of the IGI over the T simulation cycles, whereas the *worst idleness* is the highest INI observed during the T-time steps of the simulation. As emphasized by [4], the optimal strategy π is the one that minimizes the worst idleness, as $WI_\pi \geq AI_\pi$ for any strategy π.

3   Reinforcement Learning Framework

Reinforcement learning typically deals with problems where one or several agents interact with their environment to learn to perform a task. At each time step, an agent is able to (1) perceive the state of its environment, (2) carry out an action which modifies the environment state and (3) obtain an immediate reward depending on the action it just performed. After several thousands of trials, such an agent learns a policy π, which tells him what to do in every situation [8]. A reinforcement learning problem involving one agent is usually defined in terms of a *Markov Decision Process* (MDP). Several extensions of an MDP, such as MMDP [9] or DEC-MDP [10] have been proposed to deal with the problem of coordination in multi-agent systems, but these solutions are intractable when the number of agents is high. Indeed, they use joint actions whose number exponentially increases with the number of individual actions and agents involved: if there are n agents, each of which can perform a actions, then the size of the joint action space is a^n. To alleviate this problem, many approaches [3, 11–13] consider RL agents as *independent learners*. Independent learners ignore the actions and rewards of the other agents, and learn their policy using their own MDP. Although these approaches are no longer assumed to find a globally optimal solution, they still yield satisfactory results in practice. For this reason, as the patrolling problem may involve a lot of agents, we will focus in this paper on the case where agents employ an MDP learned with Q-Learning to perform its task.

4   Learning to Patrol Using Reinforcements

One of the most difficult tasks when designing a patrolling agent's MDP is the definition of its state space. As each agent uses incomplete information to find a globally optimal solution to the patrolling problem, the more features are incorporated in a state, the more precise the solution can be. On the other hand, it is well known that the size of the state space grows exponentially with the number of features. Defining the state space of an MDP is thus a trade-off between its computational complexity and the global solution approximation it can yield. In [3], the learning agents' architecture which obtained the best results was *Gray-Box Learner Agent* (GBLA), when using the idleness of the next reached node as the immediate reward. This architecture incorporates into an agent's MDP some information characterizing its environment vicinity and allows each of them to communicate its intention about its next action. As this architecture constituted the first attempt to formulate the patrolling problem in a reinforcement learning framework, it is unfortunately not perfect. In the next sections, we will discuss the drawbacks of this architecture and see how its definition can be refined.

4.1   Identifying the Dark Side of MDP

Considering that d stands for the graph degree and $|\mathcal{V}|$ is the number of nodes of the graph, the state space S in GBLA was made up of the following components :

(1) the node where the agent is ($|\mathcal{V}|$ possible values) (2) the edge from which it came (d possible values) (3) the neighbor node which has the highest (worst) idleness (d possible values) (4) the neighbor node which has the lowest idleness (d possible values) and (5) the list of the adjacent nodes which are intended to be visited by other agents (2^d possible values). The cardinality of the action set was equal to the graph degree d, each action enabling an agent to reach an adjacent node. As emphasized previously, the size of the state space grows exponentially with the number of features: with this MDP definition, the total number of states $|S| = |\mathcal{V}| \times d^3 \times 2^d$ and the total number of actions $|A| = d$. Learning several MDPs (one for each patrolling agent) with Q-Learning can therefore become rapidly intractable when a lot of agents try to patrol in a graph of high degree and a great number of nodes. For instance, with a graph with a degree of 7 and constituted by 50 nodes (the graph called *map A* in the previous works), each MDP needs theoretically to store more than 15 million scalars (used by the Q-table).

4.2   Numbering the Valid States Using the Graph Topology

Yet, among the $|\mathcal{V}| \times d^3 \times 2^d$ states, a lot of them will never be visited by an agent. For instance, let us consider the five-node graph $G = (V, E)$, where $V = \{1, 2, 3, 4, 5\}$ and $E = \{\{1, 2\}, \{1, 3\}, \{1, 4\}, \{4, 5\}\}$. Here, the MDP of an agent patrolling this graph will be potentially made up of $|S| = 5 \times 3^3 \times 2^3 = 1080$ states. But some states will never been encountered by the agent, such as the ones in which it is in node 3 and came from a node reached when performing action 2 in node 3. In fact, the number of states that will be effectively visited by an agent (the *valid states*) can be computed precisely from the graph topology. Assuming that d_i is the degree of node i, the number of valid states induced by this MDP definition is equal to $|S| = \sum_{i=1}^{|\mathcal{V}|} d_i^3 \times 2^{d_i}$. Using this formula, the size of the state space associated to this graph is reduced to $|S| = 252$, which is about one quarter of the size of the initial state space for this graph topology. Using this simple principle, since the number of states is now reduced to a sum over the total number of graph nodes, graphs with a greater amount of nodes can be dealt with. This reasoning can be pushed further by considering that only d_i actions at node i can be performed. The number of valid indices (s, a) can thus similarly be reduced when a particular scalar must be accessed through the Q-table. For instance, when dealing with map A, no more than 1.6 million scalars would need to be stored, which is here nearly one tenth of the size of the initial state space. In order to take into account only the valid states and thus avoid allocating too much memory, a variant of Q-Learning will be used to learn each MDP. This version of Q-Learning maintains an ordered list of the states that have been visited at least once. When $Q(s, a)$ must be accessed from a state s and an action a (through the Q-table), a search of the corresponding valid state s' is initiated in the *already visited states* list. If state s does not exist in it, it is added at the end. Else, its order number s' in the list is used as the first part of the index for the Q-table.

4.3 Adding More Local Information in a State Representation

We just saw that the topology of the graph to be patrolled can considerably reduce the size of the state space, so that a better characterization of the environment vicinity and of the information required to coordinate the agents' action can possibly be incorporated into a state vector. Indeed, it seems to us that the MDP defined in GBLA was incomplete. It is incomplete because the third and fourth features of a state (the neighboring node which has the highest idleness and the neighboring node which has the lowest idleness) do not precisely inform the agent about its environment vicinity if more than two edges are connected to a node. In order to allow an agent to decide which is the best action to execute in a given state using the most relevant information, we redefined the MDP associated to an agent in terms of its state space and reward function. Firstly, we suggest to represent the following features on the state: (1) the node where the agent is ($|\mathcal{V}|$ possible values), (2) the edge from which an agent came from (d_i possible values), (3) an ordered list of the adjacent nodes from node i, sorted according to their idleness ($d_i!$ possible values), (4) the list of the adjacent nodes from node i which are intended to be visited by other agents (2^{d_i} possible values). The number of valid states induced by this state space is equal to $|S| = \sum_{i=1}^{|\mathcal{V}|} d_i \times d_i! \times 2^{d_i}$. Secondly, the immediate reward given to an agent is equal to zero if the reached node was bound to be visited by other agents, else it is equal to the idleness of the reached node. This new model will be called Extended-GBLA in the remainder of this article.

5 Experimental Results

The multi-agent patrolling strategies were trained on the six graph topologies commonly used by the community (Fig. 1), with populations of 2 to 15 agents. To obtain strategies as robust as possible, the learning phase consisted of several trials. At each trial, graph statistics (the node idlenesses and the average graph idleness) were set to zero, all the agents were placed at the same starting node and they learned to patrol during several iterations. The starting node changed from one trial to the other. Patrolling strategies were trained by using GBLA or Extended-GBLA. Thus, a total of 120 patrolling strategies (10×6 for each RL method) were trained. Preliminary experiments were conducted to determine the learning parameters, such as the number of trials, the number of iterations per trial, the learning rate α, the discount factor γ and the exploration probability ϵ. The agents' MDPs were trained using 1000 trials, 10000 iterations per trial, $\alpha = 0.9$, $\gamma = 0.9$ and $\epsilon = 0.1$. Two classes of experiments were carried out to assess the robustness of our multi-agent patrolling strategies. The first ones were conducted in order to know whether the patrolling strategies trained with GBLA or with Extended-GBLA are still efficient when the node where all agents start to patrol is changed. The second experiments measure the capacity of the patrolling agents to adapt themselves from situations where some agents broke down.

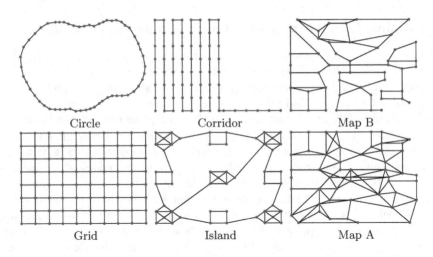

Fig. 1. Patrolling Graphs Benchmark

5.1   Comparison of GBLA and Extended-GBLA

Figure 2 presents the average graph idleness obtained after a multi-agent patrolling simulation using strategies trained with GBLA and Extended-GBLA. Each trained patrolling strategy was evaluated 20 times by changing the starting node of agents and by using 50000 cycles of simulation. Thus, subsequent results represent the average graph idleness over the 20 runs. Confidence intervals indicated on figures were computed using a risk of 5%. One can already see

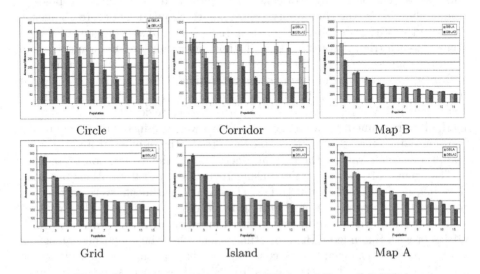

Fig. 2. Comparison results between GBLA and Extended-GBLA

that for the Map A, the Map B, the Grid Map and the Island Map, agents have learned to coordinate their actions, since the average graph idleness decreases when the number of agents increases. Despite their lowest degree, patrolling on the Corridor-shaped graph and on the Circle-shaped graph seems to be more complicated. Both RL methods give equivalent performance for the Map B, the Grid Map and the Island Map. For the other graphs, Extended-GBLA is significantly better than GBLA. By observing the agents' behavior on our simulator, we classified patrolling agents into two different classes. The first class is composed of agents that are responsible of only one region of the graph: they patrol only nodes of that region during the whole simulation. The second class is made up of agents that cross from one region to another one, especially to visit the node which links several regions, thus avoiding to decrease performances. These behaviors were only observed on the four more complex graphs (Map A, Map B, Island and Grid) with both GBLA and Extended-GBLA, and on the two lowest complex graphs (Corridor and Circle) only with Extended-GBLA. With GBLA, all the agents follow the same policy on the latter graphs: they all cross the graphs in the same direction and at the same time. This explains why the average graph idleness does not decrease when the agents' population grows. It is not the case using Extended-GBLA. We explain this phenomenon by considering that with Extended-GBLA, agents are informed about the utility to go to a given node through the reward function: if one agent intends to visit a node, the other agents will not want to visit it as it will give a zero reward. Hence, the definition of the reward function of Extended-GBLA allows agents to better coordinate their action. From this point of view, we can say that the information added by Extended-GBLA to the state space of MDPs used by agents (that is the ordered list of the adjacent nodes sorted according to their idleness) seems to have less influence than reward functions do on the performance of the patrolling strategies.

5.2   Robustness of Extended-GBLA

Figure 3 shows the influence of the removal of agents on the average graph idleness obtained after a 100000-cycle patrolling simulation using multi-agent strategies trained with Extended-GBLA. These experiments were carried out on the Corridor map and on the Map B with 5 and 10 agents. In every experiment, the first agent was removed after the 10000th cycle and each subsequent agent was removed every 10000 cycles. Results show that for both graphs, strategies are no more efficient when only one agent remains to patrol. Indeed, as an agent has only a local representation of its environment when it uses an MDP, it often forgets to visit some nodes for a while, thus decreasing performance. This forgetting behavior can also be observed when more than one agent remains to patrol (for instance on Map B where 6 out of the 10 agents are removed). In this case, it is due to the specialization of some agents that learned to patrol only in a given area of the graph. In the other cases, when a sufficient number of agents are patrolling, one can observe that agents are able to rapidly adapt to the new situations.

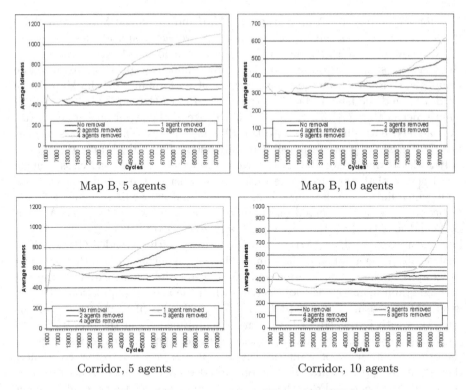

Map B, 5 agents   Map B, 10 agents

Corridor, 5 agents   Corridor, 10 agents

Fig. 3. Robustness results of Extended-GBLA

6 Concluding Remarks and Future Works

We have proposed in this article a novel definition of MDPs used by agents to
learn individually how to patrol in a graph. The RL algorithm Q-Learning was
used to give agents the capability to select the best actions to carry out in a
given situation in a dynamic environment (that is where agents continuously
move). We have experimentally shown that our RL method Extended-GBLA
significantly outperforms in several graph topologies the approach proposed by
Santana *et al.* [3]. We believe this improvement is mainly due to the redefinition
of the reward function, which allows agents to better coordinate their actions.
Moreover, results evaluating the robustness of Extended-GBLA reveal that the
patrolling strategies trained with this method are still efficient when some agents
are removed during a patrolling simulation. However, the trained strategies were
unable to cope adequately with situations where only a few agents remain to
patrol. To tackle this problem, an adaptation phase seems to be required to
allow the remaining patrolling agents to face new situations caused by a removal
of a lot of agents. Future research directions include the empirical studies of other
RL discounted algorithms for solving the problem, the use of an undiscounted

RL method, such as R-Learning [14], to solve this problem by minimizing the Average Idleness, and the comparison with other state-of-the-art techniques.

References

1. Machado, A., Ramalho, G.L., Zucker, J.-D., Drogoul, A.: Multi-agent Patrolling: An Empirical Analysis of Alternative Architectures. In: Sichman, J.S., Bousquet, F., Davidsson, P. (eds.) MABS 2002. LNCS (LNAI), vol. 2581, pp. 155–170. Springer, Heidelberg (2003)
2. Almeida, A., Ramalho, G.L., Santana, H., Azevedo Tedesco, P., Menezes, T., Corruble, V., Chevaleyre, Y.: Recent Advances on Multi-agent Patrolling. In: Bazzan, A.L.C., Labidi, S. (eds.) SBIA 2004. LNCS (LNAI), vol. 3171, pp. 474–483. Springer, Heidelberg (2004)
3. Santana, H., Ramalho, G., et al.: Multi-Agent Patrolling with Reinforcement Learning. In: 3rd International Joint Conference on Autonomous Agents and Multi-Agent Systems, pp. 1122–1129 (2004)
4. Chevaleyre, Y.: Theoretical Analysis of the Multi-Agent Patrolling Problem. In: International Joint Conference on Intelligent Agent Technology, pp. 302–308 (2004)
5. Lauri, F., Charpillet, F.: Ant Colony Optimization applied to the Multi-Agent Patrolling Problem. In: IEEE Swarm Intelligence Symposium (2006)
6. Lauri, F., Koukam, A.: A Two-Step Evolutionary and ACO Approach for Solving the Multi-Agent Patrolling Problem. In: IEEE World Congress on Computational Intelligence (2008)
7. Lauri, F., Koukam, A.: Hybrid ACO/EA Algorithms applied to the Multi-Agent Patrolling Problem. In: IEEE World Congress on Computational Intelligence (2014)
8. Sutton, R., Barto, A. In: Reinforcement Learning: An Introduction. Cambridge, MA (1998)
9. Boutilier, C.: Sequential Optimality and Coordination in Multi-Agent Systems. In: 16th International Joint Conference on Artificial Intelligence, pp. 478–485 (1999)
10. Bernstein, D., Zilberstein, S., Immerman, N.: The Complexity of Decentralized Control of Markov Decision Processes. In: 16th Conference on Uncertainty in Artificial Intelligence, pp. 32–37 (2000)
11. Sen, S., Sekaran, M., Hale, J.: Learning to coordinate without sharing information. In: 12th National Conference on Artificial Intelligence, pp. 426–431 (1994)
12. Schneider, J., Wong, W., Moore, A., Riedmiller, M.: Distributed value functions. In: 16th International Conference on Machine Learning, Morgan Kaufmann, San Francisco, CA, pp. 371–378 (1999)
13. Wolpert, D., Wheeler, K., Tumer, K.: General Principles of Learning-based Multi-Agent Systems. In: 3rd International Conference on Autonomous Agents (Agents 1999), pp. 77–83 (1999)
14. Schwartz, A.: A reinforcement learning method for maximizing undiscounted rewards. In: 10th International Conference on Machine Learning, pp. 298–305 (1993)

BSG-Starcraft Radius Improvements of Particle Swarm Optimization Algorithm: An Application to Ceramic Matrix Composites

Dominique Chamoret[1]([✉]), Sébastien Salmon[2],
Noelie Di Cesare[1], and Yingjie J. Xu[3]

[1] IRTES-M3M-EA7274, Université de Technologie de Belfort Montbéliard,
Belfort, France
{dominique.chamoret,noelie.di-Cesare}@utbm.fr
[2] Optimization Command and Control Systems, Besançon, France
s.salmon@my-occs.fr
[3] Engineering Simulation and Aerospace Computing,
Key Laboratory of Contemporary Design and Integrated Manufacturing Technology,
Northwestern Polytechnical University, Xi'an 710072, China
xu.yingjie@nwpu.edu.cn

Abstract. The thermal residual stresses (TRS) induced in ceramic matrix composites (CMCs) with multi-layered interphases when cooling down from the processing temperature, have a significant influence on the mechanical behavior and lifetime of CMCs. The objective of this work is to minimize the TRS of the unidirectional CMCs with multi-layered interphases by controlling the interphases thicknesses. A new Particle Swarm Optimization (PSO) algorithm is interfaced with a finite element code to find an optimal design and thereby significantly reduce the TRS within CMCs. This new PSO allows a faster convergence rate and gets a new effective stopping criteria based on real physical limits.

Keywords: Ceramic matrix composites · Thermal residual stresses · Particle Swarm Optimization · Radius improvement · The BSG-Starcraft improvement · Microstructure modelling · Finite element analysis

1 Introduction

The Particle Swarm Optimization (PSO) algorithm belongs to the category of swarm intelligence techniques. In PSO, each solution of the optimization problem is regarded as a particle in the search space, which adjusts its position in the search space according to its own flying experience and the flying experience of other particles [1]. The PSO algorithm has only a small number of parameters which need to be adjusted and is easy to implement. However, this algorithm has a major drawback: the number of iterations needed to find a potentially global minimum. In practical situations such as the structural optimization context, the optimization techniques may be linked to the finite element method. For

© Springer International Publishing Switzerland 2014
P. Siarry et al. (Eds.): ICSIBO 2014, LNCS 8472, pp. 166–174, 2014.
DOI: 10.1007/978-3-319-12970-9_18

this type of problems, the evaluation of the cost function for given values of the design variables requires a finite element analysis. This work can be very CPU time consuming especially when the finite element models are large and have a considerable number of design parameters. In this paper, a new stopping criterion is developed. These improvements, BSG-Starcraft Radius improvements, can drastically reduce the CPU time by avoiding needless iterations.

To test our approach, an original application to composites (CMCs , Ceramic matrix composites) is proposed. Ceramic matrix composites (CMCs) with multi-layered interphases exhibit attractive properties for thermal-structural applications [2,3]. However, in CMCs with multi-layered interphases, thermal residual stresses (TRS) are often generated upon cooling from processing to room temperatures due to extensive mismatch of the coefficients of thermal expansion between the constituents (fiber, interphase and matrix). The distribution of TRS, resulting in the cracks and separations in the matrix and interphases, has a significant influence on the mechanical behavior and lifetime of CMCs. The aim of the presented example is the optimization by PSO of TRS distribution in the multi-layered (PyC/SiC)n interphases and matrix from the point of view of the deposition thickness of each interphase layer [4] in order to achieve an excellent thermal-mechanical performance of CMCs.

2   Particle Swarm Optimization (PSO)

The two improvements of the Particle Swarm Optimization algorithm presented here have been developed by the author S. Salmon in [5] and implemented in Scilab [6]. The PSO algorithm is a global optimization algorithm described as sociologically inspired. In PSO, each individual of the swarm is considered as a particle in a multi-dimensional space that has a position and a velocity. These particles fly through hyperspace and remember the best position that they have seen.

2.1   Basis of Particle Swarm Algorithm

Members of a swarm fly in the search field (of N dimensions) and each member is attracted by its personal best solution and by the best solution of its neighbors [7,8]. Each particle has a memory storing all data relating to its flight (location, speed and its personal best solution). It can also inform its neighbors, i.e. communicate its speed and position. This ability is known as socialization. For each iteration, the objective function is evaluated for every member of the swarm. Then the leader of the whole swarm can be determined: it is the particle with the best personal solution. The process leads at the end to the best global solution.

At each iteration t , the location and speed of one particle x_i are updated as follows [1]:

$$\begin{cases} v_i^{t+1} = \omega \; v_i^t + r_1 \; c_1 \; (p_i^t - x_i^t) + r_2 \; c_2 \; (p_i^g - x_i^t) \\ x_i^{t+1} = v_i^{t+1} + x_i^t \end{cases} \qquad (1)$$

where v_i and x_i represent the current velocity and the position of the ith particle respectively (note that the subscripts t and $t+1$ refer to the recent and the next iterations respectively). p_i is the personal best previous position (*pbest*) of the ith particle and p_g is the best global position (*gbest*) among all the particles in the swarm. The parameters r_1 and r_2 are two random numbers between 0 and 1. The constant c_1 and c_2 represent trust parameters indicating how much confidence the current particle has in itself and how much confidence it has in the swarm. Theses acceleration constants c_1 and c_2 indicate the stochastic acceleration terms which pull each particle toward the best position attained by the particle or the best position attained by the swarm. Low values of c_1 and c_2 allow the particles to wander far away from the optimum regions before being tugged back, while the high values pull the particles toward the optimum or make the particles to pass through the optimum abruptly. In reference [9], the constants c_1 and c_2 are chosen equal to 2 corresponding to the optimal value for the problem studied. The role of the inertia weight ω is considered important for the convergence behavior of PSO algorithm. The inertia weight is employed to control the impact of the previous history of velocities on the current velocity. Thus, the parameter ω regulates the trade off between the global (wide ranging) and the local (nearby) exploration abilities of the swarm. A proper value for the inertia weight provides balance between the global and local exploration ability of the swarm, and thus results in better solutions. Numerical tests imply that it is preferable to initially set the inertia to a large value, to promote global exploration of the search space, and gradually decrease it to obtain refined solutions [10].

2.2   The Radius Improvement: A New Stopping Criterion

In practical situation, especially in structural optimization, there can find technological limitations on design variables. The main idea is to avoid an important number of useless iterations taking into account these limitations.

For a classical PSO, the stopping criterion is the maximum number of iterations allowed. In the context of a real physical process, the accuracy of the particle leading to the best result can not necessarily be reproduced or manufactured. Thus is it possible to imagine a stopping criterion on the precision in measuring the radius of the swarm ? This radius swarm is calculated by evaluating the distance of all the swarm of particles relative to the particle leader using a standard norm 2 . Then, if the maximum distance (Infty norm) stays less than a user-defined criterion for a number of iterations, the algorithm is then stopped (Figure 1).

2.3   The BSG-Starcraft Improvement

The question is: how to explore more quickly the search space ? The Battlestar Galactica Starcraft (BSG-Starcraft) improvement is based on two ideas inspired from the science fiction film Battlestar Galactica and a video game Starcraft. These two ideas can be formulated as follows:

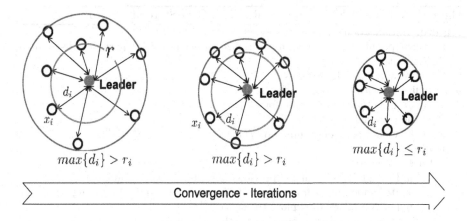

Fig. 1. The Radius improvement

- at each iteration t, the leader particle has the possibility to send randomly some new particles to fast explore the space, the raptors (Figure 2). The speed of this raptors is chosen grater than the velocity of the classical particles.
- if one raptor finds a best position than the global best then a jump vector is defined and the swarm jumps conserving the swarm geometry. The carrier location is now the raptor one.

All details of this approach are given by the pseudo-code listed in algorithm 1.

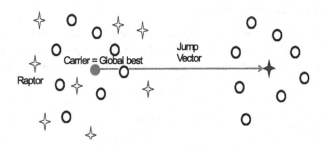

Fig. 2. The BSG-Starcraft improvement

This modification increases the number of evaluations of the objective function but a better solution is reached. To be very efficient, it means to reach more quickly the best solution, it is very useful to combine both improvements.

Algorithm 1. Particle swarm optimization : BSG-Starcraft improvement

---

Require: Initialization
1: Initialize population : randomly initialize positions of all particles distributed throughout the design space.
2: Initialize weight of all particles
3: Initialize velocities of all particles
4: Evaluate the objective function for all particles
5: Find the personal best : $p_i^0 = x_i^0$
6: Find the global best: determine min $f(x_i^0), i = 1 \cdots n$, set $p_g^0 = x_{min}^0$
7: **while** $t \leq t_{max}$ **do**
8:    **for** $i = 1, n$ **do**
9:       Find the global best of the previous iteration : it is the carrier $x_{carrier}$
10:       Create randomly with a probability $p = 0.1$, for a quite long range from the carrier, N raptors to explore the space x_k^{raptor}
11:       Evaluate the objective function for the N raptors
12:       **if** $\exists k / f(x_k^{raptor}) \leq f(x_{carrier})$ **then**
13:          Define the jump vector as $Jump = x_k^{raptor} - x_{carrier}$ and jump the swarm by the translation of vector $Jump$
14:          Evaluate the objective function for the jumped swarm
15:       **else**
16:          Evaluate the objective function of the initial swarm
17:       **end if**
18:       Update the personal best
19:       Update the global best
20:       Update velocity
21:       Update position
22:    **end for**
23: **end while**

2.4   Validation by Classical Tests

The performance of the proposed algorithm has been measured, with succes, on classical tests such as De Jong and Ackley functions. A statistically study has been realized in [6] in the conditions specified in table 1. Some results are presented in table 2.

Table 1. PSO parameters

Parameters	Values
Number of runs	100
Maximum number of iterations	400
Number of particles	20
$c_1 = c_2$	2
Radius	10^{-3}
Counter for radius	10
Number of raptors	20

Table 2. 100 runs results

	Classical PSO	Radius	BSG-Starcraft	BSG-Starcraft Radius
Ackley function				
Fitness	$m = 5.56$	$m = 4.93$	$m = 4.99$	$m = 4.73$
	$\sigma = 2.62$	$\sigma = 2.77$	$\sigma = 3.1$	$\sigma = 2.81$
Stop Iterations	$m = 400$	$m = 308.9$	$m = 400$	$m = 317.7$
	$\sigma = NA$	$\sigma = 28.8$	$\sigma = NA$	$\sigma = 26.0$
De Jong function				
Fitness	$m = 0.033$	$m = 0.025$	$m = 0.02$	$m = 0.027$
	$\sigma = 0.087$	$\sigma = 0.062$	$\sigma = 0.037$	$\sigma = 0.046$
Stop Iterations	$m = 400$	$m = 284.86$	$m = 400$	$m = 297.13$
	$\sigma = NA$	$\sigma = 19.33$	$\sigma = NA$	$\sigma = 18.31$

3 Application to Ceramic Matrix Composites

3.1 Context

The fabrication process of unidirectional CMCs with multi-layered (PyC/SiC) interphases is briefly introduced below: the architectures of CMCs consist of arranged fibers. The components of the multi-layered (PyC/SiC)n interphases and the SiC matrix are infiltrated within the porous fiber preforms. In the present study, square fiber arrays are used to model the unidirectional CMCs. Four layers of interphases are distributed around the fibers. In the longitudinal direction, the fiber axes have been assumed to be parallel and of equal lengths (Figrue 3). The optimization study is carried out on an unidirectional SiC fiber reinforced SiC ceramic matrix composite with four alternate layers of (PyC/SiC/PyC/SiC) interphases. Figure 3 shows the unit cell model of the composite. ϕ_f is fiber diameter; $d_1 \sim d_4$ are thicknesses of the interphase layers; d_5 is the thickness of the matrix layer. The finite element method is used for numerical computation of TRS. The finite element model can be seen in figure 3. Material properties of the constituents are given in Table 3.

Table 3. Properties of the constituents

Constituent	E_{11} (GPa)	E_{33} (GPa)	G_{12} (GPa)	G_{23} (GPa)	ν_{12}	ν_{23}	α_{11} ($10^{-6}/°C$)	α_{33} ($10^{-6}/°C$)
SiC fibre	200	200	80	80	0.12	0.12	3	3
PyC interphase	12	30	4.3	2	0.4	0.12	28	2
SiC interphase	350	350	145.8	145.8	0.2	0.2	4.6	4.6
SiC matrix	350	350	145.8	145.8	0.2	0.2	4.6	4.6

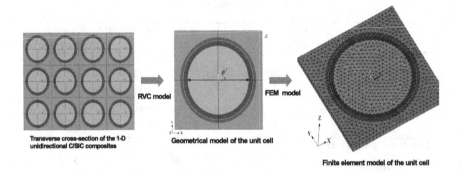

Fig. 3. Geometrical model of the unit cell of SiC/SiC composite

3.2   Optimization Problem

The goal of this work is the optimization of TRS distribution in the multi-layered interphases and matrix from the viewpoints of the deposition thickness of each interphase layer. Mathematically, the optimization problem can be formulated as:

$$\begin{cases} min \quad TRS = f(X) \\ X = (d_1, d_2, d_3, d_4) \\ 0.3 \leq d_i \leq 0.6 \end{cases} \tag{2}$$

where $f(X)$ is the objective function, i.e. the maximum hoop TRS within the interphases and matrix. The vector X is the vector defining the design variables: the thicknesses of the interfaces.

The diameter of the SiC fibre is $10\mu m$ and the thickness of the SiC matrix is $2\mu m$. The upper bound of each interphase layer thickness is $0.6\mu m$. In practice, the thicknesses of multi-layered interphases are usually limited to $0.1\mu m$ or more for oxidation resistance considerations [11] and reduction of the complexity of the CVI fabrication process. Therefore, in the present study the lower bound for each interphase layer thickness is set to $0.3\mu m$.

In this problem, the evaluation of the objective function for given values of the design variables requires a finite element analysis. So, the PSO and BSG-Starcraft Radius PSO schemes are linked to the finite element model introduced before.

3.3   Results

For all these algorithms, a population of 20 individuals is used; the inertia weight w decreases linearly from 0.9 to 0.4. The value of constants c_1 and c_2 are set to be the same and equal to 2. The maximum number of iterations is limited to 200. Radius value is set to $0.1\mu m$.

The results obtained by our approach are compared with those obtained by a classical PSO in order to evaluate the performance of the new algorithm.

Figure 4 provides a convergence rate of the optimization procedure. It can be seen that both two algorithms achieve the best solutions. The maximum hoop TRS has been decreased to $0.22GPa$ by means of handling the interphases thicknesses. The final optimized interphases thicknesses are $(0.6\mu m,\ 0.6\mu m,\ 0.3\mu m,\ 0.6\mu m)$. However, the BSG-Starcraft Radius PSO algorithm displays a faster convergence rate than the PSO algorithm in this example. It is closer to the best solution than the PSO algorithm in the early stages and hence. Besides, due to the swarm radius limitation the BSG-Starcraft Radius PSO algorithm stopped the computation after 97 iterations. Hence, the BSG-Starcraft Radius PSO algorithm requires less computational effort to find best design solutions than the PSO algorithm.

To conclude the comparison between the PSO and BSG-Starcraft Radius PSO schemes, the CPU time has been evaluated. An optimization run with the classical PSO algorithm takes approximately 12.5 hours on 7 CPU cores while the same run with the improvments takes 8.08 hours. A drastic decrease of the CPU time can be seen when the BSG-Starcraft Radius PSO scheme is used. In a structural optimization context where the optimization algorithm is coupled to a finite element analysis, the observed reduction of the number of iterations affects the number of finite element analysis and so the CPU time is strongly reduced.

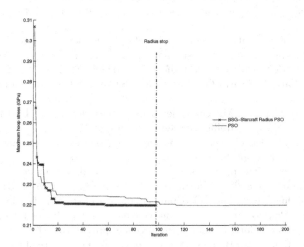

Fig. 4. Convergence rate for the optimization of hoop TRS

4   Conclusion

PSO algorithm does not use the gradient information of the optimization problem. This means that it does not require for the optimization problem to be differentiable as required by classical optimization methods such as gradient descent or quasi-Newton methods. In this structural optimization context, the optimization algorithm is coupled with a finite element analysis to evaluate the cost function. This work can be very CPU time consuming especially when the finite element models are large and have a considerable number of design parameters. That is the reason why the new version of PSO proposed in this paper is very interesting by its faster convergence rate ans its stopping criteria based on real physical limits. An original application to composite is proposed to test and validate our approach.

References

1. Kennedy, J., Eberhart, R.: Particle swarm optimisation. In: Proceedings of the IEEE International Conference on Neural Networks (1995)
2. Droillard, C., Lamom, J., Bourrat, X.: Strong interface in cmcs, a condition for efficient multilayered interphases. Materials Research Society Symposium Proceedings **365**, 371–376 (1995)
3. Droillard, C., Lamon, J.: Fracture toughness of 2-d woven sic/sic cvi-composites with multilayered interphases. Journal of the American Ceramic Society **79**(4), 849–858 (1996)
4. Xu, Y., Zhang, W., Chamoret, D., Domaszewski, M.: Minimizing thermal residual stresses in c/sic functionally graded material coating of c/c composites by using particle swarm optimization algorithm. Computational Materials Science **61**, 99–105 (2012)
5. Salmon, S.: Caractérisation, identification et optimisation des systèmes mécaniques complexes par mise en œuvre de simulateurs hybrides matériels-logiciels. PhD thesis, Université de Technologie de Belfort Montbéliard (2012)
6. Salmon, S.: Particle Swarm Optimization in Scilab ver 0.1-7 - Performance evaluations (2011)
7. Janson, S., Middendorf, M.: On trajectories of particles in pso. In: Proceedings of the 2007 IEEE Swarm Intelligence Symposium (2007)
8. van den Bergh, F., Engelbrecht, A.: A study of particle swarm optimization particle trajectories. Information Sciences **176**(8), 937–971 (2006)
9. Cristian, I.: Trelea: The particle swarm optimization algorithm: convergence analysis and parameter selection. Information Processing Letters **85**(6), 317–325 (2003)
10. Shi, Y., Eberhart, R.: A modified particle swarm optimizer. In: The 1998 IEEE International Conference on Evolutionary Computation Proceedings, 1998, IEEE World Congress on Computational Intelligence, pp. 69–73 (1998)
11. Bertrand, S., Pailler, R., Bourrat, X., Naslai, R.: Tem structure of (pyc/sic)n multilayered interphases in sic/sic composites. Journal of the European Ceramic Society **20**, 1–13 (2000)

An Efficient ACO-SA Hybrid Metaheuristic for the Synchronization of Single Frequency Networks in Broadcasting

Akram Bedoui[1,2(✉)], Philippe Debreux[2], and Thierry Schott[2]

[1] LORIA Laboratory, University of Lorraine, F-54506 Vandoeuvre-lés-Nancy, France
akram.bedoui@loria.fr
[2] TDF Company, F-57078 Metz, France
{akram.bedoui,philippe.debreux,thierry.schott}@tdf.fr

Abstract. The treasure of any radio communication network provider is the set of available frequencies and the challenge is to use the frequencies in the best possible way. Single Frequency Networks (SFNs) are broadcast networks where several transmitters send the same signal over the same frequency. They allow more efficient utilization of the radio spectrum in comparaison to traditional Multi Frequency Networks (MFNs) that use one different frequency per transmitter. SFN Synchronization Problem (SFNSP) is known to be a NP-hard problem. The aim of this paper is to present an original hybrid metaheuristic (ACO-SA) based on Ant Colony Optimization (ACO) and Simulated Annealing (SA) to solve SFNSP. Experimental results obtained with our hybrid ACO-SA on real-world benchmarks provided by the french telecommunication company named TDF[1], show drastic runtime improvement over existing approaches, and also quality improvement in comparison with existing SFN's synchronizations in the field of TV broadcasting in France.

Keywords: Ant Colony Optimisation · Simulated Annealing · Hybrid Metaheuristic · Single Frequency Network · Digital TV broadcasting

1 Introduction

Both the sectors of telecommunications and of broadcasting have to accommodate strong growth, with the sustained deployment of 3G and 4G networks, and the densification of TV networks. DVB-T, the current technical norm for Digital TV in Europe, offers the possibility to use the Single Frequency Network (SFN) technique, which consists in associating sets of synchronized transmitters. SFN's transmitters broadcast the same signal over one and only one frequency. The aim of SFN is to save utilization of the radio spectrum and allow a higher number of TV programs in comparaison to Multi Frequency Networks (MFNs)

---

[1] TDF is a french company, which provides radio and television services for telecom operators, and other multimedia services: digitization of content, encoding, storage, etc.http://www.tdf.fr.

© Springer International Publishing Switzerland 2014
P. Siarry et al. (Eds.): ICSIBO 2014, LNCS 8472, pp. 175–184, 2014.
DOI: 10.1007/978-3-319-12970-9_19

that use one different frequency per transmitter. The Quality of Service (QoS) of a SFN depends on the *extra-SFN jamming* and the *intra-SFN jamming*. The extra-SFN jamming depends on gaps in frequencies between transmitters which constitute the SFN and other transmitters not belonging to the considered SFN (i.e. transmitters on the same frequency not sufficiently far away and transmitters on adjacent channels in or in the vicinity of the SFN's coverage area). As for the intra-SFN jamming, it depends on the synchronization between the transmitters of the same SFN. In fact, the DVB-T technologies permit, in an interval of time called *Guard Interval (GI)*, to benefit from signals of the various co-channel transmitters constituting a SFN. Beyond GI, these signals are considered as interferers between them [2, 12].

In this paper, we formulate the Single Frequency Network Synchronization Problem (SFNSP) as a combinatorial optimisation problem and we present an original hybrid metaheuristic based on Ant Colony Optimization algorithm (ACO) [4, 9, 11] and Simulated Annealing (SA) [1, 3, 5–7, 10] to minimize the intra-SFN jamming of a SFN. We compare QoS of solutions calculated by our hybrid ACO-SA with operating SFN synchronizations in the field of TV broadcasting used nowadays in France.

This paper is organized as follows: in Section 2, we describe SFNSP. In Section 3, we present our hybrid ACO-SA metaheuristic. Experimental performance comparisons on real-world benchmarks provided by TDF Company are given in Section 4. Section 5 contains concluding remarks and further research aspects.

2   Single Frequency Network Synchronization Problem

SFN's transmitters are spread over the geographical area where broadcasters wish to provide the users with their services. Each transmitter covers a part of this geographical area called its *coverage area*. The area around a transmitter where transmission conditions are favourable enough to have a good reception of the signal is known as the *service area* of the transmitter. The service area is the portion of the coverage area that is not jammed by other transmitters.

The optimization of a SFN synchronization requires the adjustment of an initial transmitting delay on every transmitter so that all the signals transmitted by the SFN members fall within the *Guard Interval* (GI) on the maximum of the locations in the SFN's coverage area. If the delay spread is higher than the GI, according to the synchronization strategy of the receivers, the contributions outside the GI are considered as potential interferers and weighted with a co-channel protection ratio [2, 12].

The formal definition of the considered SFNSP is given by: let S be a SFN. Let $T = \{t_i\}_{1 \leq i \leq n}$ be a set of n transmitters distributed across the geographical area of S. Let $D_i = \{d_{i,1}, d_{i,2}, ...d_{i,m}\}$ be the set of m valid delays, that can be assigned to the transmitter t_i.

If the coverage area of a transmitter t_i and the interference area of a transmitter t_j intersect, there is an intra-SFN jamming constraint $C_{t_i \leftarrow t_j}$ between the pair of transmitters (t_i, t_j). The constraint corresponds to the amount of jamming between the transmitters for different gaps in delay $d_{i,x} - d_{j,y}$ $(1 \leq x, y \leq m)$.

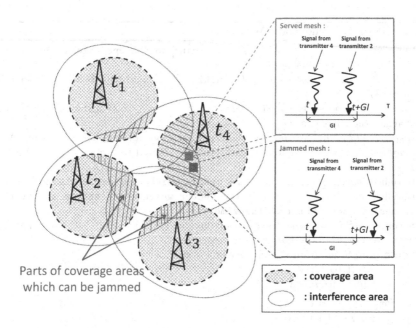

Fig. 1. Example of SFN network

A solution (i.e. synchronization) to the problem is obtained by assigning to each transmitter t_i one of the delays from D_i. It's henceforth denoted by $s \in D_1 \times D_2 \times ... \times D_n$ where $s(t_i) \in D_i$ is the delay assigned to the transmitter t_i. The optimal solution is the one which minimizes the objective function ϕ (see Formula 1).

$$Min \ \phi(s) = \sum_{t_i \in S}^{n} \sum_{t_j \in S \wedge t_j \neq t_i}^{p} \rho_{i,j} \times C_{t_i \leftarrow t_j}(s(t_i) - s(t_j)) \tag{1}$$

where p is the number of jammers of the transmitter t_i and $\rho_{i,j}$ is a weight of the constraint $C_{t_i \leftarrow t_j}$ Figure 1 shows an example of a SFN network constituted by four co-channel transmitters (t_1, t_2, t_2, and t_4). Between these transmitters, there are ten intra-SFN jamming constraints. For example, there is a constraint $C_{t_1 \leftarrow t_2}$ between t_1 and t_2 because the intersection of the interference area of t_2 with the coverage area of t_1.

A SFN network can be modelled by an oriented graph in which vertices represent transmitters and oriented edges represent intra-SFN jamming constraints. There is a strong link between graph coloring and delays synchronisation with binary interference constraints. The graph coloring problem is known to be NP-Hard [8], thus, consequently the SFNSP.

3 Principles of Our Hybrid ACO-SA Metaheuristic and Pseudo-Code

The idea of our hybrid ACO-SA (see Algorithm 1) consists in using a modified version of ACO algorithm inspired by [11] adapted to solve SFNSP combined

---

Algorithm 1. Pseudocode ACO-SA

---

1 Initialize S_0 ;   /* according to the operational delays */
2 $n \leftarrow |S_0|$; $m \leftarrow$ number of possible delays;
3 $bestcost \leftarrow \infty$; $newcost \leftarrow 0$;   /* initialization of the best and the new costs */
4 $shortStagnation \leftarrow 0$; $longStagnation \leftarrow 0$;   /* initialization of stagnation counters */
5 $restartSAThreshold \leftarrow$ nb. of stagnation iterations allowed before we run SA;
6 $stopThreshold \leftarrow$ nb. of stagnation iterations allowed before we stop ACO-SA;
7 $R \leftarrow 2$;
8 Initialize $trace[n][m]$;   /* matrix which represents the memory */
9 Initialize $sumTrace[n]$;   /* the vector which contains the sum of the values of each column of the memory */
10 $parametersSA[] \leftarrow InitialisationParametresSA(S_0)$;   /* adaptive computation of SA's parameters */
11 **while** *(longStagnation < stopThreshold)* **do**
12 | **for** $i \leftarrow 1$ **to** n **do**
13 | | $sumTrace[i] \leftarrow 0$;
14 | **for** $i \leftarrow 1$ **to** n **do**
15 | | **for** $i \leftarrow 1$ **to** m **do**
16 | | | $sumTrace[i] \leftarrow sumTrace[i] + trace[i][j]$;
17 | $i_{min} \leftarrow$ index of the component of $sumTrace$ which contains the minimal value;
18 | $S_t \leftarrow$ GenerateNewSolution(i_{min}, S_{t-1}) ;   /* computation of a neighbor solution */
19 | **if** *(shortStagnation = restartSAThreshold)* **then**
20 | | $S'_t \leftarrow SimulatedAnnealing(S_t, parametersSA[])$; /* see Algorithm 2 */
21 | | $newcost \leftarrow \phi(S'_t)$;   /* see Formula 1 */
22 | | $shortStagnation \leftarrow 0$;
23 | **else**
24 | | $newcost \leftarrow \phi(S_t)$;   /* see Formula 1 */
25 | **if** *(newcost < bestcost)* **then**
26 | | $bestcost \leftarrow newcost$;   /* updating of the best cost */
27 | | $S_{best} \leftarrow S_t$;   /* updating of the best solution */
28 | | $increment \leftarrow 1$;
29 | | **for** $i \leftarrow 1$ **to** n **do**
30 | | | **for** $j \leftarrow 1$ **to** m **do**
31 | | | | $trace[i][j] \leftarrow 1$;
32 | | $shortStagnation \leftarrow 0$; $longStagnation \leftarrow 0$;
33 | **else**
34 | | UpdateTrace($S_t, S_{best}, increment, R$) ;   /* see Algorithm 3 */
35 | | $shortStagnation \leftarrow shortStagnation + 1$;
36 | | $longStagnation \leftarrow longStagnation + 1$;
37 **return** S_{best};

Algorithm 2. SimulatedAnnealing(S_t,$parameters[]$)

Data: a solution S_t and SA parameters (temperature and α stocked in $parameters[]$)

Result: S_{best} (i.e. improved S_t)

1 $stagnation \leftarrow 0$;

2 $stopThreshold \leftarrow$ number of stagnation iterations allowed before we stop the procedure SA ;

3 $n \leftarrow \mid S_t \mid$;

4 $S_0 \leftarrow S_t$;

5 $maxFail \leftarrow \frac{n*(n-1)}{2}$;

6 $nbFail \leftarrow 0$;

7 $tFound \leftarrow parameters[0]$;

8 $temperature \leftarrow parameters[0]$;

9 $\alpha \leftarrow parameters[1]$;

10 **while** *(stagnation < stopThreshold)* **do**

11 $\quad$ $temperature \leftarrow \frac{temperature}{1+\alpha*temperature}$;

12 $\quad$ $oldCost \leftarrow \Phi(S_{t-1})$;

13 $\quad$ $S_t \leftarrow GnrerNouvelleSolution(S_{t-1})$;

14 $\quad$ $newCost \leftarrow \Phi(S_{t-1})$;

15 $\quad$ $\Delta \leftarrow oldCost - newCost$;

16 $\quad$ **if** *(($\Delta > 0$) $\vee$ ($rand(0,1) < e^{\frac{-\Delta}{temperature}}$) $\vee$ ($maxFail == nbFail$))* **then**

17 $\quad\quad$ $S \leftarrow S_t$;

18 $\quad\quad$ $nbFail \leftarrow 0$;

19 $\quad$ **else**

20 $\quad\quad$ $nbFail \leftarrow nbFail + 1$;

21 $\quad$ $stagnation \leftarrow stagnation + 1$;

22 $\quad$ **if** *(maxFail == nbFail)* **then**

23 $\quad\quad$ $\alpha \leftarrow 0$;

24 $\quad\quad$ $temperature \leftarrow tfound$;

25 $\quad$ **if** *(newCost <= bestCost)* **then**

26 $\quad\quad$ $S_{best} \leftarrow S_t$;

27 $\quad\quad$ $bestCost \leftarrow newCost$;

28 $\quad\quad$ $tfound \leftarrow temperature$;

29 $\quad\quad$ $stagnation \leftarrow 0$;

30 **return** S_{best};

Algorithm 3. UpdateTrace(S_t, S_{best}, *increment*, R)

Data: current solution S_t, best solution until now S_{best}, *increment*, and R

Result: updated matrix *trace*

1 *transmitter* $\leftarrow$ 1;

2 *curentDelay* $\leftarrow S_t$(*transmitter*);

3 *bestDelay* $\leftarrow S_{best}$(*transmitter*);

4 **while** ((*transmitter* $\leq n$) $\bigwedge$(*curentDelay* == *bestDelay*)) **do**

5 $\quad$ *transmitter* $\leftarrow$ *transmitter* + 1;

6 $\quad$ *curentDelay* $\leftarrow S_t$(*transmitter*);

7 $\quad$ *bestDelay* $\leftarrow S_{best}$(*transmitter*);

8 **if** *(transmitter = n)* **then**

9 $\quad$ *increment* $\leftarrow$ *increment* + 1;

10 $\quad$ **for** $i \leftarrow 1$ **to** n **do**

11 $\quad\quad$ **for** $j \leftarrow 1$ **to** m **do**

12 $\quad\quad\quad$ *trace*[i][j] $\leftarrow$ *increment*;

13 **else**

14 $\quad$ **for** *($i \leftarrow 1$ to n)* **do**

15 $\quad\quad$ *curentDelay* $\leftarrow S_t$(*transmitter*);

16 $\quad\quad$ *bestDelay* $\leftarrow S_{best}$(*transmitter*);

17 $\quad\quad$ *trace*[i][*curentDelay*] $\leftarrow$ *trace*[i][*curentDelay*] + *increment*;

18 $\quad\quad$ *trace*[i][*bestDelay*] $\leftarrow$ *trace*[i][*bestDelay*] + R;

---

with a modified version of adaptive SA algorithm inspired by [3] also adapted to solve SFNSP. The goal of this hybridization is to improve the quality of ants using adaptive SA algorithm (see Algorithm 2) when the search stagnates in a local minimum. Our hybrid ACO-SA metaheuristic relies on the the following main components:

- **Representation of a solution:** a solution represents a possible synchronization of considered SFN's transmitters. We represent a solution by a vector. The indices of this vector represent the transmitters and the values of the components represent the delays affected to the transmitters.
- **Initial solution:** there exist three possibilities for generating the initial solution S_0: it can be a randomly generated synchronization, or a synchronization associating a delay equal to zero to all transmitter stations, or the operational synchronization used nowadays. In our ACO-SA metaheristic we use the later possibility (see line 1 of Algorithm 1);
- **Pheromone memory:** the pheromone memory is represented by a matrix (*trace*) of dimension $n \times m$, where n is the number of transmitters of the SFN to be synchronized, and m is the number of possible delays for each transmitter. Initially, all elements of the matrix are equal to 1 (see line 8 of Algorithm 1);

- **ACO stop criterion:** the stop criterion of ACO-SA is dynamic. If the costs of a sequence of ongoing solutions continues to grow during *stopThreshold* iterations, then ACO-SA stops (see line 11 of Algorithm 1);
- **SA initialization:** the initial step of the algorithm includes also the adaptive calculus of the parameters (initial temperature, attenuation coefficient) of SA. This calculus depends on the instance under consideration;
- **SA stop criterion:** the stop criterion of SA is also dynamic: if the costs of an ongoing sequence of solutions is larger than the cost of the best solution explored until now, then SA stops.
- As long as the stop criterion of ACO-SA has not been reached, the following set of operations is executed at each iteration:
  - **Update of the vector sumTrace:** all components of *sumTrace* are reinitialized to 0, then the sum of the components of the ith column of the *trace* matrix is stored in i^{th} component of the vector *sumTrace* (see lines 12-16 of Algorithm 1);
  - **Computation of neigbor solution based on pheromone memory:** to this matrix (*trace*), we associate a vector (*sumTrace*) of length n such as $\forall 1 \leq i \leq n, sumTrace[i] = trace[i][1] + trace[i][2] + \ldots + trace[i][m]$. Based on this vector, we calculate the neigbor solution. We look for the index i_{min} of the element of *sumTrace* which contains the minimal value. Then we assign the best possible delay (i.e. delay which minimizes the number of jammed meshes in the coverage area of the i_{min}^{th} transmitter) to the i_{min}^{th} transmitter (see lines 17 and 18 of Algorithm 1);
  - **Run of SA with the neighbor solution as input:** if a stagnation of size *restartSAThreshold* is detected, then adaptive SA algorithm runs with the calculated neighbor solution and the stagnation counter short-Stagnation resets (see lines 19-22 of Algorithm 1).
  - **Update of current and best solutions:** if the cost of the neighbor solution is smaller than that of the current solution, the neighbor solution becomes the current one. The until now best cost becomes the cost of the neighbor solution. The memory matrix (*trace*) is reinitialized. The two counters *longStagnation* (this counter is in charge of stopping the hybrid procedure ACO-SA) and *shortStagnation* (this counter is in charge of restarting the procedure SA) are initialized to 0 (see lines 25-32 of Algorithm 1). If the cost of the neighbor solution is larger than the cost of the current solution, the memory matrix (*trace*) is updated according to the current solution, the neighbor solution and the two parameters *increment* and R (see Algorithm 3). The two counters *shortStagnation* and *longStagnation* are incremented (see lines 33-36 of Algorithm 1).

4   Experimental Results

We use real-world benchmarks provided by TDF and compare the experimental results obtained thanks to our ACO-SA metaheuristic with these currently obtained by TDF's software. In Figure 2, Figure 3 and Figure 4 red areas represent jammed areas, and purple areas represent service areas.

Reference service area = 9268 km^2 ACO-SA service area = 10458,5 km^2
Reference runtime = 09 min 00 s   ACO-SA runtime = 01 min 54 s

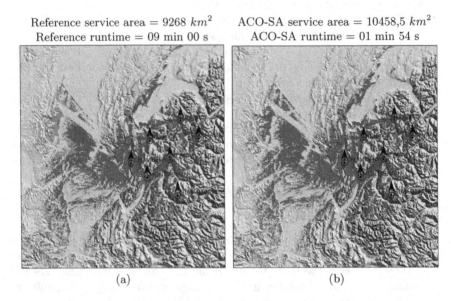

(a)   (b)

Fig. 2. QoS of reference solution (a) and ACO-SA solution (b) for Benchmark 1

Reference service area = 24506 km^2 ACO-SA service area = 25501 km^2
Reference runtime = 31 min 00 s   ACO-SA runtime = 5 min 35 s

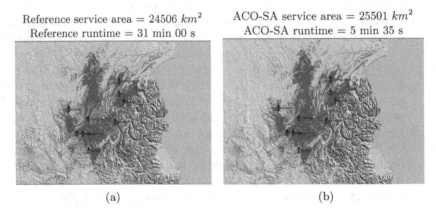

(a)   (b)

Fig. 3. QoS of reference solution (a) and ACO-SA solution (b) for Benchmark 2

Reference service area = 37167,8 km^2 ACO-SA service area = 39286,5 km^2
Reference runtime = 05 h 28 min 00 s   ACO-SA runtime = 00 h 04 min 21

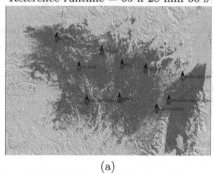 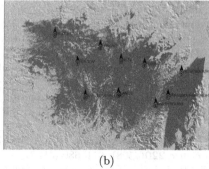

(a)   (b)

Fig. 4. QoS of reference solution (a) and ACO-SA solution (b) for Benchmark 3

- Figure 2.(b) shows that jammed areas have disappeared in comparison with Figure 2.(a). ACO-SA runs 4.7 times faster than TDF's actual software and increases the service area by 13 %.
- Figure 3.(b) shows that jammed areas have been reduced in comparison with Figure 3.(a). ACO-SA runs 5.5 times faster than TDF's actual software and increases the service area by 3.9 %.
- Figure 4.(b) shows that jammed areas have been reduced in comparison with Figure 4.(a). ACO-SA runs 75.4 times faster than TDF's actual software and increases the service area by 5.4 %.

5 Concluding Remarks and Further Research Aspects

Our hybrid ACO-SA metaheuristic has good time performances and improves (or maintains) the quality of the solutions (by at most 13%). There is still room for improvement. We are planning to explore additional hybrid metaheuristics (based on Particle Swarm Optimization, for example) and to design a non trivial, distributed version of ACO-SA.

References

1. Aouad, M.I., Idoumghar, L., Schott, R., Zendra, O.: Sequential and distributed hybrid ga-sa algorithms for energy optimization in embedded systems. In: Proceedings of IADIS International Conference Applied Computing, pp. 167–174 (2010)
2. Brugger, R., Hemingway, D.: Ofdm receivers: impact on coverage of inter-symbol interference and fft window positioning. EBU Technical Review, pp. 19–30 (1996)
3. Connolly, D.T.: An improved annealing scheme for the qap. European Journal of Operational Research **46**, 93–100 (1990)
4. Dorigo, M.: Ant Colont Optimization. Scholarpedia (2007)

5. Granville, V., Krivánek, M., Rasson, J.P.: Simulated annealing: A proof of convergence. IEEE Transaction on Pattern Analysis Machine Intelligence **16**(6), 652–656 (1994)
6. Idoumghar, L., Chrin, N., Siarry, P., Roche, R., Miraoui, A.: Hybrid icapso algorithm for continuous optimization. Applied Mathematics and Computation **219**(24), 11149–11170 (2013)
7. Idoumghar, L., Debreux, P.: New modeling approach to the frequency assignment problem in broadcasting. IEEE Transactions Broadcasting **48**(4), 293–298 (2002)
8. Jensen, T.R., Toft, B.: Graph Coloring Problems. WILEY (1995)
9. Monmarché, N., Guinand, F., Siarry, P. (eds.) Artificial Ants. ISBN 978-1-84821-194-0. Hardback (2010)
10. Gelatt, C.D., Kirkpatrick, S., Vecchi, M.P.: Optimisation by simulated annealing. Science **220**(4598), 671–680 (1983)
11. Taillard, E.D.: Fant: Fast ant system. Technical report, Instituto Dalle Molle Di Studi Sull Intelligenza Artificiale (1998)
12. Weck, C.: Coverage aspects of digital terrestrial television broadcasting. EBU Technical Review, pp. 19–30 (1996)

Floods Trajectories Modeling and Dynamic Relief Planning: A Bees Foraging Approach

Kawther Hmaidi$^{(\boxtimes)}$ and Jalel Akaichi

Institut supérieur de gestion, University of Tunis, Bardo, Tunis, Tunisia
hmaidi.kawther@live.com, j.akaichi@gmail.com

Abstract. Natural disasters represent hazards resulting from extreme geophysical events. Floods particularly are one of the most occurring disasters. They affect annually different regions of the world with varying intensities causing materiel damages and fatalities. Despite the efforts done by rescue agents in this context, inefficiencies occur yet. Thus, the need of disaster management information systems is becoming critical to mitigate the effect of natural hazards. In this paper, we aim to provide a dynamic decision making tool inspired by the foraging behavior of honey bees which assists in managing relief operations and assigning rescue agents to affected areas. We propose, equally, a trajectory data warehouse model for flood tracking and affected areas location.

Keywords: Bees foraging · Dynamic allocation · Relief planning · Floods Trajectory data warehouse

1 Introduction

The period following natural disasters represents a critical period due to various challenging factors such as the large number of casualties at stake, the time required for evacuation and the lack of rescue officers and material resources. Hence, the need of disaster management information systems is becoming critical to deliver the right information to public authorities concerned by decision making. Despite the incredible efforts done in this respect, inefficiencies in relief activities occur yet. In fact, the majority of current Disaster management systems usually are mere information systems used for graphical representation of disaster relevant data. Nevertheless, there is no efficient means which allow quick analysis of disaster information and provide rapidly an adequate planning for relief agents allocation. Moreover, when the management of a disaster extends on large scale, decision making becomes more difficult and time becomes a critical factor.

The goal of this paper is to:

- Design a trajectory data warehouse model to track the changing position of floods water waves in order to locate affected areas.
- Organize dynamically the work of rescue teams through a dynamic decision making tool inspired by the foraging behavior of honey bees.

© Springer International Publishing Switzerland 2014
P. Siarry et al. (Eds.): ICSIBO 2014, LNCS 8472, pp. 185–191, 2014.
DOI: 10.1007/978-3-319-12970-9_20

The remainder of this paper is organized as follows: In section 2, we present some research works related to bees inspired algorithms and their applications. In section 3, we propose a conceptual model for floods trajectory data warehouse. In section 4, we describe the foraging behavior of bees in nature and we provide an algorithm inspired by the latter behavior for dynamic relief management. In section 5, we will summarize the work and propose new perspectives to be done in the future.

2   Related Works

2.1   Main Algorithms Inspired by Bees Foraging Behavior and Its Applications

Over years, the computational researches have been increasingly interested to biological phenomena, as source of modeling paradigms. Particularly, the bees inspired algorithms has emerged recently and has proved its efficiency in several application domains. The main purpose was to mimic the efficiency of honey bees organization within its colonies either for establishing analogies for system functioning or for resolving renowned optimization problems. Several woks in the literature have dealt with bees inspired algorithms using different nomenclatures. We can cite briefly: bees system [5], [6], [9], Bee Colony Optimization [7], Bee Hive [11], Artificial Bee Colony [4] and Virtual Bee Algorithm [12].

The main domains are: Genetic Algorithm Improvement, Traveling Salesman Problem (TSP), Stochastic Vehicle Routing Problem, Dynamic Allocation of Internet Service, Job Shop Scheduling, Telecommunication Network Routing, Neural Network and Routing Protocol for Wireless Sensor Networks.

2.2   Models Inspired by Honeybees Foraging Behavior for Collective Decision Making in Relief Operations

Inspired by the concept of collective decision making of honeybees, Chen and Pea-Mora proposed, in [3], a decentralized and collective decision making approach for large scale disasters. In fact, it enables immediate deployment of heavy construction equipment, which supports critical lifesaving activities during urban search-and-rescue period. As well, Aldunate and colleagues presented, in [1], another distributed collaborative decision-making model which allows the system communication without any commander. Indeed, a decision making problem is modeled as the selection of one best option among available options to perform a task.

3   Floods Trajectory Data Warehouse Model

The use of remote sensing technologies, sensors and localization systems opened the way to the applications exploiting the location. Hence, the huge volume of generated trajectory data must be stored in a multidimensional model, called trajectory data warehouse. The latter, allows analysis and gives the possibility of extracting knowledge from historical data which ensures better decision making. Trajectories are stored as set points (X, Y, T) where the couple (X, Y) represents the space dimension and (T) represents the time dimension. In our context, a flood travels along a river as a wave with velocity and depth continuously changing and usually affects areas located close to it with variable levels [8]. Therefore, we consider water waves as the moving object which changes its position over space and time. Our model is presented by a star schema as illustrated below in Fig.1, composed by the fact table: Trajectory and dimensions tables:Time, Flooded area, Side, Geographic specificity, River and Flood wave. Indeed, the fact contains measures (water-level and propagation-velocity) representing analysis values while dimensions are defined as analysis axes.

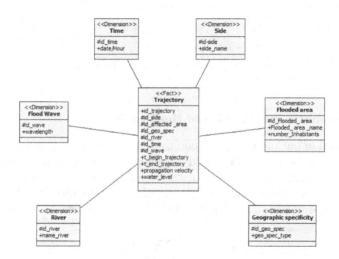

Fig. 1. Floods trajectory data warehouse Star schema

4   Dynamic Relief Planning

The aim of this work is to find an optimal allocation of relief agents to flooded areas in a dynamic way. We suppose that rescue agents are divided into homogeneous teams, where each team is composed of a predetermined number of agents with different rescue skills. Every relief team is equipped with a mobile device. Once a relief team finished an evacuation task, he changes its state to available and then either he indicates the number of evacuees or he indicates that this area does not request relief yet if all inhabitants are evacuated. Iteratively, considering areas not served yet and areas served but still requesting relief, the system has to choose which area to serve based on a probability with which relief teams are assigned. In order to save the biggest number of evacuees, the relief demand may correlate highly with the number of survivals trapped in the flooded areas. During relief operations, a relief team may have the different states as illustrated below in Fig.2.

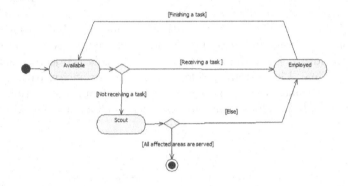

Fig. 2. Different states of a relief team

4.1   Mathematic Formulation of the Problem

The main goal of our model is to maximize the number of evacuees by assigning relief teams to flooded areas. Inspired by generalized assignment problem where the objective function aims to assign a set of tasks to a set of agents, we formulate the problem as an integer programming model with the objective to maximize the number of evacuees. The objective function is as follow:

$$maximize \quad \sum_{i=1}^{n}\sum_{j=1}^{m} E_{ij}x_{ij} \tag{1}$$

subject to

$$x_{ij} \in \{0,1\} \tag{2}$$

$$\sum_{i=1}^{n} a_{ij}x_{ij} \leq b_j \quad \forall j:1\cdots m \tag{3}$$

Where E_{ij}:Number of evacuated inhabitants in flooded area i by relief team j; x_{ij} : Variable decision =1 if flooded areas i is assigned to relief team j ,0 otherwise; n : Number of flooded areas i:1..n ; m: Number of relief teams j:1..m; bj: Capacity of relief team j ; ai : Relief resource needed by flooded area i. Constraint (3) specifies the maximum capability associated with each given relief team.

4.2   Bees Foraging Behavior in Nature

The foraging behavior of honey bees in nature designates the search of food. During this process, the forager bees are divided into employed: they are engaged in exploiting a food source, and unemployed: They are continually at look out for a food source to exploit. There are two types of unemployed foragers: scouts: searching the environment surrounding the nest for new food sources and onlookers: waiting in the nest and establishing a food source through the information shared by employed foragers. The communication is insured through the waggle dance in order to recruit the nest mates and send more follower bees to more promising patches [2].

4.3   Correspondence Between Honeybees Foraging Behavior and Relief Agents Allocation

At the outset of our research, it was immediately obvious that the relief teams allocation and foragers allocation problems were similar. We note that the set of relief teams having to be assigned to flooded areas is analogous to bees foragers allocated to multiple flower patches. Both of them aim to choose the most profitable sources in term of either flowers nectar or number of trapped people in affected areas. Table 1 illustrates the previous correspondence.

Table 1. Analogies between honey bees foraging behavior and relief agents assignment

Bees foraging behavior	Relief teams allocation
• Food sources	• Flooded areas
• Fitness of food sources: Nectar amount	• Severity degree of affected areas : Number of trapped inhabitants
• Forager bees	• Relief teams
• Employed bees	• Relief teams assigned to flooded areas
• Onlookers bees	• Available relief teams
• Scout bees	• Relief teams finishing a task and not receiving a new one
• Objective: Maximize the total nectar amount collected from different flower patches	• Objective: Maximize the total number of evacuees from different affected areas by assigning relief team i to flooded area j

4.4   Dynamic Relief Allocation Algorithm

As detailed previously, the aim of the proposed model is to dynamically allocate rescuers.Hence,the algorithm Relief-Alloc has to check, iteratively, the list and choose the flooded areas to serve in order to maximize the total number of evacuees.For each area, a probability with which relief teams are assigned is computed by the procedure Compute-probability.Thus, as the number of trapped persons increases, the number of assigned relief teams increases too.

Algorithm Relief-Alloc

```
Input: Nbr flooded areas , Nbr  relief teams, Nbr trapped people in area i
Output: Dynamic allocation of relief teams to flooded  areas
Begin
 While (List of affected area not empty)
  For each flooded area i
   Compute  probability()
  End for
  For each relief team j
   If state j  = available then
      Assign available relief teams to flooded areas having max pi
      Set state of assigned relief teams to  employed
   Enf if
  End for
  If task accomplished then
   Share information about number of evacuees
   Set state of relief team to available
  End if
  Compute the number of remainder trapped people in each served area i
  If number of remainder trapped people = 0 then
   Remove areas from list of flooded areas
  Else
   Update list of flooded areas
  End if
 End while
End
```

Procedure Compute-probability

```
Input:L: list flooded areas, n: Nbr flooded area, nbrtr : Nbr trapped people
Output: Lprob: list flooded areas with relative p
Begin
  For each affected area
```

$$\frac{nbrtr_i}{\sum_{i=1}^{n} nbrtr_i} \tag{4}$$

```
  End for
End
```

5   Conclusion and Future Work

Floods have been considered as one of the most devastating disasters throughout the last century either in terms of property damage or human causalities.

Thus, in order to improve relief operations and save the biggest number of victims, our work focused on analyzing floods data and organizing the work of relief teams.By drawing analogies from the foraging behavior of honey bees in nature, we have provided an algorithm to dynamically allocate relief to flooded areas. We have equally modeled the trajectories of floods through a trajectory data warehouse schema.As part of our future work, we aim to include fuzzy logic to locate flood waves positions.As well,we propose to improve the allocation of relief by considering the nearest flooded zones to choose when assigning rescuers

References

1. Aldunate, R.G., Pea -Mora, F., Robinson, G.E.: Collaborative Distributed Decision Making for Large Scale Disaster Relief Operations: Drawing Analogies from Robust Natural Sys-tems. J. Complexity **11**, 28–38 (2005)
2. Bitam, S., Batouche, M., Talbi, EL.G.: A Survey on Bee Colony Algorithms. In: 2010 IEEE International Symposium on Parallel and Distributed Processing, Workshops and Phd Forum (IPDPSW), Atlanta, pp. 1–8 (2010)
3. Chen, A.Y., Pea-Mora, F.: Decentralized Approach Considering Spatial Attributes for Equip-ment Utilization in Civil Engineering Disaster Response. J. Comput. Civ. Eng. **25**, 457–470 (2005)
4. Karaboga, D., Basturk, B.: Artificial Bee Colony (ABC) Optimization Algorithm for Solving Constrained Optimization Problems. In: Melin, P., Castillo, O., Aguilar, L.T., Kacprzyk, J., Pedrycz, W. (eds.) IFSA 2007. LNCS (LNAI), vol. 4529, pp. 789–798. Springer, Heidelberg (2007)
5. Lucic, P., Teodorovic, D.: Bee system: Modeling Combinatorial Optimization Transportation Engineering Problems by Swarm Intelligence. In: Preprints of the TRISTAN IV Triennial Sym-posium on Transportation Analysis, Azores Islands, pp. 441–445 (2001)
6. Lucic, P., Teodorovic, D.: Transportation Modeling: An Artificial Life Approach. In: ICTAI 2002 14th IEEE International Conference on Tools with Artificial Intelligence, pp. 216–223 (2002)
7. Markovi, G.Z., Teodorovi, D.B., Aimovi-Raspopovi, V.S.: Routing and wavelength assignment in all optical networks based on the bee colony optimization. J. AI Communications **20**, 273–285 (2007)
8. Mujumdar, P.P.: Flood wave propagation. J. Resonance **6**, 66–73 (2001)
9. Sato, T., Hagiwara, M.: Bee System: Finding Solution by a Concentrated Search. In: IEEE International Conference on Systems, Man, and Cybernetics, Orlando, pp. 3954–3959 (1997)
10. Teodorovic, D., Davidovic, T., Selmic, M.: Bee Colony Optimization: The Applications Survey. J. ACM Transactions on Computational Logic **12**, 1–20 (2011)
11. Wedde, H.F., Farooq, M., Zhang, Y.: BeeHive: An Efficient Fault-Tolerant Routing Algorithm Inspired by Honey Bee Behavior. In: Dorigo, M., Birattari, M., Blum, C., Gambardella, L.M., Mondada, F., Stützle, T. (eds.) ANTS 2004. LNCS, vol. 3172, pp. 83–94. Springer, Heidelberg (2004)
12. Yang, X.-S.: Engineering Optimizations via Nature-Inspired Virtual Bee Algorithms. In: Mira, J., Álvarez, J.R. (eds.) IWINAC 2005. LNCS, vol. 3562, pp. 317–323. Springer, Heidelberg (2005)

Author Index

Printed in the United States
By Bookmasters